W9-AXH-999

"The relation of love to pain is one of the
most difficult problems, and yet one of
the most fundamental, in the whole range of sexual psychology.
Why is it that love inflicts, and even seeks
to inflict, pain? Why is it that love
suffers pain, and even seeks to suffer it?"

—Havelock Ellis, "Love and Pain"

S-M
The Last Taboo

Gerald and Caroline Greene

BALLANTINE BOOKS • NEW YORK

Library of Congress Catalog Card Number: 74-7680

ISBN 0-345-27160-2

This edition published by arrangement with Grove Press, Inc.

Manufactured in the United States of America

First Ballantine Books Edition: March 1978

CONTENTS

What Is Sadism?   1

The Growth of Study   5

Havelock Ellis   17

The Spanking Setting   29

America and Masochism   45

Who Was de Sade?   63

The Role of Fantasy   95

The Role of Woman   113

What is S–M?   127

S–M in Daily Life   133

The Problem of Encounter   139

S–M in Marriage   157

The Structure of the S–M Experience   171

The Scenario   175

"Water Sports"—Undinism and Enemas   189

B & D   205

S–M Materials   211

A "Tidy" Pain   215

APPENDIX: From the Fields of Infamy   221

  Charles Baudelaire, *The Damned Women*   223

  Charles Baudelaire, *To Her Who Is Too Gay*   224

  From George Colman, *Squire Hardman*   227

  From Aubrey Beardsley, *Under the Hill*   237

  From Edith Cadivec, *Confessions and Experiences*   243

  From Edith Cadivec, *Eros, The Meaning of My Life*   261

  From Pauline Réage, *Story of O*   273

  From Anonymous, *Harriet Marwood, Governess*   285

  From *Oh! Calcutta!*

      "Who: Whom"   301

      "St. Dominic's, 1917"   305

  From *The Tutor*, P.N. Dedeaux, ed.   319

  From Françoise des Ligneris, *Fort Frédérick*   327

  From Blake Tremaine, *New At It*   333

WHAT
IS
SADISM?

It is a sunny afternoon at a busy intersection in Middletown, America. A man runs over a child returning from school. "The sadist!" we hear. That night, in desperation at his deed, the same man kills himself—"What a masochist!"

The example is scarcely too extreme. Embedded in our laws are reactions to "sadomasochistic practices" that are equally preposterous, were they not so dangerous. Rigor of enforcement coupled with vagueness of definition is the classic situation calculated to make any lawyer shudder; and it could be said of some of our state penal laws that under the classification "sadism" has been collected almost everything our society most fears.

This width of terminology itself is enough to arouse feelings of insecurity. Few people are agreed as to what "sadism" means, any more than they are agreed as to what the sister term "masochism" means. We are told by one authority that the suicide is in reality a sadist since he is killing someone else, and by another that the painful growth of teeth in infancy is the true physiological basis for masochism. Drug addicts and political radicals are frequently referred to in our press as masochists, while a delightful dividend of any etiological research into the activity is to learn, from yet another learned and degree-bedecked authority, that a sadist is really a miser as well as being, on the side as it were, a

vegetarian, to say nothing of Freud's "explanation" that sadism
originates from "the rage of the mouth-thwarted child." Also the
sadist, it seems, blows up offices.

Unless we are involved in clinical psychiatry, our reaction to
these ingenuities must be to yawn. In order to acquire meaning a
word or term must mean that same thing twice. We suggest sadism
has become, therefore, a catch-all for any form of behavior the
user dislikes, fears, or wants to discredit in general. The nomenclature requires reform. At the present moment it is a construct of
what we can only call popular psychopathology. Why?

The term "sadism" was a neologism first used in England in
1888, from French *sadisme,* derived in turn from the name of the
Comte (usually called Marquis) de Sade (1740–1814), to whom we
shall, inevitably enough, revert below. The term "masochism" was
adopted by a professor of neurology at Stuttgart, Richard von
Krafft-Ebing, from the name of the Austrian novelist Leopold von
Sacher-Masoch (1836–1895), a prolific journalist as well as a
teacher. Sadism came to cover *sexual* pleasure in the infliction of
pain, masochism *sexual* pleasure in its reception; we shall only
pause to observe here that de Sade contained elements of masochism within him, and Sacher-Masoch of sadism. Freud then
coined the term translated as "sadomasochism" perhaps since he
did not come to understand the subject (modestly admitting as
much), and felt the existence of one tendency in a human being
presupposed the existence of the other.

Other investigators into what was considered abnormal behavior preferred yet other terms. Havelock Ellis, for instance,
found "algolagnia," from Greek *algos*-pain and *lagneia*-enjoyment,
"a convenient term [devised by Schrenck-Notzing] to indicate the
connection between sexual excitement and pain, without reference
to its precise differentiation into active and passive forms." It was
an omnibus term, in short, which made it unnecessary to codify
down to sadism and masochism in each instance, and also brought
into its ken a wide variety of phenomena (e.g., not only flagellation).
Recently we have seen professionals in the field using the term
"sexual sadomasochism," evidence of the manner in which its
original sense has been drained from it.

Furthermore, though convenient, algolagnia may possibly create more terminological inexactitudes than it solves. Masochism isn't simply sadism turned inside out. This was well brought out by Gilles Deleuze, a philosophy professor at the University of Paris and author of a work called *Présentation de Sacher-Masoch* (1967, translated as *Masochism* in the United States). "In order to interpret masochism," Deleuze writes, "it is not sufficient to reverse the pattern obtaining in sadism . . . The etiological fallacy of the unity of sadism and masochism may perhaps be due to an erroneous interpretation of the nature of the ego and the superego and of their interrelations."

We do not wish to clutter the present survey with these semantic modulations, more particularly since we are advancing our own. But anyone who thinks about it for a moment will acknowledge that the self-complementary definition sadomasochism may, in fact, leave out more than it relates together, while the man in the street probably uses "sadism" more often for cruelty unconnected with direct sexual satisfaction than otherwise. Indeed, the confidence with which supposedly intelligent people recently talked of the British "Moors murderers," young morons who used to cut up animals before they molested humans, as sadists is considerably surprising; it is, indeed, to fall into just those clichés de Sade mocked himself. Meanwhile, the widest description of all might be that of Geoffrey Gorer who calls sadism "the pleasure felt from the observed modifications on the external world produced by the will of the observer."

Any terms as blurred at the edges as these can nearly always be justifiably suspected of acting as a general blanket for taboo, with accordingly wide correlative claims. By this we mean that if the diacritica of definition are sufficiently fuzzy you can always see a source fear lurking underneath. The "Moors murderers" and Neville George Heath, to whom we will also come back below, are repeatedly held up as model examples of *le vice anglais,* with de Sade's "insanity" as the root of all evil; these are the pet witches of the contemporary unconscious.

Such people, it is said, were sadists. Their reading, their imaginative fantasies, the argument runs, erupted into overt behavior—

and they killed. Similarly, in America, child abusers—often barely-conscious drug addicts or alcoholics, numb to any sexual impulse —are conveniently lumped under the category of sadists. (Cp. the Kinsey Institute *Sex Offenders.*) It is not allowed that they were psychopaths first. In a sense, the burden of this book could be said to be that if there is one thing a "sadist" is *not,* it is a rapist. He knows too much about pain, for one thing. As a matter of fact, it was the contention of Magnus Hirschfeld that it is the woman who is the real sadist.

For these reasons alone—to avoid the opprobrium of the terminology and to get away from the stigma of aberrance by which such terms are constantly dogged—we intend throughout this study to use as much as possible the new popular coining "s-m." It comes conveniently to hand, is briskly American, and as yet remains relatively uncontaminated. It can be used to cover what we want it to cover, a vivid, erotic response to one of the purest and most beautiful and esthetic of human sexual relationships.

Having said as much, we must confess that the intersexual nature of our subject matter makes it extremely difficult to write about; and this may even have affected Freud's vocabulary. One point about s-m is that it is beyond biology so that in writing about it there is the difficulty of ascription of gender. The sado-masochist can be either male or female. Or, in a sense, both at once! A lot has been written lately about "desexing the language," even to the extent of using common gender terms (like *tey, ter,* and *tem*), but by this stage of English we are stuck with a grammar, willy-nilly. Male-oriented it may be. S-m is not. It can include both genders. Clear communication, however, makes it impossible to write something like he/she as a pronoun in its every mention.

If what we are proposing, then, is a sort of supreme sexual art form, why has our society feared it for so long?

THE
GROWTH
OF STUDY

In our society, an advanced technology in the second half of
the twentieth century, almost every aspect of human sexuality has
been explored and tabulated. For instance, the Institute for Sex
Research at Indiana University found that about 20% of males
and 12% of females report some degree of sexual arousal by sadomasochistic stories.

The Kinsey research is by now nearly a quarter of a century
old. Masters and Johnson have succeeded the marriage manuals.
Every sexual act has been objectified, mechanized, detached from
libido. In Susan Lydon's apt words, "Man becomes a spectator of
his own sexual experience" (*Ramparts* magazine). Is it not especially ironic that the one enhancement of sex which is always
intimately linked with love and tenderness and, especially, awareness of the feelings of one's partner, namely s-m, has not only
never been examined with care or respect, but has lingered so
long in the deepest dungeons of ignorance and superstition?

To begin with: Although Freud returned to the subject in
three important papers, he could not square up masochism with
his pleasure-principle. First, if we are motivated by desire for
pleasure why inflict pain on ourselves? Second, his system was
biologically structured—a face exposed by recent women's lib
attacks on it—so that, while sadism could to an extent be subsumed

under the pleasure-principle, masochism was impossible for him to swallow since it occurred in both sexes. Unlike Krafft-Ebing, Freud seems to have had little interest in s-m, and neither man examined any real practitioners. If Freud had known more about sadism, he would probably have been baffled to have found it, too, intersexual.

He came back to masochism in his 1919 paper "A Child is Being Beaten" (note the ubiquitously defenseless infant of the popular myth). Here he made his famous proposal that punishments may be agreeable as relief of guilt. Most mothers might nod in agreement to this as a surface judgment, but it begs the question: What is our guilt, and why? Freud then seems to have more or less thrown up his hands at the whole mess in a final return to the problem in "The Economic Problem in Masochism" of 1924, where we read: "For, if mental processes are governed by the pleasure-principle, so that avoidance of 'pain' . . . is their first aim, masochism is incomprehensible." If you think like Freud, it is.

Again, we do not wish to clog a book that is intended to be about joy with a lot of abstruse theory. Yet ignorance of the true nature of the subject forces us to clarify the background somewhat, before proceeding to practice. In surveying almost any other field of sexuality, such would not be necessary. This task of exegesis speaks for itself.

For we are a "scientific" culture, given to attaching electrodes to nipple and navel and thereby hoping to verify something called sexual response. To date, however, there has been no equivalent investigation into s-m, nor could such seem anything but remotely possible. Writing in the magazine *Sexual Behavior,* for September, 1971, Professor Eugene E. Levitt states categorically: "A survey of professional writings on sadomasochism for the past thirty years failed to unearth as many as ten scientific articles." We are venturing into a topic about which there is no empirical but the vaguest theoretical, information available.

Most of the latter, even, is anthological (Krafft-Ebing, Hirschfeld, the neo-Freudians, and the anthropologists). All of it is extremely vague, based on what an interested psychologist, Judson Brown, terms "casual report," while a lot of the so-called findings are frankly contradictory. Thus Freud found women naturally masochistic, whereas Havelock Ellis, though akin to Freud in many respects, roundly declared: "Masochism is more especially found in men." This was in *Studies in the Psychology of Sex* but in *The Sexual Impulse in Women* and in the most important paper (for our purpose) "Love and Pain" he voiced the same bias.

Quoting "Bloch," and bringing Rousseau's Mademoiselle Lambercier and England's inexorable Mrs. Brownrigg to the fore, Ellis here states: "Although masochism in a pronounced degree may be said to be rare in women, the love of active flagellation, and sadistic impulses generally are not uncommon among them. 'Bloch' believes they are especially common among English women." Krafft-Ebing's tentative observations, hilariously developed by James Joyce in the Circe section of *Ulysses*, would seem to side with the latter, with all three, or four, men regarding the response as firmly deviant.

Here is our point. The analytic litany which succeeded Freud simply shored up, by so many catalogues, the attitude that s-m was an aberration. At points Ellis alone rises above this attitude, and may have been a practitioner, or at least strong sympathizer, himself. One finally gets the impression that almost any rare state of being comes to be regarded, by such pseudoscientific "researchers," as aberrant, to be guided back into the mainstream of a given society by psychoanalysts.

Krafft-Ebing's voluminous *Psychopathia Sexualis* is precisely what its title suggests—extreme cases of cathection, often in petty criminals. Put beside Magnus Hirschfeld's *Sexual Anomalies* of 1936, and supported, out of literature, by a work like Mario Praz's *The Romantic Agony*, it furnishes the yardstick by which the s-m person has to date been measured and judged. By its canon most of the British male upper-class should have been impotent a century or more by now, instead of furnishing what, for a small state, may be said to have been a fairly effective civilization.

The legacy such writers left has been that the sadist is nearly always, in embryo, a violent criminal, what the French call an *obsédé*. Hirschfeld had the theory, which hits several nails on the head, if only inadvertently, that female sadism is necessarily total-

itarian. The *Gauleiterin* of the German concentration camps are
at this point usually sprung out of their horror closet. At the other
end of the spectrum we sense a blink of disbelief from the many
happily married, sexually potent s-m individuals of both sexes and
all ages, who have been good husbands, wives, lovers, mothers,
business and working people, but *who are told by their society they
are aberrant*.

Ashley Montagu writes:

> The English public schools, as is well known, were breeding-
> grounds for homosexuality, for these were all-boy schools and all
> the teachers were males, and usually the only love a boy ever
> received was from another boy or a master. The parental inadequa-
> cies from which many of these boys suffered produced a high
> rate of homosexuality. Such famous figures as Algernon Swinburne,
> J. A. Symonds, Oscar Wilde, Lord Alfred Douglas, and numerous
> others, were all products of such parents, and such schools.

Such is the glib stereotype, and one would like to test it by the
tools of contemporary sociology. Was in fact the "high rate of
homosexuality" in the Victorian public schools (to which the
"public" was not, of course, admitted) any higher than that of the
contemporary American public schools (to which it is)? And does
it matter? Of the four mentioned, as dreadful examples, three had
lively heterosexual lives when young and at least three were men of
great brilliance. Society would have been poorer without them. It is
the old mashed-potatoes syndrome (some murderers ate mashed
potatoes). Monckton Milnes, like Swinburne an ardent flagel-
lomane, seems to have been securely and contentedly oriented to
his society, a century ago. What happens is that cultural patterning gets embedded in our laws, and all the etiological research
comes to seem tangential to it. Rape is a social result.

Indeed, once more barring Ellis, the early clinicians seem to
have known no real s-m people. Even contemporary well-wishers
seem hopelessly at sea. The sympathetic Professor Duane Denfeld,
for instance, of the University of Connecticut's Sociology Department, blandly writes that "Analysis of the s-m correspondence
publications suggests a relatively high incidence of female interest

in sadism—particularly in the areas of domination, bondage, and discipline."

This all sounds very scholarly, until you realize that in many of these publications the majority of the s-m ads are written by one person, the editor, not uninterested in receiving the $2 forwarding fee charged by his magazine. Furthermore, the "high incidence of female interest" may be an equally high interest in the quick buck, such correspondents being from the profitable sorority of the professional dominatrix. Some of these termagants have crowded traveling schedules, flying from city to city with whip and strap in their Gucci bags. They are frequently immune to and bored by true s-m and are generally disliked by the devotee as giving the diversion a bad name. Some of Krafft-Ebing's "cases" seem, indeed, to have copied their fantasies from books.

A certain evidential insecurity is germane to this whole field, of course. In his excellent *Art and Pornography* Professor Morse Peckham comes to a long analysis of b & d (bondage and discipline) materials, in particular a set of drawings in the files of the Indiana University Institute for Sex Research; these were of "pony-girls," viz. young women domesticated into the roles of horses pulling a light carriage (or made to carry men). He observes "the lavish care spent on the mechanical details," i.e. of straps, bits, spurs, and the rest of the appurtenances of the slave stable. "Nowhere is there a hint of genital stimulation." He concludes that "the elaboration of the mechanical details" is evidence of "loving care" on the part of the self-indulgent artist. But unless the latter was the celebrated "John Willie," to whom we shall also return below and whose ideal fetish this was, the artist may simply have been acting under orders from a patron, and the elaboration of the effects have had no stimulus at all, remaining simply part of the design.

In fairness, a resumé of s-m theory should pay some tribute, however small, to the late Alfred C. Kinsey, and, in particular, to his associates Dr. Wardell B. Pomeroy and Dr. Paul H. Gebhard. They again still had to be extremely tentative, Kinsey himself citing the "fragile base of clinical commentary and casual report" that had come down on the subject. In sum, the Kinsey researchers found themselves faced with an impossible position. What to do with all these atypical individuals, these "deviants," handed down by Krafft-Ebing, Hirschfeld, Stekel, Schrenck-Notzing, and the rest of the great unpronounceables? Could it possibly be that a Southern Senator who wanted to be beaten by his typist was as American as apple pie? In his day Kinsey had no battery of electrodes to which to fly for refuge.

His Institute's findings were summarized by Gebhard. Leaning heavily on Ellis, the latter seems to have understood the cathection, if such it must be called. He found *true sadists* extremely rare, despite the advertisements in the pulp magazines. He responded to the important idea of helplessness and power, and understood Ellis' understanding of ritual, the *sine qua non* of any s-m worthy of the name:

> Accidental pain is not perceived as pleasurable or sexual. The average sadomasochistic session is usually scripted; the masochist must allegedly have done something meriting punishment, there must be threats and suspense before the punishment is meted out, etc. Often the phenomenon reminds one of a planned ritual or theatrical production . . . When one appreciates this one realizes that often in the relationship the sadist is merely servicing the masochist. The sadist must develop an extraordinary perceptiveness to know when to continue, despite cries and protests, and when to cease.

This is about as close as "research" has come to s-m, rather than sadism. The great cataloguers made no real effort to sort desired from undesired pain, or even to dissociate pain from cruelty (as in Ellis' "Love and Pain"). To the true s-m person, cruelty is anathema, he dislikes it more than anyone. But because cruelty involves pain, the tautology gets set up that since s-m people share some feelings shown by the famous case histories, all s-m addicts are psychotic. As well say that since most people have some s-m tendencies, we may conclude that almost everyone is deranged.

Language is self-reflexive. You cannot toss class terms like this around with impunity. If you blithely define someone as an alcoholic, a junkie, a hippie, the chances are that the character will come to act out the label. It is the *post hoc, ergo propter hoc* fallacy. Such feedback certainly seems to have been the case with several of Krafft-Ebing's supposed deviants. To those anxious boys he reports as having masturbated with special materials, like fur or velvet, a modern world might simply shrug: "Why not? Go ahead." They do not seem to have harmed anyone, let alone over-populated the globe. Even his pathetic baker's assistant in whose room 446 ladies' handkerchiefs were found only committed, by contemporary standards, the mildest of crimes, lightening a lady's pocket of a tiny morsel of linen. Yet he is described as "wet with sweat" for fear of detection simply because his society, and his society's physicians, made him feel he was deviant (Case 110).

During the writing of this book Manhattan's liberal *The Village Voice* announced a meeting of an s-m group (more m than s, as it transpired) called the Till Eulenspiegel Society—anyone wishing to see a collection of "slave freaks" was urged to attend. The authors of this book did so, together. Sure enough, there were the predictable responses to the term in evidence, clad in straps and chains, together with a number of marginal men and women (a high proportion of amputees and the generally disfigured was observed). Society simply gets the classifications it desires. This is another way of saying that as members of a culture we return to it what it gave us in childhood.

So the axis on which the early researchers rotated was a social gift. This makes their monumental compilations intensely sad— "Has it ever been your experience, as it has mine," Charles Baudelaire asks his readers, "that after spending long hours turning over a collection of bawdy prints, you fall into a great spell of melancholy?" Until World War II, with the exception of Ellis, we lose all sense of spectrum in the experience and simply have to pick up fragments from what Vladimir Nabokov nicely calls "the garbage cans of a Viennese tenement."

Frankly, the Austrian investigators were not themselves brought up in a society conceding women much psychic freedom and s-m demands complete equality of the sexes. In "Love and Pain" Ellis saw this paradox, while in *Studies in the Psychology of Sex* he made a considerable effort to examine the social substrate which gives deviation its very name, and to differentiate the love bite from the raging of a frothing epileptic:

> Every normal man in matters of sex, when we examine him carefully enough, is found to show some abnormal elements, and the abnormal man is merely manifesting in a disordered or extravagant shape some phase of the normal man. Normal and abnormal, taken in the mass, can all be plotted as variations of different degree on the same curve. The loving woman who exclaims: "I could eat you!" is connected by links, each in itself small, with Jack the Ripper. We all possess within us, in a more or less developed form, the germs of atrocities.

But the importance of Ellis to our argument is that he observed that *we do not all become* Jack the Rippers. Sexual atrocities are performed by an infinitesimally tiny percentage of the general population. Ellis thus strongly questioned both the classificatory techniques and the strong latency assumptions of the hard-breathing Austrians.

In his essay on eonism (transvestism or cross-dressing) Ellis properly challenges Hirschfeld's flat-footed classifying of Richard Wagner as a TV, or transvestite, on the basis of the great musician's love of silks and satins later in life. Ellis sensibly suggests that this was no more than was the same with Haydn, the natural inclination of "an artist who, after an early life of hardship, was at length able to gratify the repressed cravings of his physical and psychic sensitivity." If stuff fetishism is evidence of a latent condition, what on earth would Hirschfeld have done on the streets of New York or London today, let alone in an eighteenth-century drawing room?

No. For this kind of "investigator" something always is really something else. You have never shown the slightest sign all your life of wanting to be a cockroach, therefore you are a latent cockroach. By this canon of judgment we are surely all latent corpses, and Ellis took a giant step forward in firmly opposing it. For instance, when examining an elaborate analysis of a female TV called "Elsa B." made by Stekel's assistant Emil Gutheil, under

the former's direction, Ellis finds such a fantastic farrago of
fictional suggestion read into the objective events that he virtually
gives up:

> Certainly it would hardly be possible to pile up a greater number
> of complexes and perverse fantasies on to Elsa B.'s devoted head.
> They seem to be plentiful enough to account for anything. Yet one
> can well understand the sceptic feeling that the psychoanalyst is a
> kind of spider who spins his pathological web-complex so widely
> and so elaborately only in the hope that somewhere, at all events,
> the fly must become entangled.

Significance drawn out of study of complex human beings by
an analyst can sometimes become so subjective that one under-
stands what H. J. Eysenck meant of Freud in saying: "He was a
very great writer—he would have made a great novelist. In fact
I think he *did* make a great novelist." Ellis refused this direction,
writing in the same essay on eonism:

> We are not entitled to classify a group of cases in relation to a con-
> dition which for the most part they never reach. To do so is a
> regression to precisely the same kind of error as Krafft-Ebing made
> when he classified his interesting case of eonism in relation to in-
> sanity. We all, however normal, possess latent possibilities. But it is
> quite unprofitable, however correct, to classify the general popula-
> tion under the three heads of masked thieves, masked murderers,
> and masked adulterers, especially when we have to add that the
> same person may belong to all three groups.

Sadomasochist desires may arouse extraordinary intensity of
sensation, but that a baker becomes "wet with sweat" for stealing
a pocket handkerchief not much bigger than a postage stamp is
the responsibility of a social taboo. Society deeply fears any cur-
tailment of potency in a man—even more than the man may fear
it himself. One repression leads to another. In her sensible little
handbook *Any Wife or Any Husband* Joan Malleson puts it:
". . . potency in a man is limited *because a sadistic element linked
with it requires also to be repressed.*" (Italics hers.)
Certainly, the repression of s-m feelings may carry this danger.
If we could lift its need, we might truly advance the sphere of

sexual relationships. Frankly, there are times when the fears of the clinics about potency seem pretty pathological, as well as plain silly, themselves; it must surely be a rather odd type of woman in the first place who could choose to cohabit with a man who was impotent. But to admit as much would be to destroy the whole Freudian set-up.

So it is still not unusual to find the most permissive sexologists, even the Kinseyites, fearing to allow the unlocking of the cell door on this, our last limping taboo. Erich Fromm is, of course, the most distinguished total opponent (in *The Art of Loving*), but even the liberal Swedish Dr. Lars Ullerstam proposes, in his *The Erotic Minorities* of 1964, a sexual bill of rights for virtually every conceivable deviation *except* sadism—"Active algolagnia is the only erotic deviation I do not want to encourage without reservation." A few years later, that flippant little bestseller *The Sensuous Woman* followed up with frantic yips in favor of every form of heterosexual activity, again excepting s-m: "If he wants to resort to whips and chains or have you urinate on him or something of that nature, I agree with you, I think he's sick—and he should let you alone and go find a simpatico sickie or, better yet, get professional help" (the end of the spectrum represented here as representative is not without significance). Finally, *Screw* magazine, though priding itself on being sensationally liberal, has to date shown little but derision of s-m, while openly condoning the use of drugs.

What are Dr. Ullerstam's reservations? They turn out to be penal, indeed, no less than censored s-m under controlled conditions in organized brothels, presumably like those of erstwhile Egyptian or Mexican persuasion:

> Therefore the sadist should be helped, in my opinion, to achieve his special brand of happiness, provided that his wishes are not too bloodthirsty. The most suitable place for this is the brothel, where the execution can be controlled. Such a safety valve for this energy ought to be valuable both to the sadist and society. It could be argued that if one habituates the sadist to such satisfactions of his urge, one might thereby create a sexual compulsion, with unfortunate consequences. The sadist could always get into the predicament of not having enough money to afford a visit to the brothel, just

when the urge makes itself felt. But I think we ought to take this
risk, considering the values of human happiness that lie in the
balance.

Well-intentioned as this is, it has little to do with genuine s-m.
The latter is invariably predicated on a relationship between human beings which prostitution, by its nature, negates. In s-m pain
is both given *and accepted* as a token of love. Prostitution could
not supply this need, and probably only sullies it.

Once again, the anthropologist Ashley Montagu, equally
judicious and liberal as Dr. Ullerstam, devotes several pages of
his useful book on tactuality, *Touching* (1971), to the phenomenon
and treats it as plain sexual pathology: "Flagellation, generally on
the buttocks and thighs, has been a most frequent form of sexual
perversion." Nor have we either space or inclination to consider
here what is now a vast library of slander of the mode, ranging
from the lucubrations of D. H. Lawrence to the fury of his followers (like David Holbrook) which certainly reads as pathic.
Such scarcely constitutes study at all, being mainly diatribe. Read
George Steiner on de Sade ("sheer nonsense . . . pedantic frenzy
. . . inescapable monotony"). High-level intellectuals have been
notoriously inhospitable to a trend which they sense as too close
to them for comfort, and the reactions of a Steven Marcus or an
Irving Kristol to the subject are really too predictable to need,
or bear, quotation here.

Two statements must serve to complete our summary, and its
plea for a new terminology, before passing on to the man whose
life ran beside Freud's, but whose vision of the reality of this relationship was far more whole. The first is drawn again from Joan
Malleson's guide and is perhaps a hopeful sign (despite the customary context of impotence) of a new enlightenment concerning
this much-abused love play:

> The extent to which sadomasochistic activities permeate a sex-
> ual relationship is obviously a personal matter. A man who needs to
> beat a woman before intercourse is open to no condemnation pro-
> vided the woman consents; a masochistic woman often seeks to be
> beaten. But without this chance fortune in the choice of a partner,
> the lot of a highly sadistic person may indeed be wretched.

Our second citation is unusual since it comes from a self-confessed devotee and would itself have been lodged, presumably, as some sort of case history in the lumbering lexicons of Hirschfeld and Krafft-Ebing. Yet almost every writer we have reviewed, with the possible exception of Ellis, has viewed the subject from without. In *The Village Voice* for May 13, 1971, Terry Kolb, a significantly pseudonymous co-founder of the Till Eulenspiegel Society, writes:

> Surprising as it may seem, the high intellectual character of many masochists is only to be expected when you consider how intellectual the s/m mystique really is. Reik states categorically that a person with a weakly developed imagination cannot become a masochist. In the eyes of the public, a sadomasochistic scene is a very sordid affair with a "sex fiend" brutalizing an equally weird victim. It is seen as a scene without sensitivity or any aesthetic feeling. The exact opposite is the case. The s/m relationship is the most democratic that exists!

HAVELOCK
ELLIS

Of all those writers on or collectors of sadomasochism mentioned so far, Henry Havelock Ellis (1859–1939) alone studied with interest, and some sympathy, what we have termed s-m. In this respect he was truly a pioneer.

His life ran almost exactly beside that of Freud (1856–1939), but his reputation was for long eclipsed by the celebrated Austrian investigator, to whom he paid generous tribute. At times Ellis could write a leaden style, he was not gifted with Freud's fluency of pen, but he is differentiated from Freud, Adler, and even Jung, in not presuming to hand down a system. The least dogmatic of sexological writers, he was never one to call something like masochism "incomprehensible" because it didn't fit into a schema. He approached his subject in a spirit of real inquiry rather than, as appears to have been the case with Krafft-Ebing, thinly concealed distaste. "All living things," he wrote in "The Discipline of Pain," to be found in *My Confessional*, "are perpetually haunted by the fear of pain, for the fear of pain is but another aspect of the love of life."

It is indeed possible that this curiosity had a personal origin. It has been said that he himself had a "tortured adolescence." Was it such? There is the famous story of the boy who, at the Poplars School at Tooting (perfect s-m names!), rode "H.E." like a horse round and round the dormitory, using spurs fashioned from pins.

Taken out of context, this naturally sounds like the kernel of a maiming experience. But the truth is that nearly every British boy of the time knew his bully at school (and not only every British boy). The judgment is as American as Edmund Wilson's on Kipling's allegedly wounding experiences at United Services College. Wilson tells us that "Stalky & Co." is "a hair-raising picture of the sadism of the English public-school system," with the masters "constantly caning the boys in scenes that seem almost as bloody as the floggings in old English sea stories." To judge by contemporary U.S. standards like this is perfectly absurd; the truth is probably that Kipling had a rather mild public school education when compared with what went on at Shrewsbury, Rugby, and, especially, the Scottish schools.

Further, Ellis was blessed with a beautiful and strong-minded mother, on which much store has also been set. But there is little connection we can see between his love for his mother and the uneven tenor of his own matrimonial life later. Did Ellis really write *Gynecocracy* and *Sadopaedia?* The suppositions that he penned clandestine pornography seem unlikely. Indeed, far from turning on his mother as a dominant figure (even over her rather weak sea-captain husband), as Samuel Butler turned on his in *The Way of All Flesh*, Ellis was actually stimulated to exert himself on behalf of womanhood by her. "Throughout life," he was to say, "I have possessed an instinctive and unreasoned faith in women, a natural and easy acceptance of the belief that they are entitled to play a large part in many fields of activity. The spectacle of my mother's great and unconscious power certainly counted for much in that faith and that belief."

Still, whatever the motivations, immaterial to us, Ellis was into s-m, certainly into urolagnia. And the whiff of clinical ether is lifted from his pages as a result. Part of his helpfulness in the field was doubtless due to his instinctive understanding of the role of fantasy in life, to which we shall come back below. He was well read, edited Elizabethan dramatists, published studies of Nietzsche and Zola. He knew how to distinguish fantasy from reality, and he had a strong respect for the artistic imagination.

Frankly, a general public seems loath to do either where s-m is at issue. Reading a letter in, say, a magazine as glossily successful as *Penthouse* appears to be, we fail to play fair to s-m's essential fantasy. A woman writes in to explain that her "family physician" has pierced her nipples by which her husband now ties her up; another expatiates at length on being painfully bound by her lover for forty-eight hours in a single position.

Such excesses might well result in real damage (as would the same with food or drink). Any obsessive mania is scarcely "normal"—a housewife could indulge in such a passion for cleanliness that her home became uninhabitable as a result—and only a psychopath would try to put these patent fantasies into effect. Yet reading such letters, a non-initiate sees them as so much offered reality. (This is what s-m people do?) Their repudiation is then immediate and violent partly because T. C. Mits (The Celebrated Man in the Street) feels himself suddenly threatened by powerful subconscious urges he is reluctant to admit as existing, least of all in a contemporary technology.

Ellis clearly sensed the human potential that would be liberated if all these psychic energies could in some way be harnessed and eventuated. His hypotheses are often crudely reduced to so much stimulation of weak or flagging sex drives. On the contrary, in the "Love and Pain" monograph, where Ellis set out what is the most insightful psychosexual explanation of s-m prior to World War II, he studied animal courtship as a mock-combat since it was only a *semblance* of combat, and an *appearance* of cruelty. While the love play of some animals, therefore, undeniably resembles a minor pugilistic contest, both male and female are in fact seeking the same end, that of sexual union at the joint pitch of highest excitement.

Bolstering himself up with (almost unnecessary) anthropological detail, Ellis then collects for our edification specimens of much the same from savage or semi-savage societies, where courtship is by mock-conquest (not invariably male, one instance being of the Kirghiz maiden who is armed with a whip against unwanted suitors). Margaret Mead's *Sex and Temperament* could have helped out further.

In all these instances we see a dynamic inter-relationship of will and imagination. Ellis then proceeds to lead us into the copious and extremely fortunate correspondence he seems to have had with sadomasochistic women, for the first time in this literature surreptitiously enjoying themselves. Despite the proviso, evidently inherited from "Bloch"-Dühren, that "pronounced masochism seems to be much rarer in women than sadism," the speculation is at stake: Can the paradox of pain be converted into the dynamics of love? "We can see, therefore," Ellis writes, "how, if pain acts as a stimulant to emotion, it becomes the servant of pleasure by supplying it with surplus stored force."

This is crucial, even if the realization is possibly prompted by Nietzsche ("One ought to learn anew about cruelty," *Beyond Good and Evil*). Modern Apollonian man finds himself deeply tempted by this animal anima of Dionysiac intoxication. How can he return to nature, in the deodorant civilization? How re-unite the animal and spiritual?

By the end of "Love and Pain," then, s-m comes to seem something of a civilized re-enactment of natural courtship combat (the emphasis on the buttocks being present in both modes). By implication, biology is transcended, the sexual dichotomy lulled into aesthetic union. The cruelty of nature is allowed into the arena, solved and resolved—at least for a moment of ecstatic love play, and human wisdom.

A consequence is that the true s-m individual is likely to be one who is highly sensitive, even hypersensitive, being so intensely aware of (and aghast at) the cruelty of nature and the power of the animal instincts. Ellis himself unequivocally states that s-m occurs typically in "highly sensitive" children. Hence the true paradox that the s-m person is usually one of the most tender of beings. Again, Ellis proposes as much (here relying on Montaigne):

> The strong man is more apt to be tender than cruel, or at all events knows how to restrain within bounds any impulse to cruelty; the most extreme and elaborate forms of sadism (putting aside such as are associated with a considerable degree of imbecility) are more apt to be allied with a feminine organization.

In other words, sadism is not, as previously considered, excessive masculinity. Nor is the masochistic person necessarily one who gets any enjoyment out of being hurt and/or humiliated in daily life. So the atavistic element (rather reluctantly admitted by Krafft-Ebing) is suddenly "placed" by Ellis, allowed into life to be handled by the imagination.

Mental representations may be extreme to the point of utter impossibility. This can be a thorny matter. In de Sade they were doctrinally so, in order to call out a reciprocally intense activity by the imagination in their transcendence. If you can get enjoyment out of eating excrement, say, you have demonstrably overcome the animal (which is another way of saying returned to the animal under controlled conditions—a cat eats its own vomit). We are not recommending either activity here, and would strongly disrecommend both for s-m love play!

But aphrodisiac literature can sometimes function in this way, while in life very strong emotions—anger, hate, fear—have a notorious overflow effect, triggering off sexual response. Hence the fetishists and extremists, those who want to see blood or drink urine, who are offered up to us on the Viennese sexual smörgasbord as so many typical warning Cases. "Ivan Bloch"-Eugen Dühren goes about de Sade in this spirit.

We shall have to deal with the s-m milieu in more detail below, but it can here be asserted, with the confidence of the authors' own experience, that no boy or girl prefect at any British school got or gets any sexual pleasure *during* the actual infliction of a caning. (A monitor watching possibly might.) Basically, justice is at stake, and God is always right. The schoolchild may well reflect on the scene *later* and be stimulated by it. And this is why T. C. Mits gets led astray by s-m manifestations in public print, either those famous "Letters to the Editor" or plain pornography.

Secondly, as Ellis observed, "memory can only preserve impressions as a whole; physical pain consists of a sensation and of a feeling. But memory cannot easily reproduce the definite sensation of pain, and thus the whole memory is disintegrated and speedily forgotten." It is probably true in general that a boy who has known the cane at school might make a mental picture of a more severe type than a girl who had only known the infliction of a slipper. Indeed, most girls might well be satisfied for masturbatory purposes with images of the ritual involved, bending over, raising the skirt, rather than of any pain at all. Similarly, Americans who were knocked around by a parent, rather than chastised with love, tend later to think of s-m fantasies of the most brutal kind imaginable—all bike-boys, chains, straps, and whips.

Just as s-m, a transmuting agency, seems particularly prevalent in clean countries (Sweden, England, Denmark, and—yes—Switzerland), so we would venture to hazard the generalization that crimes against the person are higher in those milieux which have no s-m in their psychic background (compare Italy with England). Obviously, one can juggle with statistics as one wishes, especially when they are non-existent, but it is still a fact that in 1971 there were over 1,500 homicides in New York City as against 75 in London, a figure which in England caused widespread concern. Ellis himself conjectured that the courtship period is today the highest in "crimes of blood," which he thus designated as carrying "a kind of tertiary sexual character."

Just so. If he was right, and s-m is atavistic, there seem less and less overt outlets for love play of the nature in our hyperrationalized society. The adolescent is in this sense in a state of permanent frustration. We ourselves are not making ridiculous pretensions at this stage of history that all our sexual ills could be cured if teen-agers would indulge in spanking, or something of the sort. You cannot reverse the course of a civilization in a day. But the history of ferocious wars in this century (the technological century) is scarcely very encouraging.

Moreover, Ellis' whole attitude in this direction seems remarkably healthy. Sadomasochist tendencies can manifest their appearance in the individual long before puberty, as the experience of both writers of this book can attest. It is easier to think of this as atavistic than as originating in treatment in a pram at the age of two—in every instance. Lists of confessional biographies, elicted later in life, bemuse the reader with the idea that sight of some early spanking scene turned an otherwise "normal" development (whatever that may mean) aside into "deviant" channels (whatever that may mean). There are the good ladies Ellis himself lists who confess to being turned on by, respectively if not necessarily in order, bullfights, vomit, and crushed frogs—scarcely scenes they would have seen in a pram.

One of the authors of this book attended an ultra-liberal weekend sponsored by CSIES, a sincere organization for the dissemination of information about sex (now sailing under the abbreviated acronym CSI). Counselors answer telephone questions. Amid the pornographic movies, and psychedelic light effects, there was one brief vision of s-m. A young girl, sprawling barefoot on the obligatory mattress, was heard to mutter to her neighbor, "What a hang-up!" The next stage in the itinerary is then conceived to be, on one hand, the Englishman the Goncourts report as getting sexual stimulation out of watching executions and, on the other, Tolstoy's heroine who hoped that her husband would hang her over a precipice (leading Ellis into some fairly pointless philosophizing about suspension and sex).

Surely it is more comforting to look human personality full in the face and frankly admit what Ellis put as follows:

> While in men it is possible to trace a tendency to inflict pain, on the women they love, it is still easier to trace in women a delight in experiencing physical pain when inflicted by a lover, and an eagerness to accept subjection to his will. Such a tendency is certainly normal.

It is all at once possible that Krafft-Ebing's trembling army of Cases, "wet with sweat," who seem to have made a sterling contribution to society as dentists, soap manufacturers, "merchants," whose first crime was to masturbate, their second being to visit a prostitute, were far from what we call "kinky" today. Pain is another aspect of love, Ellis wrote. It behooves us to make it so.

In this slight summary of an undoubtedly great man we have not tried to set "H.E." up as some sort of new sexological luminary. He was distinctly limited. He saw sex, to an extent, as propagation of the species, but he was a kind and enlightened person who also wrote, "There is no finer task in life than to let a little

light and sunshine into those parts of it which have so long been
shut up to fester in darkness."

The consequence of his curiosity, personally motivated as it
may have been, is for us highly germane. To utilize fear, apprehension (anger, even) as sexual overflow devices could be truly
creative. Perhaps, by Ellis' tentative probings (and they were little
more), s-m might come to be considered as an aristocracy of sex.
"The day for academic discussion concerning the 'subjection of
women' has gone by," he declared. "The tendency I have sought
to make clear is too well established by the experience of normal
and typical women—however numerous the exceptions may be—
to be called in question." Women, he well saw, are simply not
imperfect men. They "have the laws of their own nature; their
development must be along their own lines, and not along masculine lines."

Pain, Ellis insisted, should be differentiated *toto caelo* from
cruelty. Sadism and masochism could be seen "as complementary
emotional states." De Sade was not Judge Jeffreys. "Any impulse
of true cruelty is almost outside the field altogether . . . In algolagnia, as in music, it is not cruelty that is sought; it is the joy of
being plunged among the waves of that great primitive ocean of
emotions which underlies the variegated world of our every day
lives." Pain then becomes "intense emotional excitement," a stimulus sought as well as given: "the real object throughout was to
procure strong emotion and not to inflict cruelty." Just as some
birds call out courtship cries at sight of an enemy (some women
find anger in a man turning-on), so our parched sexual instincts
could be aroused to new heights by a recognition of the true relationship between love and pain.

Ellis' female correspondents apparently told him as much.
One woman wrote: "The fascination of whipping, which has
always greatly puzzled me, seems to be a sort of hankering after
the stimulus of fear . . . Excessive fear is demoralizing, but it seems
to me that the idea of being whipped gives a sense of fear which
is not excessive. It is almost the only kind of pain (physical) which
is inflicted on children or women by persons whom they can love
and trust, and with a moral object."

Another lady of his acquaintance—she has been referred to in print (of course) as a patient, but does not seem to have been so—described these circumstances with the precision of the s-m addict:

> *Actual* pain gives me no pleasure, yet the *idea* of pain does, *if inflicted by way of discipline and for the ultimate good of the person suffering it* . . . I only get pleasure in the idea of a woman submitting herself to pain and harshness from the man she loves when the following conditions are fulfilled: 1. She must be absolutely sure of the man's love. 2. She must have perfect confidence in his judgment. 3. The pain must be deliberately inflicted, not accidental. 4. It must be inflicted in kindness and for her own improvement, not in anger or with any revengeful feelings, as that would spoil one's ideal of the man. 5. The pain must not be excessive and must be what when we were children we used to call a "tidy" pain; i.e., there must be no mutilation, cutting, etc. 6. Last, one would have to feel very sure of one's own influence over the man.

The passage is particularly compelling since it suggests so much control, i.e. art. A Sadean fantasy frequently has the infliction of punishment accompanied by a mandatory smile on the face of the victim of it. Outside the sexual sphere pain is condemned. One of Ellis' lady correspondents who seems to admit an atavistic element ("why should a child of six do such things unless it were a natural instinct?") recounts how excited she used to become by visiting an old Australian convict ship, "where all the means of restraint are shown." The Museo Criminale in Rome (and other European criminal museums) had roughly the same effect on the authors of this volume. *There,* one realized, were the actual instruments and appurtenances of genuine fustigation. At the same time, the photographs and depictions of outright brutality in such museums probably horrified us more than most.

So s-m is a personification of the imagination. In his fine paper "Masochism in Modern Man" Dr. Theodor Reik remarks that "individuals with weakly developed imagination show no inclination to become masochists," and again, "I only wish to stress here that the importance of the fantasy as the very essence of masochism has not yet been appreciated in analytical theories." But, as

he amusingly, if somewhat mischievously, adds, it has not neglected to take its revenge, in the fanciful nature of the notions
propounded.

"The technique of sex," Ellis himself presciently observed,
"is not necessarily the art of love and may be antagonistic to it."
When he wrote that "all living things" were haunted by pain as
an aspect of love of life he was saying a great deal. He was proposing an attitude towards aggression that transcends Freud and
indeed sounds like an echo in advance of current English object-
relations theory. "Aggression is not necessarily destructive at all,"
Clara M. Thompson writes, in *Interpersonal Psycho-Analysis*. "It
springs from an innate tendency to grow and master life which
seems to be characteristic of all living matter." There is, thus, a
spectrum of behavior, of civilization, and control, which separates
the man in the street from Jack the Ripper. In Anthony Storr's
wise words, "No sharp dividing line can be drawn between such
individuals and the 'normal' man, since the same psychological
mechanisms are operative in both." In truth, in all of us—and
Ellis recognized this.

Yet if it is fairly clear that infliction of pain on another is common to the animal species, meditative toleration or even enjoyment
of it is a uniquely human property. Animals manage to be cruel
to each other without being self-destructive, principally by those
conventional displays of aggression Ellis himself alluded to: subsequent studies of animal societies have simply proved him right.
Aggressive behavior against a political foe in something like Congress or the House of Commons, an adversary to be a dining
companion later perhaps, or the ritual squaring-off of two at-
torneys in a law court, are the best we can do, in a democratic
technology, to simulate such conventions.

But man's greatness and his terror are that he alone is able to
imagine what his victim feels. This is what a lot of Baudelaire is
about. In one magnificent, agonized poem Baudelaire is both executioner and criminal. This the animal may not be. "No one,"
writes Anthony Storr, "would have been concerned to free slaves
or to prevent child-labor unless, imaginatively, he could put himself into the shoes of a slave or an ill-treated child." This is well

seen. In humans altruism is what is exacted by cruelty; we have witnessed spectacular examples of this rule in American liberalism of late.

Such considerations logically bring us to the next stage in our exposition, the vexed problem of locale. Is there, in fact, a correlation between what is dubbed "the child-whipping milieu" and what Ellis' charming correspondent called "tidy" pain in adults, viz. s-m?

THE
SPANKING
SETTING

In every Englishman's subconscious, claimed the French writer Pierre Daninos, lurks a cat-o'-nine-tails and a schoolgirl in black stockings. More portentously, Hirschfeld postulated a "national perversion" for every country and flatly stated that "historians and sexologists are unanimous in regarding England as the classic land of flagellation." This has become a prime sexual myth of our times, despite the fact that when Hirschfeld wrote the above there were virtually no "sexologists" extant at all.

What, one wonders, is the "national perversion" of Poland? Biting bananas while standing on the head? In *The Second Sex* Simone de Beauvoir recounts the story told her by a prostitute of "a German officer [who] wanted her to parade naked around the room with an armful of flowers, while he imitated a bird taking flight." It is parenthetically interesting that, although this odd client treated the girl concerned with the utmost "generosity and politeness," paid highly for his vagary (which gave her no trouble), she disliked the business, preferring the routine in-out. Imagination had made her momentarily uncomfortable.

In any event, whenever the question of culturality comes up in any discussion of sadomasochism, England always rates first mention. It is traditionally viewed as the s-m center, and sadism has

been called *le vice anglais*.* Thus at the start of his Appendix to
The Romantic Agony Mario Praz finds it in him to state with
ringing confidence:

> It seems to be an assured fact that sexual flagellation has been prac-
> ticed in England with greater frequency than elsewhere—if, at least,
> we are to believe Pisanus Fraxi and Doctor Dühren, who have
> made special researches into the subject. Their conclusion appears
> also to be confirmed by the fact that literature on this subject comes
> mainly from Anglo-Saxon sources.

We do not mean to argue this unanswerable semantic trap all
the way down the line here, so much as to try to suggest some
helpful qualifications. In any event, you cannot finally pigeon-
hole these interlinking problems; or, as Gilles Deleuze puts it,
"Sadism and masochism are confused when they are treated like
abstract entities each in isolation from its specific universe." Praz
is referring to "Bloch"-Dühren's remarks that "It is well known
that England is today the classic land of sexual flagellation" (*Der
Marquis de Sade und Seine Zeit*), and "in no land has the passion
for the rod been as systematically developed and cultivated as in
England" (*Das Geschlechtsleben in England*).

Countless commentators since have easily inherited this heady
opinion, based on similar "special researches." In *The Other
Victorians* Steven Marcus taps the Pisanus Fraxi or Ashbee collection in the British Museum, finds a major portion of it flagellantine, understandably assumes it to have been the purlieu of the
Victorian male upper class, and equally understandably completes
the syllogism—the British ruling class was highly responsive to
sadomasochism.

Such is the general stereotype. Just as the English love animals,
they also cane children. We have instanced Edmund Wilson's
reaction to reading about Kipling; when the same critic came to
review for *The New Yorker* the six-volume edition of Swinburne's

---

* The only example we found, in the course of perusing a huge literature, of this
term being used to characterize male homosexuality was in Stephen Barlay's *Bondage*
(New York: Funk & Wagnalls, 1969, originally published in England by Heinemann
under the title *Sex Slavery*); this usage is quite atypical.

correspondence, in which we see the great Victorian poet, indirect donor of *Anactoria* and *Dolores* in prize editions to generations of diligent British schoolgirls, commissioning birching pictures from the painter Simeon Solomon, Wilson was simply horrified. How could this happen? Such a civilized race . . . and then all those distressing entries in the Index under "flagellation."

After which, Professor John McLeish of the Psychology Department of the University of Leeds bustled forward to remind us that England has lately been the only country with a popular movement to restore the corporal punishment of criminals (ironically enough, it was a black dictator who, when the Caribbean island of Grenada recently became independent of Britain, restored the ancient Flogging Act).

Now, before grappling with some of the swarm of arguments, counterarguments, rejoinders and surrejoinders which bristle instantly to the surface here, we must clarify that we are dealing in the dark. "Bloch" does not seem to have made any "special researches into the subject" at all, at least by any form of contemporary standards. S-m pornography is hardly indicative of class. We ourselves, both brought up in England, feel quite sure that the lower classes there were and are also extremely interested in the subject, sexually. For a starter, take a look at the correspondence columns of the pre-war *London Life*, which we know to have been generally genuine, at least for many years.

If the lower classes had had the money a century ago to buy the expensive pornography Professor Marcus insists on as typical, they might well have purchased its s-m exempla. Furthermore, there was and is a mass of sadomasochist aphrodisia published in France and Germany—and not only for rich British tourists, either. The recent *ballets roses* revelations in France were pure s-m. And it is rather odd, when you come to think about it, that the founders (as it were) of sadism and masochism were French and Austrian respectively.

In a word, the facts are far too sparse to make any analysis anything but superficial. We are in the realm of total conjecture. As Professor Levitt admits,

Thus far, the lore of sadomasochism has come largely from the offices of practitioners from the verbalizations of patients, the narratives of anonymous correspondents, and from diverse hearsay sources. Analysis of heterogeneous data collected in unstandardized situations can be informative to a degree, but it is only a preliminary to scientific investigation. It does not substitute for it.

Since conjecture can be total, the theories about *le vice anglais* have been truly rococo. We hear that there is a correlation between the need to suffer and depression; hospital admissions for depression (i.e. masochistically inclined people) are nine times more common in England and Wales than in the United States (Professor Aaron T. Beck, University of Pennsylvania). But yet the diagnosis of depression is notoriously vague. Psychological terms vary widely, even within the same language; "constitutional inferiority," in England an anxiety ailment thought benign, was once grounds for finding an alien inadmissible to America.

Next we learn, from another learned authority, that since sexual relations were inhibited in British boarding schools (though evidently not in the same kind of establishments elsewhere), the resultant guilt evoked by resultant homosexual attachments set up a craving for correction. A craving, we might add, that neither of the present authors recollects as a feature of their English childhoods.

Frankly, we would like to lay these restless demons of the psyche to rest once and for all. The interpretations almost invariably suggest masochism, rather than sadism, since the arbiters are usually American; moreover, as a "sadistic" nation, England has been conspicuously moderate in its international relations. However, if we permit ourselves one sweeping generalization of the sort, it shall be that the characteristic s-m spectrum in England is dominant male/submissive female, while in modern America it is the reverse. We will try to develop this helpfully in our next section.

First and foremost, the term "child-whipping milieu" is unfortunate. Children are not and were not *whipped* in England, they were chastised. We also want to make it quite clear that neither author of the present volume is in the slightest in favor of corporal correction of children; in fact, in our experience, s-m people are unanimously against it. The Till Eulenspiegel Society held a debate on the question and all attending felt strongly the same way. It is simply that one has inherited an imagistic background . . . and it is *not* of "whipping." Exposed in the London *Observer,* the recent Hyde Lees case of a schoolmaster who exceeded the ritual amount of cuts in an Approved (or Reform) school aroused no less than national horror, and the anonymous boy's wealed buttocks were shown in several publications, not simply for the sake of sensation. A few years ago we strolled through the City, the financial section of London, to see cool yellow canes on sale at newsstands; a month later, driving through country districts in France, we saw merciless leather martinets, with tough biting thongs.

It is true that England long retained public flogging, that of women only ceasing around the turn of the eighteenth century. We remember reading with avidity in our own youth of the three "Mayfair playboys" in the *News of the World,* then the newspaper with the largest circulation in the world; these young men who had assaulted an old lady were sentenced to and given eight strokes with the cat. Of course it was interesting reading, though not nearly as much so as was the story of a girl bending over in tight knickers for six of the best with a cane in *Nursery World* (impounded off the lap of a dozing governess.) In other words, there is a distinction in *kind,* not merely in degree, between child and criminal punishment in England (and under the latter head we would also designate military and naval floggings of adults).

We believe Ellis. Flagellation is by its nature so intimately sexual, atavistic if you will, its sexual links are so strong that it should really only be eventuated under extremely controlled, Apollonian conditions (i.e. by consenting adults). S-m is essentially, for us, an adjunct to intercourse on the part of those who want to do it. Now, to introduce such a potentially powerful aphrodisiac into the lives of children is dangerous since unrelated: it raises an emotion only to abort or veto it. An intense psychic frustration, a sort of minor *coitus interruptus,* results.

Still and all, the child is punished by someone interested in its welfare. The criminal, on the other hand, is a grown adversary, self-declared. The cat-o'-nine-tails was accordingly administered by a stranger, who would never see his victim again, was originally even masked, and who laid on as hard as the human arm would permit (to such an extent that one of the three mentioned above had his score of strokes administered in two sessions, separated by a week).

This was so much social retribution, revenge. In the case of the child it was usually the parent who chastised, and the point was that the punishment was administered with love, with interest in the other's being, and with moderation. In our opinion this was assuredly the case in the British lower as well as the upper classes, despite the horror stories to the contrary, usually involving alcoholic parents.

What, then, of the teacher? The teacher was no relative. Well, in a sense the best were. They were parental delegates, given mandates by fathers and mothers whom they sometimes, we recall, telephoned for permission to punish corporeally (generally to be urged on to be more severe than they themselves had ever wished to be). Was this the case in Germany, France, Sweden? From what we have read and heard, private schools in Switzerland, certainly those for girls, have perpetuated c.p. (corporal punishment) for children far more zealously than has modern England. Has the "child-whipping milieu" been a sponsor of s-m in those countries and cultures? Why not *le vice suisse*? Professor Levitt claims that "there appears to be some connection between a child-whipping milieu and the occurrence of sadomasochism in adulthood." We definitely need to refine this down a bit, since there is simply no empirical data at hand for the conclusion.

We have said that children were not "whipped" in England, despite Dickens. This should be qualified. The great birching headmasters, Keate of Eton and Busby of Westminster, appear not to have been governing schools so much as fighting back anarchic child ghettoes. The *Nicholas Nickleby* stereotype was later, and other. In Keate's day there were few masters at Eton at all and, rather like a New York City high school now, the pupils regularly threatened to assert their own authority, letting loose large rats during prayers and the like. As Lytton Strachey tells us of Keate, "Every Sunday afternoon he attempted to read sermons to the whole school assembled; and every Sunday afternoon the whole school assembled shouted him down."

This is scarcely an s-m situation. Headmasters like this did not know their pupils or, rather, only knew their backsides, which they spent whole mornings birching to blood. In fact, the cane was brought into these so-called public schools because it could inflict as intense a pain within a shorter period. At the girls' schools it was different. Helen Burns was very lightly birched at the beginning of *Jane Eyre* and we now know, from the researches of the Brontë Society, that Charlotte exaggerated the discipline of Cowan Bridge School in her fictional Lowood. But long birchings at the boys' schools took up so much time. Strachey describes it as follows:

> It was a system of anarchy tempered by despotism. Hundreds of boys, herded together in miscellaneous boarding-houses, or in that grim "Long Chamber" at whose name in after years aged statesmen and warriors would turn pale, lived, badgered and over-awed by the furious incursions of an irascible little old man carrying a bundle of birch-twigs, a life in which licensed barbarism was mingled with the daily and hourly study of the niceties of Ovidian verse.

This potentially explosive combination of freedom and terror was brought to book, and reduced to some order, when the headmastership of Rugby fell vacant in 1827 and Thomas Arnold accepted the position. *Tom Brown's Schooldays* was destined to become a sort of darling of the clinics, with David Benedictus' *The Fourth of June* doing the same for Eton a century later. Hazing underclassmen in front of the fire came to be accepted as characteristic of British schoolboy sadism.

In fact, the creation of equality among peers within the school (and a hierarchy outside it) was extremely genial, and is little understood in America, it seems. In America it is looked at, we believe, from the other end of the spectrum. By making every boy in the Sixth Form automatically a Praepostor, Arnold hoped to turn his school into "a place of really Christian education," i.e. of

individuals as simulacra of the civilized human race . . . and God
always right. A few years ago we found that at Eton as many as
sixty boys could cane without the necessity to consult a master for
approval first. Very few of these actually did so, and the Benedictus
stereotype was entirely exceptional. There would have been instant
complaints from parents if it had not been, particularly since the
liberal headmaster, Anthony Chenevix-Trench, was then closely
scrutinizing the whole system. And of course every British schoolboy knows it is far preferable to be caned by a master, often
antique and doddering, than by a knowing peer.

The peer-punishment system, which Arnold certainly ordained
if not originated, is nuclear to s-m which we must repeatedly stress
is a relationship among equals. It directly responds to Ellis' lady
correspondent: "The pain must not be excessive, it must be deliberately inflicted, in kindness and for the woman's improvement,
not in anger or vindictively. She must have complete confidence
in her lover's judgment and ability to control himself." What an
echo of Arnold who, in Strachey's educated accents, "was particularly disgusted by the view that 'personal correction,' as he phrased
it, was an insult or a degradation to the boys upon whom it was
inflicted; and to accustom young boys to think so appeared to him
to be 'positively mischievous.' "

The accepted cliché is that all factory workers used to strike a
child about the head rather than go through what Gebhard well
describes as "a planned ritual or theatrical production," but the
records are meager. The great Victorian reformers like Ruskin
simply show control coded into the culture with a very high valuation at all levels of society, an apogee of this admiration appearing
in the kind of schools presided over by the Dr. Arnolds of England.

Almost certainly there were, much later on, the Dr. Arnolds
of Germany, too. But the emphasis inherited, if not inherent, in
Germany was on the production of a warrior class. England's was
on a mercantile administrative class. The Mensur scars were supposed to make a man attractive in Germany, but their infliction
had little sexual reverberation (and thus goes unrepresented, so
far as we can find out, in German pornography). The reputation
England gained as the principal locale for s-m owes its inception,

in our opinion, to the simple fact that in the British Isles it was, until recently, highly visible.

In other words, ritualistic child punishment was quite normal. This is what the French call "*exact*." A girl's fantasies literally were reality (knickers, skirt lifting, six of the best). Girls told each other such stories even where they didn't exist, and they spanked their dolls. Boys showed each other their caning marks in changing-room or dormitory. As they grew up, English women even of the interwar period knew no immense guilt about being turned on by spanking. Men may have been somewhat more reticent, but men always were so in England, the land of the male club where no SILENCE sign ever had to be posted in any room. Besides, they were on the giving end of the bargain—you don't boast of beating your wife.

However qualified, the idea was neither deviant nor even peculiar. Krafft-Ebing might well have found his clients "wet with sweat" over masturbating at the idea of a girl bending over for the cane, but we do not frankly feel that an English girl of the past would have been so at all. Corporal punishment was allowed, condoned by family and state alike, encouraged, talked about—*in the open*. Consequently, an atavistic urge (*pace* Ellis) was to an extent located in society, and given a form.

At this point we are in danger of being accused of a serious contradiction: We are against c.p. for children, yet would seem to admire certain aspects of it. This is an oversimplification, to the point of tautology, and we would prefer to decline it. What we should like to see freed are certain life qualities. Anyone who admires civilized behavior must admire control, which is to say self-control. In this respect, the British upper-class school system enjoined a certain highly qualified admiration, but it was formally undesirable. The system allowed, as it were, the top of the iceberg to show through, then rigidly denied what lay under the surface. *This* is the contradiction. S-m in sex might well be *one* way for freeing resultant guilts for *some* people. We must make it quite clear that we do not counsel it for all, or even most. In this book we simply hope to make people less afraid of it than before.

The anthropologist Ashley Montagu sets a lot of store in this

regard on the Anglo-Saxon being a "non-contact" culture. "For
example," he writes, "in a crowded vehicle like a subway, the
Anglo-Saxon will remain stiff and rigid, with a bland expression on
his face which seems to deny the existence of other passengers. The
contrast of the French Métro, for example, is striking. Here the
passengers will lean and press against others. . . ." Americans, he
surmises, have to some extent inherited this repression, with the
result that "While waiting for a bus Americans will space themselves like sparrows on a telephone wire, in contrast to Mediterranean peoples who will push and crowd together."

To which one can but add—And how! Or—would that Americans would! Tactuality in an infancy pattern almost certainly
makes for psychic health (though its brusque withdrawal in adulthood, as in prewar Japan, can cause alarming frustrations and conflicts, the brutal Japanese treatment of helpless enemies being
attributed to such denials by more than one authority). Yet in
small overcrowded countries like Japan, England, Switzerland, life
would be unbearable if a certain distance between people were not
respected, even if only symbolically. New York City teaches us
the same. Here, too, in the subway, "the passengers will lean and
press against others," and there are those of us who wish they
wouldn't. Many women who are gratuitously pressed on in morning and evening rush hours every day would be grateful for a little
more of the much derided Anglo-Saxon distancing, and even see
the "blank expression" as a sort of apology for the unwanted and
involuntary proximity. Those who saw wartime queues in England and their total travesty, resulting in regular mayhem, in a
country like Sicily at the same time will quickly get the point.
Writing in *The New York Times* of April 1, 1972, Anthony Lewis
quotes an American lady tourist's reactions to a delay on the London Underground (subway) due to a suicide on the tracks in front
of the train she was in: "We sat there for twenty minutes or half
an hour and no one gave any sign of recognizing that anything
unusual had happened. The train was quite crowded and there
were men standing all around us flicking the pages of their *Financial Times* as if we were moving right along." The woman then
got into conversation with a fellow traveler, who remarked, "Some

people call the English complacent. I don't know what you'd call it. I call it patient. Can you imagine the Paris Métro under these circumstances? By now there would be ten dead Frenchmen."

The cultural conditioning of England, and of Germany, came to have its compensations in this respect. Why, then, Nazism and the German concentration camps? No pat answer to this complex and thorny problem is possible here. But we would again tentatively suggest that punishment in British schools, and not only upper-class schools, was more involving of control, ritual, in short of the Apollonian. This was not nearly as generalized in Germany and was probably fairly inexistent in the last, Bismarckian century altogether. Hence the savage surge of Dionysiac forces from the underworld of the German psyche was able to topple the whole German *Geist*. Thomas Mann's work tells us as much again and again, while Edith Cadivec actually calls one of her first schoolgirl submissives Dionysia, in her celebrated *Confessions and Experiences* (see Appendix).

Let us once more reiterate that corporal punishment was not the easy vehicle of repression in England that most American psychologists seem to have taken it for. At least, the repression came much later than in most other countries. Stekel is helpful here. At the start of his *Compulsion and Doubt* he admits that "All children show a predisposition to compulsions." Many of these (like not stepping on cracks in a sidewalk) are perfectly harmless and evaporate after puberty. If they persist they may take on the nature of an obsession. Characteristic of an obsession or "compulsion neurosis" is "a pecular division of thinking processes."

This dissociation understandably occurs "whenever moral categories are involved." Thus England builds stoicism, the "grin and bear it" philosophy, into its conduct and as a result many of its children may excusably have a predisposition to a sadomasochist compulsion, when quite young. If the adult culture then entirely impedes these feelings, you clearly get a conflict that could be as damaging as that instanced concerning Japanese tactuality above. In France we note that s-m is a *vice*.

Well, we can only reiterate that it was not nearly as much so

in England. Men may not have talked about it a lot to each other in
adult life, but then Englishmen don't talk to each other a lot about
anything (resulting, for one critic, in the strength of their scrip-
tural culture). Arnold's "personal correction" was for years a way
of life, virtually a style. (This can be checked out side by side with
the French in Canada.) The Ward-Profumo investigations brought
out what everybody already knew anyway, that every English
prostitute has her cane (in Hogarth's day it was a birch). And in
the more civilized homes and schools this punishment was almost
never cruel.

We have insisted that the British are normally kind to animals.
Surely this is beyond dispute. One of the present authors, while
serving in North Africa in the last war, saw an ordinary British
soldier, no member of the upper class, become so incensed by an
Arab's cruelty to his donkey that he untethered the galled and
bleeding beast and forcibly haltered the Arab between the shafts
of his own cart. There is nothing edifying about seeing an Arab
belaboring his nag, in fact it is disgusting. To cuff a child on the
ear is almost equally so. If it is true that s-m has been the prerogative of the upper rather than lower classes in Britain, it may simply
be that the latter did not have the time and leisure, even if they
had the desire, to perfect a ceremonial scenario. Eton did.

Montagu is doubtless so correct about contact and non-contact
cultures that we risk repetition:

> Among the upper classes of England relationships between par-
> ents and children were, and continue to be, distant from birth
> till death. At birth the child was usually given over to a nurse, who
> either wetnursed it for a brief period or bottle fed it. Children were
> generally brought up by governesses and then at an early age sent
> away to school. They received a minimum amount of tactile expe-
> rience. It is, therefore, not difficult to understand how, under such
> conditions, non-touchability could easily become institutionalized as
> part of the way of life. A well-bred person never touched another
> without his consent. The slightest accidental brushing against an-
> other required an apology, even though the other might be a parent
> or a sibling . . .
>
> The English public schools, as is well known, were breeding-
> grounds for homosexuality, for these were all-boy schools and all

the teachers were males, and usually the only love a boy ever received was from another boy or master. The parental inadequacies from which many of these boys suffered produced a high rate of homosexuality. Such famous figures as Algernon Swinburne, J. A. Symonds, Oscar Wilde, Lord Alfred Douglas, and numerous others, were all products of such parents, and such schools.

Meanwhile, one longs to rejoin, Walt Whitman, Henry James, and Hart Crane weren't? Despite the fact that the usual American contention here is that sadists and masochists "are generally suffering from a latent homosexuality" (L. R. O'Conner in *Sexual Intercourse*), Montagu is correct, and could be reinforced. Much of what he writes applies to girls as well as boys in England, and he does not identify the separation of parents from children in this class as frequently being forcible. Both authors of this book had childhoods in England with parents at times stationed in the East, from which return to the "home country" was at that time slow.

Having conceded as much, one must also admit that corporal punishing is a form of touching, even in as cold a climate as that of England. Children may find it more reassuring than a scolding voice. It is certainly testimony of more interest! In hand spanking skin is touched by skin. And Montagu himself, opposed as he is to our point of view, cannot help but acknowledge the intensity of control involved in British chastisement, and so admired by children, as a kind of taming of the barbaric itself:

> The canings, usually administered by senior prefects, customary in English public schools, during which any display of emotion on the part of either the caner or his victim was strictly tabooed, undoubtedly served to produce a dissociation between pain and emotion.

Our own summary, then, is offered in the spirit of humility with which we hope it will be received. It is: That the data here remain unusually speculative, the subject being a free-for-all; that sadomasochist arousal is probably omnipresent, though respondents are far more likely to reply affirmatively to questions about masochism than about sadism, thanks to the social stigma attached to the latter; that guilt feelings about s-m arousal later in life at least show instinctive deference to a dominant moral code (a clod would not care); that such guilt feelings could and should be relieved.

Two decades ago the Institute for Sex Research at Indiana University found 20% of male and 12% of females conceding arousal by sadomasochistic stories. The 1969 Manfred DeMartino interviews (published in *The New Female Sexuality*) went far higher for women. A University of Miami survey did the same. Then, moving outside America as well as within it, the Eleanore Luckey/Gilbert Nass University of Connecticut survey gave 8% of male U.S. students and 5% of female actually admitting "whipping or spanking before petting or other intimacy." Now this was literal, overt behavior. The last-mentioned survey is especially interesting since it sampled students also in England, Norway, Germany, Canada, and Italy. The British, of course, won hands down, 17% of men and 33% of young women reporting such experiences.

Commenting on this survey, which he helped to initiate, Vance Packard, author of *The Sexual Wilderness*, asks: "Is it possible that the use of over-stern discipline pervaded English life during the eighteenth and nineteenth centuries because of the straining to hold together history's most far-flung empire?" The idea is far from far-fetched. The great public schools of England were organized to provide a class—civil servants, policemen, statesmen—to rule what was, after all, at the date of our own birth, close to a third of the world. Control obviously had a high valuation.

Thus, the real point about the "Englishness" of our vice is that a cultural pattern was set for fantasy. England was originally a Germanic country, settled by Angles, Jutes, and Saxons, and the mother was subordinate to the father. We are not saying that this was good, simply that it was so.

Consequently, the British school, with its emphasis on restraint and control, ceremony and ritual, formed a perfect scenario for s-m. The individual was respected, as he was not in a purely military ambience. The masochist contributes as well as the sadist. Neither is a digit in the love play. A boy from a modern German Eton who spent a term in a leading British public school between the wars told us that at his school the military, or officer training, program had been infinitely stricter than he found it to be in the English equivalent (where it was looked on as more of a joke than anything); but in every other department of daily school life—chapel, hall, meals, classes—where *ceremony* had been injected rather than inherited, the British school was ten times stricter.

The German milieu was far more one in which force ruled. The ceremony was mostly quasi-military, which is to say based on killing people. Quite the contrary was the case in a British public school of the past and near-past. Rape statistics are notoriously higher in the former than the latter background. As Hans Toch (among many others) has demonstrated in *Violent Men*, the s-m setting is the opposite of a crime-inducing one. The sex murderer is seldom a sadist.

If then we may agree on one point, namely that in England corporal punishment is more likely to be arousing, to elicit sexual response, than elsewhere, we can logically proceed to its corollary: What about America? What is its "national perversion"? For in one sense America began as so much exported England, as did Australia, uncongenial as the idea may be to the citizens of both.

Despite its paranoiac optimism, considerably tempered by current events, contemporary American civilization can be termed a "depressive" culture, one in which the true aggressive drive natural to men is institutionally *depressed*. With everyone equal, and institutions organized to soften out all differences of strength and intelligence (cp. urban schooling), aggression is disposed of, it is hoped, like so much unpleasant garbage.

This creates considerable problems of social structure. It is hardly necessary to point out that in the ultra-egalitarian state eruptions of personal violence are seen as so many periodic illnesses. "He's sick" is said of someone who shows abnormal aggression, and this would not be said in a confident black culture in the Caribbean, say. If "he's sick," then we're all really guilty by tacit consent and, as a result, we appoint the policeman for the teacher as authority figure in the classroom.

The resultant frustration takes many forms. If you hate yourself for having been, in a previous existence, beastly to blacks, you will love blacks for punishing you: hence the Black Pearl "model" agency of dominant black "masseuses." If there is no one you can hate in a socially accepted or directed way, you hate yourself. In Orwell's *1984* only a socially licensed enemy could be genuinely hated—cp. "commies." But since such absolutes grow increasingly vague, and intellectually dissatisfying, anyone of intelligence finds it hard to compensate for the essential deprivation. The result seems to be truly "ambivalent," in the Freudian sense: either overt violence or a strong drive toward self-punishment and self-hatred.

President Kennedy took the bullet-proof bubble off his car. Murder in America is frequently followed by suicide. With aggression bottled up, no longer admitted as serving the species, only allowed in pecuniary activities (a "killing" in the stock market), America seems ripe for masochism.

AMERICA
AND
MASOCHISM

"*Submissive male*, 30, 5'6", shy and inexperienced. Needs dominant women to teach proper respect for females through humiliation . . . *Male slave*, 31, obedient but untrained, seeks goddess to train, discipline, and humiliate me. Let me live under your feet . . . *Young slave*, good-looking, 23, masculine, could dig hearing from young butch . . . Photos appreciated."

These are typical ads from a typical American s-m publication of recent date. Despite what we have said above about such ads, and such publications, there is a strong consensus of statistics, experience, and inference that s-m in America is quite different from what it is, or was, in England. (We will come back to one of the most celebrated of these samplings at the end of this section.) Namely, that U.S. s-m is in a high degree, and this order, masochistic, male-masochistic, homosexual male-masochistic, and—so the cliché generally goes—usually indulged in by those, of both sexes and all genders, in whom the sex drive is moderate.

Actually, the homosexual quotient need not imply any weakness of sexual impulse here at all; Ellis was only one of many to remark that when men can't find women for the practice of s-m they naturally seek out other men. And we shall conclude our summary by suggesting that if s-m in America does have a considerable homosexual content, then it doubly rejects the national norms.

For those of us living in America in the latter half of the twentieth century the problem of its "national perversion" is not merely important but all-important—sexually, culturally, socially, in every way. Suddenly we find that, although both England and America are at base Puritan cultures (wherein the woman, as temptress, is punishable), the dominant male/submissive female structure of the former country's fantasy, as to some extent that found by the prewar European researchers, has in the United States a lower erotic arousal valence than its reverse. T. C. Mits, in short, thinks of chains, whips, and women wielding them over men, whenever he hears the term s-m, or its twin b & d; he thinks of high-booted Monique von Cleef (a Dutch Jewess) and her Newark "house of torture," visited by an evidently prominent clientele. A British equivalent would summon up, instead, Neville Heath who whipped his good-looking girlfriends and whose trial, in 1946, filled the gallery of a London court with, mainly, women. Furthermore, the notion that sadomasochism is a composite receives some chilling shocks in America. Why is this so?

The problem—why America has opted for masochism in the relationship—is enormously complex, and the findings once more thin. Gradings of photographic erotica for arousal value by young people can be made to prove almost anything, but in everything American on the subject we have read there is invariably a high response by men to the fantasy of being beaten by a woman. It is virtually a cliché of the U.S.A. Our clichés become our politics and the matter carries with it, indeed, such wide affects in the society at large that almost any relatively intelligent speculation about it could be useful if productive of enlightenment. We are dealing here not so much with a national perversion as a potential world disaster.

For every American is daily made more conscious of the fact that technology cannot come to terms with its antithesis—violence (to which add sex to the pot and stir). In every American city, every day and every night, to say nothing of the battlefields of Vietnam, we witnessed the deepest, most vile and evil aspects of the psyche erupting and flourishing, simply because they were denied rather than invited to co-operate from the first. Unfortunately, as Jung once wrote, "the spirit of our time believes itself superior to its own psychology." My-Lai should have taught us to the contrary, but scarcely seems to have done so.

This failure of a society's myth to redeem its own unconscious results in ennui, the reverse of the aroused optimism; this is what in social terms Durkheim called "anomy" and Marshall McLuhan, in our case, "narcissus-narcosis" (becoming mesmerized by ourselves). So we have made ourselves spectators of sex and, as a result, spectators of bloodshed. The mass slaughter of Asian peasants is nudged nightly off the television screen by the latest hemorrhoid ad.

Now we are not the only country to fail to "code" its unconscious. The location of magic, mystery, the so-called primitive in modern society, poses perhaps insuperable problems. We have mentioned Nazi Germany in this context. Schiller saw a similar failure in the France of his day, the revolution beginning by reason, proceeding to a bloodbath, and culminating in a military dictatorship. Let us once more quote Jung, out of *Psychological Types,* bearing in mind the barbarism inflicted recently by a vast technology on a tiny, impoverished, peasant country in Southeast Asia:

> The damned-up instinct-forces in civilized man are immensely more destructive, and hence more dangerous, than the instincts of the primitive, who in a modest degree is constantly living his negative instincts. Consequently no war of the historical past can rival a war between civilized nations in its colossal scale of horror.

The comment makes us uncomfortably conscious of the fact that, as a society, we have lately had our *authorized* Moors murderers. Which is another, shorthand, way of saying that we are, as a culture, terrified of sadism because we are regularly committing it with such relish. We retreat from the mirror in alarm. In the widest sense, of course, a technology fulfills its sadistic drives in dominating its environment, the end-product of which seems to be dropping gelled gasoline fluid on Asian peasants, and calling the activity "pacification" by napalm, incendigel, or whatever the scientific neologism of the moment may be.

In short, with the increase of what we call civilization (a definition declined by Claude Lévi-Strauss) there is an increasing tendency to masochism, or demand for punishment. In his admirable book on pornography Morse Peckham points out that suffering is usually the symptomatology of someone at your mercy. De Sade saw that what we all yearn for is *mastery*. Such is a social directive of the American economy, just as it is a taboo of its ideology. You are not supposed to be socially a master of someone else in a "democracy." Yet the only security we can climb to, in the jungle warfare of contemporary capitalism, is that pinnacle from which we can assure ourselves that others are suffering. Consciousness-raising sessions at more than one s-m group we have attended have always raised this anomaly of our culture, truly a crippling one.

In a penetrating paper on "Sex and Art" in *The American Journal of Psychology* Colin Scott tells us that in the secondary law of courtship, as he terms it, the female becomes aggressive and the male proportionately attentive to her demands, both physical and mental, conscious and unconscious. To most European observers it has seemed quite astounding that a new wave of aggressive feminism should lately take root in, of all places, modern America, so far in advance of most other countries in sexual equality (a fact admitted with equanimity in Simone de Beauvoir's *The Second Sex* nearly a quarter of a century ago). Surely it could only have done so in a truly masochistic society.

Again, the parallel with England may help to clarify this tangled and retangled issue. For, after all, Britain was the technology of the nineteenth century, was it not? Why no Reikian masochism there?

To answer satisfactorily would demand a book. Probably a little library. Let us first of all remember the racial background and the ideals of the society. England has inherited a far more rigid and hierarchical social and sexual patterning than America. Margaret Mead once expressed as much in a nutshell by saying that Americans have substituted anthropology for history. Being unable to make depth comparisons, we Americans make them in width; we forever test, poll, sample, check and countercheck our new phenomena with a scrutiny seldom known before. The shelves of our "public opinion" periodicals groan with such statistics; fed by computers, our "information" banks grow bloated. The true horror of the Orwellian National Data Center proposed in Washington, with its computerized dossiers on every living American, is that at a flick of a switch it will regurgitate petrified classifications (grades in school, military service, religion, race) *on the same level of cognition*. Kinsey's famous report might be subtitled *How They Do It In Oshkosh*. De Sade's agonized inquiries were in depth, into what differentiated man from nature; as Geoffrey Gorer well put it, "De Sade would probably have had least sympathy with the taxonomic work of Kinsey and his ilk." Television has been far less disruptive of family life in England to date partly thanks to this inherited historical perspective. If you wanted to be nasty, you could say it's about all England's got left these days.

This patterning obviously leads to an acceptance, in the most general terms, of authority. With the father traditionally the head of the family this conduces in turn to male dominance and female submission on the fantasy level. The latter becomes simply a repetition of the social mores. There was a very definite sense—certainly in upper-class English families before the war—that criticism of your father was some sort of criticism of your country, too. Furthermore, the bachelor was never looked upon as a deviant, or opter-out, as in modern America (where he is harshly penalized by the tax laws), and he certainly never was regarded as of low sexual horsepower. On the contrary, he was accorded a real role in society. During the writing of this book the Prime Minister of England (another Heath) was a bachelor, evidently a contented one.

America started out by rebelling against authoritarian England and had such anti-establishmentarianism written into its Constitution. With subsequent polyglot immigration, rapid social mobility, and *laissez-faire* capitalism, the dominant myths came to carry as central to them a clear injunction to rebel—if not against the government, against family, age, sex, and so on. This has been underlined so clearly of late as to require no further exposition here;

what we must be concerned with is the resulting psychosexual dynamic.

America destroys its "father" in the form of England (today politically the most despised minority in the U.S.A., even if surreptitiously admired; the English make statistically the worst of our immigrants, i.e. those investing the least amount of psychological capital in the culture). The replacement—Uncle Sam—is, we observe, a fairly decrepit myth figure. At all levels, and in all representations, the Uncle Sam image is easily eclipsed by that of America as Magna Mater, or great mother. America is woman, tempting us with a fecund largesse of being. Archibald MacLeish makes but one of hundreds of similar apostrophes in this vein when he describes his country as a huge woman lying "on her left side her flank golden" ("She has brown breasts and the mouth of no other country"). No culture has ever quite matched America's breast (milk-giving) fetishism. In microcosmic form this comes down to Mom.

But America the absolute has violated her bountiful Gea-Tellus, and has deep guilt feelings as a result. The recent breast-beatings about damage to the ecology struck so sharply on this by now exacerbated nerve that they were readily transferred into new laws. Over our technocratic dynamic, indeed, might be put de Sade's maxim, from *Aline et Valcour*, "Let us dare do violence to this unintelligible Nature, the better to master the art of enjoying her." So America rapes its mother and craves punishment, from a woman, as a result—it is, after all, a fairly unnatural, or antinatural, orientation for a strong man to want to be whipped by a woman, at this stage in history.

You can of course Freudianize all this and come up with something as suggestive as Gilles Deleuze's summary: "The beating woman represents the superego superficially and in the external world, and she also transforms the superego into the recipient of the beating, the essential victim. This explains the conspiracy of the mother-figure and the ego against the father's likeness. *The father's likeness represents both genital sexuality and the superego as an agent of repression: the one is expelled with the other.*"

(Italics his.) Yet, does this get us any closer to the functional reality?

It would indeed be convenient if we could leave it at the above, a sort of slick manifestation of the Electra complex. Unfortunately, there is far more to the problem. For a much wider understanding of masochistic motives in modern society at large the reader is referred to Theodor Reik's study "Masochism in Modern Man," in that writer's *Of Love and Lust*. In what we call America we are dealing, we must remember, with a vast collective civilization of great disparity (Ellis at one point quotes with dismay an estimate of our population as 154 million by 1990!). This inexorable collective is, we hear on all sides, suppressing individuation and producing functions rather than people. By our schooling, our jobs, our life roles and "other-directed" ideals the society appears to be a sort of homogenizing hopper into which our tots are tossed in order to become mere functions. Mainly functions for making money.

Now making money is not really a "conversion" ideal, any more than is a military pretension. It is a habit rather than a way of life. Nazi Germany and Napoleonic France had objective social glory at stake: this was no better and, in one case, it was far worse. The Apollonian element in a civilization is its "conversion" or transmuting device. Nietzsche, whom part of de Sade anticipated, is repeatedly misunderstood (e.g. by Kassirer almost entirely, on this point) as having postulated the Apollonian, in civilizations as in men, as a sort of policeman of the intellect. Not so. In *The Birth of Tragedy* Apollo, it is true, "demands self-control," but Apollonian culture is the force of illusion (too esthetic for Jung's taste, to be sure) transmuting and converting subjective chaos.

In Nietzsche's words, it must "always triumph first over titans, kill monsters, and overcome the somber contemplation of actuality, the intense susceptibility to suffering, by means of illusions strenuously and zestfully entertained." In the Hellenic mind at its "ripest" Nietzsche saw "the Dionysiac and Apollonian elements, in a continuous chain of creations, each enhancing the other." Reverting to America with this in mind, and witnessing a cultural ideal of the absolute validity of the rights of man, we suddenly recall with a jolt that these come at once into conflict with a highly Dionysiac slave culture; we can only marvel that the famous "melting pot" has not boiled over more often than it has.

For, if every individual has inalienable and imperishable rights, if this is the ideal in order, then what are we doing with slaves? Now almost every country seems, at some time, to have been enslaved to another. The British certainly were to the Romans and their Queen Boadicea is said to have killed herself after being publicly flogged (the true origin of *le vice anglais* perhaps?). The Greeks produced an upper-class culture by suppression of the majority populace. This happened centuries ago. The point about America is that you aren't supposed to have slaves *at the same time* as you are trumpeting the worth of individual rights. American literature shows us that its psyche could not, in fact, stomach this split.

In England of the last century and a half an upper-class school system allowed the subjective some external form on the boards, as it were. Not much, but some. It was a kind of play-acting, with a suppressed majority (of lowerclassmen, junior boys, etc.) governed by an elite (of prefects), all in the sterling service of the nation's "conversion" ideal, which was not simply one of making money (though it later became far more so). Most British public schools were intensely religious, with some form of chapel at least twice a day and three times on Sunday. Talking in chapel was one of the most severely punished faults going.

The process we are sketchily tracing is summarized with some brilliance by Jung, who asserts, in so many words, that our slavery has by now been driven back into the soul (we obviously do not follow Jung on the political implications of a correction of this condition):

> The external form of society in antique civilization was translated into the subject, whereby in individual psychology an inner condition was produced which had been external in the older civilization, namely, a dominating, preferred function, which became developed and differentiated at the expense of an inferior majority. By means of this psychological process a collective culture

gradually came into existence, in which *"les droits de l'homme"* certainly had an immeasurably greater guarantee than with the ancients. But it had this disadvantage, that it depended upon a subjective slave-culture, i.e. upon a transfer of the antique majority enslavement into the psychological sphere, whereby collective culture was undoubtedly enhanced, while individual culture depreciated. Just as the enslavement of the mass was the open wound of the antique world, the enslavement of the inferior function is an ever-bleeding wound in the soul of man today.

Applied intelligently, and without undue prejudice, to America's racial heritage this tells us a great deal. There is, as these words are written, an agency in the New York area called Black Pearl Unlimited, supplying female black dominants at a very high price indeed.* When the radical feminist Shulamith Firestone tells us, in *The Dialectic of Sex,* "the obvious: that white men have a thing for black women . . . that white women have a secret sympathy and curiosity about black men," we confess to some bafflement; this judging the whole human race by one part of it, the American, seems to us quite astonishingly arrogant. Neither of the present writers ever saw a black until the age of twenty or so, except on the screen, and none of their multiple brothers, sisters, aunts, uncles would have looked other than quite blankly at the above claim. Add American optimism, that of the dominant technology, to the brew and quite a lot gets solved.

The violated mother must punish, and you deserve your punishment on the racial level, as you also desire it on the personal, where it is a rebellion against digitary existence, and the hortations to procreate. For there *is* an unconscious optimism in the masochistic attitude. This is clearly brought out by Reik, in his description of the masochist's "victory through defeat." That is, the masochist voluntarily submits to punishment and thereby pays for the right of sexual satisfaction, which he feels is not permitted before it (he hardly wants to be punished afterwards).

As we shall try to expose in detail below, the most thrilling

* "BIZARRE 'N' BLACK—Dominants featured this week at our ultra-private office/studios: LORITA, the Black Pearl, Lovely Excitement in leather. 5′ 5″ . . . We offer English massage by these models. Beginners welcome. Rate: $40 for up to one hour. No tipping required. BLACK PEARL MODEL AGENCY."

elements of sexual play for a masochist are, rather than the actual reception of pain, often the waiting, the apprehension. "This suspense is dreadful," as a lady in an Oscar Wilde play puts it, "I do hope that it lasts."* There is, in short, pleasure awaiting somewhere beyond this agonizing, yet so delectable, anticipation. In his "Love and Pain" monograph Ellis caught this clearly: "It would appear to be a purely psychic fantasia founded on the elementary physical fact that restraint of emotion, like suspension, produces a heightening of emotion."

This restraint conjoins the masochist with the sadist who must also exhibit restraint, control, to be effective. Reik puts this well, if at length:

> This secret feeling of superiority draws its power from a fantasy that denies the laws of time and that keeps extending the suspense . . . A young man's daydream assumed an increasingly masochistic character by the accumulation of retarding and obstructing elements which had gradually entered into it . . . Just as in sexual masochism the mounting pain announces the arrival of the pleasurable discharge, in collective suffering the deepest distress and oppression become signals of imminent redemption and triumph.

Both Jung and Reik are, however, admittedly schematic, and it is not always possible to see individuals prefigured as nations in one as diversified and plural as modern America. It is, rather, a continent. Yet a masochistic one.

Here the dominant woman (Mom) clearly substitutes at nearly all phases for father, becoming preternaturally powerful while remaining sexually desirable. (In truth, the latest wave of emancipatory feminism may be an understandable reaction against the anxieties induced by all these cross-pollinating demands, kept active by commerce.) The extroversion of the culture at large, its optimistic collectivism, produces or is married with a fantasy of

---

* Cp. "It's most dangerous nowadays for a husband to pay any attention to his wife in public. It always makes people think that he beats her when they're alone" (Lady Plymdale in *Lady Windermere's Fan*); and nb. "the art of suspense always places us on the side of the victim" (Gilles Deleuze, in a long analysis of Masoch's novels).

introversion, viz. masochism. In England you have had a highly
introverted male at all class levels, a man of reticence and taciturn-
ity, whose fantasy was therefore likely to tend to be extroverted,
viz. sadistic.

Law itself, as Stekel explains, is a form of compulsion, based,
as with the child, on fear of punishment and the resultant blocking
of the pleasure principle. As a matter of fact, Stekel suggests on
the side that all new philosophies may have been created by men
suffering from compulsion neuroses, since their genesis is usually
a protest on the part of the instincts against culture. "Any real
change," writes James Baldwin, "implies the breakup of the world
as one has always known it, the loss of all that gave one an identity,
the end of safety."

In England we can still to a considerable extent see an inner
assimilation of the retributory system; the populace as a whole
agrees with most of its laws, which have thereby become convictions. Public and personal morality to a degree illide. The individual who doesn't concede either is likely to be truly criminal.
So British s-m basically recognizes, faces up to, and collaborates
with its culture. We are not saying that this is necessarily "good,"
simply that this particular fantasy in fact follows its culture, and
so gets less hurt en route.

In the United States the law seems to be regarded quite dif-
ferently . . . if indeed regarded at all. There may be external
concession to it, partly for fear of consequences, but it is not nearly
so internalized. It could hardly be so with the plurality of race and
religion available. So its s-m is contra-cultural and natural heir to
the rebel mission.

As a result, it is not considered as deviant in America for a male
to be masochist as it is in England. On the other hand, it hardly
dare be breathed in America today what Ellis considered normal
and healthy, namely that women are. The 1969 DeMartino survey
of a strange sample of women, including nudists and lesbians,
came under fire from Women's Lib since when a reaction was
invited to the idea of "a sexual experience in which the female is
overwhelmed and forced to submit, but *without* any threat to her

of bodily harm" [italics sic], over a third of the sample answered
positively.

Unpopular as such findings may be with Women's Lib, they
cannot simply be swept under the carpet as so much political
refuse. The psychodynamics of the situation must be understood.
The masochist is not an inferior. Quite the contrary. Kate Millett
brushes off female masochism as a male invention, one which
"justifies any conceivable domination or humiliation forced upon
the female." Joan Nicholson, editor of *Do It Now!*, the organ of
the National Organization of Women, opines that: "Reflected in
the pin-up is the masculine view of woman as passive—an object
to be pinned up—and masochistic—existing for men's pleasure
in whatever form it might take." She adds, "Underlying much
literature and openly expressed in many other forms, including
psychoanalytic theory, is the male fantasy that women desire to be
dominated—raped—by men."

Being dominated is *not* being raped, nor is being masochistic
"existing for men's pleasure" alone. It may well be that the fully
eventuated female masochist gets one of the strongest charges available in human sex, and is one of the most powerful controllers of it.
We are going to have to confront later what meets us in every psychological study of recent date, what Ellis' famous Florrie and
Charlotte Brontë's Jane Eyre told us alike, that it is the strong
woman who is so often the true sexual masochist.* "It is just
those few women who show no signs of the culturally expected
attitude of deference to men in whom we find what seems to be a
much more truly masochistic attitude (in a psychological rather
than a cultural-conventional sense)," wrote Abraham Maslow in
a complex article in *The Journal of Social Psychology* in 1942.
When we take what is required of Mom into account, then, we see
that the American masochist of *both* sexes is a society-disowned
rebel as well as self-proclaimed misfit, an outsider who refuses to

---

* Glimmers of understanding now come through the political fog, e.g.: "I believe that
most women want to be sexually dominated by men and that male dominance doesn't
necessarily imply male superiority or female masochism. I'm not saying that women
want to be dominated and protected by men *all* the time. But, based on my researching
and personal experience, it seems they do want it *some* of the time, as evidenced by
their fantasies." (Mary Reinholz, "Mission-Submission?", *Forum*, October, 1972.)

recognize the laws of society, defies the manly myths and, finally, by so often being homosexual, declines to breed the race.

In conclusion, what use is it to know all this for those stuck with sadomasochism in their souls? For them the foregoing may excusably have been faintly boring. What are they supposed to do with the end result of a national trauma? Masochism has been made into a compulsion neurosis by an aggressive culture which, with the ever more violent and destructive policies of its government, is feeding back ever more and more guilt into the social substrate. As the official slaughter of distant Asians continued year after year (fewer troops on the soil but bigger and more terrible bombs from the sky), as this became the daily diet of our radio news, so did those crimes on the police blotters in which force was used "to gratify carnal desires." Here is the true correlation: force is condoned and surreptitiously given the rank of a social ideal. American masochism seems to be aggression turned guiltily against the self.

The Kinsey Institute found 14% of institutionalized sex offenders had been convicted of felonies involving aggression. Denying that such could be called sadists, in any sense of the term, Stanton Wheeler, a Professor of Law, commented that it is "more valid to view their offenses as part of a broader behavior system in which force may be used to attain their goals."

In this resume of and speculation on the roots of masochism in modern America we have tried not to run into elements often occurring in relation to the subject: religion and infantilism. Frankly, confrontations here would lead us into so many bypaths, none of which would serve to assist the practicing or would-be practicing s-m person. Reik among others has seen the ideal of heaven as a perfect future state corresponding with those sexual postponements of pleasure, equally charged with imagination, indulged in by the true masochist.

As regards the infantile quotient, we must freely admit that there is a powerful latent issue here. If s-m is to any extent a complex web of reminiscences of an individual's past, then it must involve something of a reactivation of the parent-child relationship. The spanking stories nearly always begin this way, as a result. So the masochist is, for Freud, arrested or fixated in childhood, in a way the sadist is not—animals and savages practice courtship sadism and while this involves pain for the partner, we do not know how eagerly this pain is sought out, if at all.

If we are still children, repression then arises through resistance to incest. Actually, Freudian repression starts directly we are born, and could be said to be intensified by the incest taboo. It would be tempting to compare this with what happened on the racial scale, in Nazi Germany, where a father-figure required the devotion of a child on the part of his populace with catastrophic results (the incestuous self-worshiping of an elite class being presciently parodied in Mann's early story "The Blood of the Walsungs"). But frankly, the Freudian interpretation seems to mistake, or underestimate, the role of fantasy altogether; it takes symbol for sign. We will come back to this below.

To see your lover as your father, or mother, or God, may well be disturbed and disturbing behavior. It would be to see the symbol as the thing (in the case of God a concept). In actual fact the use of background reminiscence works the other way and can represent a most healthy resolution of everything Freud gathers under incest, of which the s-m partners compose almost a parody. The dramatic love play of s-m, far from repetitiously imitating childhood, actually represents a psychic act of great emancipation and independence. Jung put his finger on this when grappling with the infantile theory in *Psychological Types*:

> Characteristically, it is the symbols of the parents that become conscious and by no means always the images of the actual parents; a fact which Freud explains as the repression of the parent *imago* through resistance to incest. I am of the same mind upon this interpretation, and yet I believe it is not exhaustive, since it overlooks the *extraordinary significance of this symbolical replacement*. Symbolization in the shape of the God-image means an immense step forward from the concretism, the sensuousness, of reminiscence; inasmuch as the regression to the parent, through the acceptance of the "symbol" as a real symbol, is straight-way transformed into a progression; it would remain a regression if the so-called symbol were to be finally interpreted merely as a sign of the actual parents and were thus robbed of its independent character.

We wish to make it clear that nowhere in this section have we said that masochism in America is either desirable or healthy. We have felt, however, that given the dominant culture of the country its high incidence gives touching tribute to the resilience of man's psyche and to his undying imagination.

But in saying as much you are also indicting the dominant society which makes this reaction necessary. In his admirable book *Human Aggression*, dedicated to another pioneer in this field, Konrad Lorenz, Anthony Storr, an Englishman, assumes "sado-masochistic" fantasies to be those "concerned with male dominance and female submission." He instances the perennial popularity of the Rhett Butler or even King Kong image in which "A *frisson* of fear of the more dominant male reinforces rather than inhibits erotic arousal in females."

He then adds, "it is less easy to understand why men also may have masochistic fantasies in which they are at the mercy of dominant females." If we ourselves, then, have ventured to suggest eventuation of s-m on the adult plane as a kind of psychic conquest, male homosexual masochism, evidently prevalent in America, would seem to be regressive in the true sense of the term.

Storr explains "the regressive wish to be cared for by a power-ful figure" as common to both sexes but sees it as more normal in a woman since she requires protection in our society. Now, since single males take on elements of the other sex, as do single females (spinsters), the fastidious and effeminate fairy or gay of popular legend and life is simply playing the female to the point of real regression—that is, playing the role in daily life. "No doubt," Storr concedes, "this is partly genetic; for we all spring originally from a conjunction of male and female cells, and every cell in our body contains chromosomes derived from both sexes." Being pun-ished and rendered helpless in various ways could thus be regarded, in one sense, as a continuation of the basic homosexual isolation.

The need for security in an anxiety-torn, dynamic, ever-altering society such as is ours today forces this over-compensation on both women and men. They are scarcely to be blamed for it. Over and over again Havelock Ellis reminds us that we cannot understand sadomasochism until we are willing to admit that it is invariably motivated by love: "The impulse to inflict pain, whether on others or on oneself, whenever it arises from a sexual motive, must never be regarded as a manifestation of hate and cruelty. Whenever it so arises we can safely eliminate any genuinely sexual impulse." In a ruthless, dominant technology like modern America, continually raping its environment, single males are going to crave ever more and more for some psychic stability. They are ordered by their society to marry; they are penalized by its tax system if they don't. No wonder they rolled up in droves to Monique von Cleef's so-called "Torture House," first on Staten Island and then in Newark, to be whipped and degraded.

Evidently regarding herself as a sort of combination social worker and psychiatrist, Mrs. von Cleef showed considerable understanding of what was amiss in her clients (if the remarks attributed to her are to be trusted). "They come to me to find what is missing in their lives," she told an interviewer in 1971, six years after the arrest which took her for three months to the Caldwell, N.J., State Prison. "I think it's probably love. They feel on some level that to be beaten and humiliated is to be loved . . . I only know I do a service in that I help the people who come to see me. They can cope with the world better after they see me."

The feeling of being what Monique termed "a leather social worker" received corroboration from call-girl *par excellence* and self-confessed madame, Xaviera Hollander, author of *The Happy Hooker* (1972). Conceding an "eight to ten" percentage of her customers as male masochists, she added, "I almost feel like a psychiatrist in certain cases, and I did work with psychiatrists that had cases." Monique clearly substantiates Ellis when she remarks, "Most masochists are sadistic in their work. They are tyrannical bosses and foul to work for. They trample on people, and yet with me they want the roles reversed.

Terry Kolb neatly summarizes both the regressive and the infantile dilemma in one:

> Psychologists have challenged the immaturity theory in relation to homosexuality. I do not know of any who have done so in respect to masochism. It is true that most of us have had fantasies dating back to early childhood, which would tend to support the immatur-

ity theory. However, it is equally true that, whatever the origin of the *need* for masochism (i.e. whether or not it arises from an infantile situation), the *solution* of masochism is not primitive or childish or regressive. It represents a sort of transcendence over the human dilemma, and one that involves the most human part of our natures.

WHO
WAS
DE SADE?

The name is like a knell. Was he a Bluebeard or a genius? A monster of infamy or the father of psychoanalysis? A crazy, perverted tyrant, progenitor of the anarchy on our streets today, or a great moral investigator, like Baudelaire and Gide?

De Sade was both more and less than all these, and the trouble was that he often was so at the same time. Not only did he himself clearly go in for a sort of Rimbaudian derangement of the senses, he wrote mainly fictive works from which it is quite impossible to sort any truly systematic philosophy, though some clever and courageous attempts have been made to do so. Finally, pirated wherever possible, his *oeuvre* has come down to us in a more disheveled state than that of almost any writer. Why, it has only recently been learnt, thanks to the indefatigable Gilbert Lély, that *Zoloé*, the work which ridicules Napoleon and Josephine and may have prolonged if not provoked the incarceration in the Charenton asylum, was not by de Sade at all. Large chunks of his canon have only been published in this century.

There is frankly so much in de Sade: blasphemy, *galanterie* as well as filth, Gothic romanticism alongside agnostic determinism, Don Juan and Quixote joining arms to elbow the old feudal class off the stage to derisive squirts of sperm. He has more than once been called a one-man Krafft-Ebing—"an eighteenth-century *Psy-*

chopathia Sexualis" (Havelock Ellis), "the first *psychopathia sexualis*" (Geoffrey Gorer). He certainly was an investigator; according to Simone de Beauvoir, author of a perceptive study of his thinking, "Sade must be given a place in the great family of those who want to cut through the 'banality of everyday life' to a truth which is immanent in this world."

All too often reception of his work has told us more about the judge than the judged; it has ranged from venomous contemporary detraction (Restif de la Bretonne, a personal enemy), through disdainful revulsion (Mario Praz), to enthusiastic re-discovery (Apollinaire) and discipular regard (Pierre Klossowski), with a vein of polite boredom proceeding at one side. Often enough, too, as Gorer well observes, "it has been the gallants, the lady-killers, the successful amorists who have attacked de Sade with the greatest violence and have been the most distressed by his debunking their behavior." If there was one thing de Sade was not, it was a sexist.

As with sadomasochism, then, so with de Sade. He was most widely reviled by those who hadn't read him (as was demonstrably the case with William Beckford, author of *Vathek,* who seems to have been blessed with prior vision of the contents of both *Justine* and *Juliette*). He was "*le monstre-auteur*" (Restif), a blasphemer and satanist dripping with the blood of the Revolution which he had so perversely urged into being. Throughout the nineteenth century this seems to have been the prevailing stereotype, opposed by only a few voices, such as those of Petrus Borel (who called de Sade a "martyr"), Baudelaire, Swinburne, and—one of the calmest—Sainte-Beuve. Lastly, the Berlin analyst Dühren publishes his life of de Sade and the thirty-nine-foot roll of thin paper, in microscopic hand, which is the manuscript of *The 120 Days of Sodom,* around the turn of the present century. The philosopher in chains (to crib from Camus) became the prisoner of the clinics.

The neglect, if not sheer hatred, with which de Sade's work was treated until recently is perhaps partially attributable to the fact that until recently there was no decent text to work on (it is to de Beauvoir's credit that her essay was so comprehensive without one). After World War II, the situation was somewhat remedied by relatively full editions in Belgium and France, though the complicated censorship laws in the latter hardly helped. Both Jean Paulhan and Georges Bataille assisted in the work of restoration. The 1952 Pauvert edition, in its small crown octavo format, was impounded by the French Ministry of the Interior before it could go the distance. In 1966 Claude Tchou had another shot, a number of detailed, beautifully bound volumes going out to subscribers of his *Cercle du Livre Précieux* (subsequently to pay equally beautiful homage to Balzac and Zola). Now Pauvert has returned to the fray, with a lavish 25-volume edition, including material not in Tchou, so that de Sade is in danger of passing from ignorance and ignominy to inflation by the centipedes of scholarship. The penalty, no doubt, for being so disreputable a literary specimen for so long.

Above all, every student of s-m owes a debt to a gentle, learned Frenchman called Maurice-Henri Meyer-Heine (usually known as Maurice Heine) who undertook a restoration of de Sade's reputation during the 1920's onwards. Born in Paris in 1884 Heine strayed from a medical career and sojourn in Algeria to a literary life in the capital after World War I, when his socialist interests of the time brought him near the surrealists, also flirting with what they knew of de Sade. A frail, courteous little man, Heine was a scrupulous scholar and in touch with the latest sexology as well as literature (he praised Ellis as early as 1926). In 1940 penury compelled him to take a modest teaching position near Paris; he died May 26th of that year, one week before the bicentenary of de Sade's birth at a moment when, in the words of his friend Gilbert Lély, European behavior was justifying Sade's most pessimistic views about "the incurable algolagnia of the human race."

Heine's mantle in this matter fell on Lély, who had been given access by de Sade's descendant, the Comte Xavier, to what were left of the family archives after the German ransacking of them in 1942. Lély spent most of the war years in Provence and then gave us his *Vie du Marquis de Sade*, published in two volumes by Gallimard, in 1952 and 1957. It rapidly acquired the reputation of being a work of whitewashing.

Lély then expanded this biography into what we now have as the vast volumes I and II of the Tchou edition; the first of these is 657 pages long and the second 695, both in small type. The whole took Lély over ten years to compile, and no wonder. For Volume I is virtually an anthology of documents, depositions, letters, doctor's reports, bills, hearings, the like (one footnote fights off the text for two whole pages); if it was to Heine's credit to straighten the record of the famous Marseilles affair (that of the allegedly poisoned and/or aphrodisiac candy de Sade experimented with), it is to Lély's to have provided us with almost every document we would want to have in connection with de Sade, and more. Unfortunately, Lély's expository and critical abilities are not of the same level as his anthological.

In the section that follows we are not going to presume to lock horns with the numerous theories and countertheories aroused by all this recent speculation and scholarship. But it would be a cop-out, in a book on s-m, to deny paternity to de Sade, whose work will always exert an irrational fascination on any true devotee of *le vice anglais*. What we shall try to do is brush off a few cobwebs and single out those elements truly conducive to a full eventuation of the s-m situation. If we provoke a certain confidence in handling de Sade, as well as giving a useful glimpse into the wellsprings of our *vice*, we shall have done all we hoped.

The first thing we observe, therefore, is that de Sade wrote about the unspeakable. He brought every conceivable sexual taste to the light of day and did not shirk their consequences. To the contrary, as de Beauvoir puts it, "He made of his sexuality an ethic." And he dared to do so because he took a new view of sex.

Indeed, although his attitudes altered, became (understandably) more and more misanthropic, sex was for him simply a positive sensation. It extended over all life and was closer to what was to be called, by the Freudians, libido. This is extremely important to a recognition of s-m. Though de Sade is miles from Tolstoy, Barbara Hardy claims that for the great Russian master also, "No single emotion of pure love exists, no separation of sexual from non-sexual vitality." Similarly, of the Italian novelist Alberto Moravia, R. W. B. Lewis writes, "Everything other than sex is, in the stories of Moravia, an extension of sex."

But while the Freudians used anthropological study in order

to demonstrate repression, and the need for social restraint on sex (as in Freud's own *Totem and Taboo,* for instance), de Sade himself would have found a far more congenial locus in Herbert Marcuse's *Eros and Civilization,* where libidinal forces are invited to expand over all life: "The regression involved in this spread of the libido would first manifest itself in the reactivation of all erotogenic zones and, consequently, in a resurgence of pre-genital polymorphous sexuality and in a decline of genital supremacy. The body in its entirety would become an object of cathexis, a thing to be enjoyed—an instrument of pleasure." One at once thinks of de Sade's extraordinary experiments with child-like anality and coprophilia in *The 120 Days,* a true investigation into taboo which has probably turned more readers off than any other single element. Basically, then, de Sade would have agreed with Marcuse's call for an "erotization of the entire personality" and "a spread rather than an explosion of libido—a spread over private and social relations which bridges the gap maintained between them by a repressive reality principle."

It will at once be objected that the Sadean scene culminates in a veritable vertigo, if not farrago, of genital orgasm. So it does. But here he is of course giving witness rather than propounding. De Sade was not saying that we should live like this, simply that we do. And his characters are frequently based on fact. His heroes torture and degrade women—so does our society. It would be a complete mistake to see women as sex objects in his work (except in the Butua section of *Aline et Valcour* where he holds a mirror of Swiftian satire up to his times); everyone is an object, a natural one in a co-fraternity of equals, including male homosexuals (a buggering bishop calmly comments, "The crime committed with a creature completely like yourself seems greater than that with one who is not"). There are of course whole pages of de Sade that might have been written by Betty Friedan. ("Must the diviner half of humankind be laden with irons by the other?")

Secondly, de Sade extends to the cerebrum. The philosophical needling of a victim can be as great an aphrodisiac as the actual torture. In truth, it needn't be needling, simply an idea will do it. Thus de Sade's whole orientation is fundamentally s-m. He insults society which at the same time he wants to re-order. Indeed, it is probably only in these past few years that de Sade's work has sunk into any sort of decent literary perspective at all. With the mass-production of pornography in America today de Sade is no longer read for arousal properties. Why, before the last World War even Joyce was used as jerk-off literature. With such provisoes in mind, then, we can look, just as briefly, at the man's life.

It was, if anything, almost more of a nightmare than his work. Indeed, the correlations can be acutely disturbing. As Ellis himself put it, "Many scenes of the Revolution were the embodiment in real life of de Sade's imagination; such, for instance, were the barbaric tortures inflicted, at the instigation of Théroigne de Méricourt, on La Belle Bouquetière."

The man whose prison cell (at Picpus) overlooked a guillotine to which 1,800 men and women lost their heads during a single month of his incumbency is scarcely likely to turn out an ardent supporter of capital punishment. De Sade nearly lost his own to this bloody instrument and probably had to assist in the burial of the corpses. As a matter of fact, the Fouquier "*réquisitoires*" (printed anew in Tchou) show a far more ferocious lust for blood on the part of the Accusateur Publique of the time than was ever exhibited by any fictional figure in de Sade.

It has similarly been pointed out that the Duc de Charolais was more bloodthirsty than any Sadean hero and de Sade evidently used him under his own name in the lost *Journées de Florbelle* (of which the manuscript notes vanished in the last World War, the original having been burnt by the Napoleonic police; fortunately Heine photographed these fragmentary, tempting notes and left a facsimile at the Bibliothèque Nationale). Finally, we know that de Sade himself declined a post in the provinces which would have licensed him to torture and kill. ("They wanted me to commit an inhumane act. I have never wanted to.") When he did hold office as a revolutionary *commissaire*, he helped his mother-in-law who had persecuted him relentlessly to escape the guillotine.

Donatien Alphonse [Aldonse] François de Sade was born on June 3, 1740, in Paris in the house or *hôtel* (i.e. palace) of the great Condé family. He was the only child of Jean Baptiste Joseph

François, Comte de Sade, Seigneur de Saumane et de La Coste and Co-Seigneur de Mazan, a cavalry colonel and governor-general of several provinces. The family pedigree, given in detail in Tchou, shows it ennobled in the twelfth century, with the husband of Petrarch's original for Laura as a direct forbear. De Sade's mother was a lady-in-waiting to the then Princesse de Condé, one of the first families of the land the last of whose line, Louis Henri Joseph, Duc de Bourbon, was found dead in suspicious circumstances in 1830 (officially a suicide, almost certainly an assassination organized by the English mistress he had brought back with him to Chantilly on the Restoration).

De Sade's youth was uneventful, culminating in the standard cavalry commission in the King's Guard, and subsequent service in Germany. Royal permission was given for an equally standard *mariage de raison* between de Sade and Renée-Pélagie Cordier de Launay de Montreuil, daughter of the President of the Board of Excise at Paris. Disaster started. De Sade didn't really know or like his intended and fell in love with her sixteen-year-old sister, Louise. However, he was made to marry Renée on May 17, 1763, in the presence of the King and Queen. On October 29th of the same year the King committed de Sade to prison in Vincennes. The *Ordre du Roi* was laconic; signed simply LOUIS, as was the custom, the sentence was indefinite, as was also the custom. De Sade had probably been betrayed by some girls he had attracted into his *petite maison* in Paris. This is about as close as we can get. The offense remains vague; the police may have been suborned. Why was the King interested in the matter? We do not know. But de Sade was at this time close to the Court and from this point on he was what we might call today in and out of prison, mostly in solitary confinement.

He was let out after two weeks, but this seems to have been sufficient to have branded him, at any rate in the eyes of the Paris Police Inspector of the day, Marais. De Sade's father died in 1767 and he succeeded to the title of Comte, indulging in some extravagance. In the following year occurred one of two sexual escapades of which we have fairly detailed depositions: this was his flagellation of Rose Keller, a thirty-six-year-old commoner. Enticed

somehow into his house, the woman escaped and complained. De
Sade gave her a huge indemnity, was detained at Saumur, admitted
much of her charge and was fined and released. The whole scandal
is given in detail in Tchou, even down (or up) to the doctors'
contentions about the kind of instruments used. These medical
pedants seem positively to have pored over the good woman's ample
buttocks in order to decide if such-and-such a contusion had been
caused by *verge, martinet,* or simple *bâton.*

The case was the Profumo affair of its day. Instead of keeping a
low profile after it, de Sade seems to have behaved with reckless
lack of prudence, virtually eloping to Italy with his beloved sister-
in-law Louise, while his wife was pregnant with what was to be
his second son. His behavior earned him the virulent and undying
enmity of his mother-in-law, the *"présidente"* or plain Madame
de Montreuil (a name reminiscent of Choderlos de Laclos' fictional Madame de Merteuil). From this point until his death she
persecuted de Sade systematically, and was responsible for his
major imprisonments (often from debt).

In June of 1792 de Sade went to Marseilles with a letter of
credit (viz. to raise funds). Once there he sent out a favorite servant
called Latour (*"il chasse pour le marquis,"* as a witness later put
it) to procure some girls for his pleasure. This led to the second,
and far more interesting, of his overt experiments with s-m. Everyone of his class had orgies, but de Sade had a thorough one. Those
of Charolais were bloodier, but de Sade staged a research session.
He whipped and was whipped, buggered and was buggered (by
Latour). It was this episode more than any other in his life or
work that gave his name to the perversion. Yet it was more than
mere hedonism (he appears to have suffered acutely himself). It
was a search for liberty, total self-understanding.

During the festivities he may have given some, or one, of the
girls sweetmeats. One of them, Rose Coste, age eighteen, declared
herself seriously ill as a result. The others then complained, made
hostile depositions, and the Public Prosecutor issued a warrant
for the arrest of de Sade and his valet. One incidental result of this
was a search of his Château de la Coste, and a minute inventory
of all his effects of the time (given in Tchou I). We even have the

examination of stool and vomit of the suffering maidens, as made by master apothecaries (one was called Rimbaud). It is doubtful that some of the girls in fact ate anything. Looked at from one point of view they were tough whores given a glorious chance to blackmail.

Another useful side-product was to bequeath us a physical description of de Sade at thirty-two. He was a small man with a small mouth, ruddy face, and piercing blue eyes. De Beauvoir describes him as "of medium height," but tallness is culturally coded, and she writes this on the same page that she gives us two testimonials of de Sade's height as five feet one.

Well, sodomy was a serious crime. Sometimes called *"biribi"* in de Sade's day, from a then popular song, it had in fact long carried the death penalty, and even today is looked on askance in our Southern states. Despite withdrawal of some of the charges, de Sade and Latour were sentenced to be executed for poisoning and sodomy, de Sade by decapitation and Latour by strangling. The document is given entire in Tchou and it is a grim one. The culprits wisely absenting themselves, both were burnt in effigy in nearby Aix.

We have said that the Marseilles affair was interesting. It certainly was, not only for the intimate descriptions of de Sade's repertoire of flagellatory instruments (including, in this case, a parchment cat garnished with hooked pins). De Sade seems to have acted as a sort of manic one-man Masters and Johnson sex team, indeed anticipating the parody of such presented in *Oh! Calcutta!* He whipped while being buggered. He buggered while being whipped. Having birched Mariette Borelly, the oldest of the ensemble, de Sade then instructed her to birch him, marking off the number of cuts he had received with a knife on the mantelpiece. Marianne Laverne, an eighteen-year-old Lyonnaise, lacked heart when de Sade told her to lay into him with the barbed martinet— *"elle ne put luy en donner que trois coups parce que le coeur luy manquait."* De Sade urged them to hit on and hit hard. In the spirit of a genuine sexologist he sniffed Marianne's anus, evidently hoping to have flavored her farts with his bonbons. He then buggered her while Latour buggered him.

A great deal is going on here, in every sense. We are watching a disciple of Holbach and La Mettrie, author of *L'Homme-Machine* (1748), push secular determinism on to parodistic proportions. Dashing around that Marseilles room like some Marx Brother of philosophy, one part of de Sade was saying: The mechanical philosophy is not going to satisfy man, and it might run amok. Now that we see that it has done so, we can surely agree with de Beauvoir that in this sense de Sade was, if somewhat inadvertently perhaps, a very great moralist—"if he seeks support in determinism, he does so, like many others, in order to lay claim to freedom."

In that modest third-storey apartment, 15 *bis* de la rue d'Aubagne, de Sade struck a real truth. Sex isn't what we call sex. It is a spread, rather than an explosion. It is everywhere, infusing and informing all we do with significance. So what is a perversion? What is normality? Perhaps even the lowest form of life can be transformed by the imagination; even a turd could be interesting, not through its intrinsic qualities, but by a meaning conferred upon it. ("The greatest pleasures are born from conquered repugnancies.") Give the world a new meaning, and even time and space could be overcome. So de Sade set himself to explore every possible anatomical possibility, a prophetic doctor or, better, semi-derisive father of the psychoanalytical couch.

We touch here, of course, on the reality principle. A human being has but a limited number of orifices. In his work written in prison, in his fantasy, de Sade created situations, sexual positions, which are probably impossible. Perhaps even deliberately so. The crescendic frenzy of the uncontrolled Sadean scene was brilliantly spoofed in a charming, but little-known, Olympia Press porno called *The New Organization,* by "Harriet Daimler" (Iris Owen). "This is the logic behind *The 120 Days,*" George Steiner writes. "With the pedantic frenzy of a man trying to carry *pi* to its final decimal, Sade labored to imagine and present the sum total of erotic combinations and variants. He pictured a small group of human bodies and tried to narrate every mode of sexual pleasure and pain to which they could be subject. The variables are surprisingly few."

All right, already. The point is de Sade's, before it is Steiner's. The precision of our civilization is mocked by the sexual encyclopedist, who is experimenting with sex as a relationship with a subject, not a thing. Facing up to coprophilia in *La Nouvelle Justine,* de Sade tells us, in de Beauvoir's apt summary, "that the truth of a thing lies not in what it is but in the meaning it has taken on for us in the course of our individual experience." On the way, we have learnt a lot about psychophysiology. America discovered the clitoral orgasm via its laboratory lovers, with the assistance of the Masters and Johnson electrodes. The same is to be found on every second page of *Juliette,* and in a context of ecstatic enjoyment there.

Obviously de Sade is not offering a marriage manual. That is the point. But if in the complex of feminine sexuality a chief pleasure is that "of being penetrated and filled by a man" (Susan Lydon), then let us see, de Sade was saying in Marseilles, if she can be buggered and fucked at the same time (she can, though it is not to be recommended for any or all of the participants).

The number of whip strokes administered in some of de Sade's stories would seem to be enough to hospitalize the victim for weeks. Yet it is to be noted that the police reports record the following counts listed one under the other on that Marseilles mantelpiece:

215

179

225

240

It is usually assumed that these have included cuts de Sade gave the others.

In his fiction this kind of high itemization is, anyway, part and parcel of nascent realism in the novel, which had already, in England, become the tool of a rising class. Deprived of his patron, the English writer could sink himself into society since his existence depended on receipts and sales rather than on an aristocratic employer who was also an esthetic arbiter (Lord Halifax tried to impose improvement on Pope's Homer). Partly because England had killed its monarch in 1649, it had by de Sade's day developed a certain political liberty (Voltaire envies such in *Candide*); in France and Germany there was still a court art. Rousseau's *Nouvelle Héloïse* netted the author almost nothing, the protection of a patron was essential.

Not so in England. Crusoe's contracts and computations have been shown, *chez* Defoe, to be pretty absurd, perhaps paranoiac, yet equally accurately predictive of the end of the feudal class which was displaced by the upper bourgeoisie via contracts as against inheritances (de Sade himself suffered embezzlement of his own). When we come to Balzac, we get this monomaniacal objectification again; there are certain books of *The Human Comedy* from which you come away with a sense of almost continuous screwing, killing, or making money, in a perfectly grotesque social burlesque (e.g. *Cousine Bette*).

The organs of sex, de Sade realized, are those of excretion. Money is said to be anal—or copophragous, so much dung we feed on. De Sade's work is nearly as littered with digitary computations as that of Balzac or Zola, where they do carry, we must admit, a cash-register monotony at times. Again, we note de Sade spreading sex over this, as de Beauvoir rightly remarks: "Theft appears in his work as a sexual act, and the mere suggestion of it is enough to cause orgasm." Today we know that kleptomania is often accompanied by a high state of sexual tension.

Thus, indirectly, Marseilles starts de Sade's long series of imprisonments. His mother-in-law intercepts his letters, gets him imprisoned at Chambéry, in Savoy. With the help of his remarkably long-suffering and faithful wife Renée (who may even have procured for him—small as he was, de Sade seems to have been highly attractive to women) he escapes through a lavatory window. But in 1778, after the death of his own mother, de Sade is arrested by his old enemy Marais, roughed up, and incarcerated at Vincennes, the first of many cold, damp cells through the doors of which food was pushed in to him "like a wild beast." In 1784 he was transferred to the Bastille.

De Sade was kept in these prisons by *lettres de cachet,* given to the complainant, usually his mother-in-law. The nearest modern equivalent might be something like committing someone to a mental hospital. He was not formally accused (though he begged to be), he was simply slowly destroyed incommunicado, or almost, his wife's visits, like his own exercise, being severely rationed. In his last years at the *maison de santé* of Charenton-Saint-Maurice he was all but blind, vastly fat, and suffering agonies from the gout.

He had already started his prison writings by the time he got to the Bastille, though the "philosophy" seems to have cohered later. The first version of *Justine* was written around 1787, coming out *"En Hollande"* (viz. Paris, Girouard), in two octavo volumes in 1791. Seventeen works in all came out by de Sade in his lifetime, excluding those erroneously attributed to him. Of these seventeen, nine are fictions, or fantasies, including under this head the drama *Oxtiern* (in which he acted). The rest were political petitions, discussions, reports. *Dorci* was published posthumously in 1881, with a notice by Anatole France, while *The 120 Days* was given us by "Bloch"-Dühren in 1904. We do not mean to pause over these here.

The legends of de Sade in the Bastille abound. He apparently incited the populace against the prison, using a sort of tube-and-funnel loudspeaker system he had himself set up. On July 4, 1789, he was therefore transferred to Charenton, ten days before the Bastille was stormed by the mob. Seals were found affixed to his cell door. *Lettre de cachet* prisoners were then amnestied by the Constituent Assembly and de Sade was released on April 2, 1790.

During the "Terror" de Sade was initially in with the revolutionaries. On August 30, 1792, he did twenty-four hours guard duty at the Tuileries and a few days later, as the massacres started in earnest, he seems to have been elected Secretary of his Section des Piques, or ward district. On the 21st of this month the Assembly handed over authority to a new body, the National Convention, which immediately voted for the abolition of the monarchy. Citizen de Sade's ward papers, some reporting on hospital conditions, have come down to us.

It must have been an incredible time for him, enough to turn any man's imagination. He himself had purloined the butcheries in his books from those of men like Charolais, Richelieu, in real life, only to find fact now savagely surpassing his wildest fantasies therefrom. On September 6, 1792, de Sade wrote a letter to his law-yer Gaufridy filled with disgust at the fact that three days earlier 10,000 prisoners had been butchered in a single day—"The former Princesse de Lamballe was one of the victims. Her head, stuck on a pike, was shown to the King and Queen and her poor body was dragged through the streets for eight hours after being subjected to the most savage debauchery." He had the tact not to itemize the last, which included the slicing off of her mons by an executioner and sticking it on her upper lip as a mustache.

The Section des Piques to which de Sade was elected by the revolutionary regime was the most democratic imaginable (for-merly the Place Vendôme Ward), as can be seen by the nature of the "*commissaires*" other than himself elected to it (listed, inevitably, in Tchou). But he was clearly disgusted by the "Terror" and, on suspicion of moderantism, put into a series of prisons by the police. From these he was let out penniless, destitute, and sick. After a period trying to live in a garret, he went into a state hospital for a while "dying of cold and hunger." In 1801 he and his publisher were arrested for pornography (*Justine* and *Juliette*). Thrown into Sainte-Pélagie prison (of his own short stay in which, some years later, Gérard de Nerval wrote a poem) de Sade found it the worst of all. He implored the Minister of Justice either to release him or sentence him properly.

Instead, he was returned to the asylum at Charenton, suffering from "sexual dementia." This was a method by which Napoleon stifled likely dissidents, and the Emperor remained deaf to all pleas. Barely able to walk, occasionally visited by his family, de Sade died on December 2, 1814. The world's subversive had been in various prisons for twenty-eight years and we do not even know who accom-panied him to his last, under a cheap and nameless slab in Saint-Maurice cemetery.

"To sympathize with de Sade too readily is to betray him," wrote Simone de Beauvoir. This was in her famous *Temps Mod-ernes* article "*Faut-il brûler Sade?*" which remains one of the most perceptive summaries of his thinking, though its first part (which appeared in December, 1951) is marred by High Existentialese. This jargon blemished the same author's brilliant *The Second Sex* far less, since application of the existential principle of The Other seems more stable, and can be much more helpful, in a man/ woman setting than in a sadist/masochist where the sexes fluctuate and interchange. In fact, existentialism in the former is a genuinely useful tool and *The Second Sex*, which had come out two years before the essay on de Sade, contains admirable pages on what masochism means to a woman. Once again, it is no surprise to find a leading feminist sympathetic to de Sade. But de Beauvoir is right: to call de Sade "the first reasoned socialist," as does Gorer, is really to draw his teeth. He exceeds the label.

Moreover, admiration of de Sade tends perhaps to qualify somewhat his true strength, which was to understand horror. Addressing himself to "the anxious man whose first reaction is to de Sade as his daughter's potential murderer," Georges Bataille, in his 1954 Preface to *Justine* (elaborated in his later *Death and Sensuality*) puts this paradox poetically:

> Certain minds are fired by the thought of turning the most securely established values topsy-turvy. They are thus able to say gaily that the most subversive man who ever lived—the Marquis de Sade—was also the man who rendered the greatest service to humanity. Nothing to their mind could be more certain; we shiver at the thought of death and pain (even the death and pain of other people), tragic or unspeakable events cut us to the quick, but that which inspires us with terror is like the sun, no less glorious if we turn our weak eyes away from its blaze. Like the sun at least in being intolerable to the naked eye, the figure of de Sade fascinated and terrified his contemporaries: Was not the very idea that the monster was alive revolting?

When we approach de Sade's thinking (by which we mean his feeling), we realize that we have to cull the majority of it from the mouths of his fictional characters. Many—even most—of these are women. Justine is generally spoken to (as befits the relationship), whereas Juliette recounts, in the first person feminine, as had evidently also been the plan for much more of *The 120 Days;* in the length and relish of the *Juliette* redaction it is tempting to see, with Klossowski, destruction by a mother virago (de Sade's Madame de Montreuil). But we must not forget that de Sade was a writer, if not a very good nor careful one, and that a character's dialog is not invariably an author's thought. For instance, de Beauvoir calls Dolancé (in *La Philosophie dans le Boudoir*) "Sade's mouthpiece."

It is true that he does, at one point, resume de Sade's known political ideas but to endorse in the same way statements by characters as different as Noirceuil, Blangis, and Gernande can be risky. It is done on the assumption that such characters shared sexual tastes with their creator.

This is far from certain. We know now that de Sade was making a *catalogue raisonné* of so-called sexual perversion. Thus Geoffrey Gorer writes: "I do not think that there is a single unconscious wish or fantasy painfully recovered from themselves or their patients by Sigmund Freud, Melanie Klein, and their numerous associates and followers which is not described as being performed in at least one of de Sade's surviving novels."

There is no evidence that de Sade went in for the sort of massive blood-letting indulged in by Gernande as a turn-on device (unless we take Rose Keller's highly suspicious testimony that de Sade cut her back in places with a knife against that of the doctors who examined her; and he used no knife in Marseilles). There *is* evidence, however, that such people as Gernande exist in our State mental hospitals today, where their cathection is a pitiable conflation of what society has almost ubiquitously fantasized as the vampire myth. Only a year ago a Puerto Rican was discovered in the Bronx buying buckets of blood from a butcher; this he splashed on the floor of his apartment before he could make it with his wife. In 1949, John George Haigh confessed in London to the murder of nine people, drinking blood from the jugular vein of each; Peter Kurten, the celebrated Düsseldorf murderer beheaded in 1930, was driven to ejaculation by the sight of his victims' gore.

So, to start with, de Sade's philosophy comes down to us in fantasy. This is the essence of s-m. The pantomimic nature of the Sadean scene is all-important here, for it calls forth the imagination. That children are also polymorphous perverts in this way, playing with feces and fetishizing objects (as Baudelaire saw in his essay on toys), scarcely invalidates the love play; you can term it regression if you like but, as we have suggested, you can also call it conquest. We note that *The 120 Days* has a perfect s-m structure: *the scenario is narrated before being enacted.* Hence the lover becomes an actor or magician; de Beauvoir well observes: "The world of the masochist is a magical one, and that is why he is almost always a fetishist." She continues:

> By means of this duplication the act becomes a spectacle which one observes from a distance at the same time that one is performing it. It thus retains the meaning that would otherwise be obscured by solitary animal excitement. For if the debauchee coincided exactly with his movements and the victim with his emotions, freedom and consciousness would be lost in the rapture of the flesh. The flesh would be merely brute suffering, and the rapture merely convulsive pleasure.

As Gérard de Nerval was to put it, "Animals love close to, minds from a distance." For this reason, indeed, sadism has come for the man in the street, Mr. T. C. Mits, to be virtually some sort of sorry synonym for cruelty, while we observe that France, the culture of intellect, has given us some of our outstanding s-m documents (de Sade, *O, The Image,* etc.).

There is another initial proviso to make in this context. All de Sade's works without exception get involved at some point with religion; his first work was an apology for atheism, *Dialogue entre un prêtre et un moribond* of 1782. A large part of *Justine* takes place in a Rabelaisian anti-monastery. This prompted Huysmans, much later, to an analysis of sadism as the left hand of God:

> This strange and ill-defined condition cannot in fact arise in the mind of an unbeliever. It does not consist simply in riotous indulgence of the flesh, stimulated by bloody acts of cruelty, for in that case it would be nothing more than a deviation of the genetic instincts, a case of satyriasis developed to its fullest extent; it consists first and foremost in a sacrilegious manifestation, in a moral rebellion, in a spiritual debauch, in a wholly idealistic, wholly Christian aberration . . . The truth of the matter is that if it did not involve sacrilege, sadism would have no *raison d'être.*

As has been said, there is a great deal at issue here. De Sade's venom against the Church—for us today surely a fairly harmless institution—seems excessive, a mania. His blasphemy knows no bounds, and indeed makes for considerable monotony, though sometimes the level of his prose rises within it. This vein in his work may have been, in fact, what made the fictional form more congenial to him than poetry or drama, since the novel was an increasingly secular force. De Sade wanted a God he could respect.

In de Sade's day the Roman Catholic religion was a repository of ritual and fetishism. Tempting to any creative mind (as illustrated in England at the end of the nineteenth century), this religion requires a creative effort for escape from its harness. Huysmans was in a sense right; the overthrow of religion meant for de Sade a real moral rebellion, and it took him into the depths of man.

So he gleefully—if over-lengthily, for modern tastes—ridicules this lost magic, because he has found another. He gives us a rambunctious sexual Black Mass, in which Justine is fucked on the altar, as in the convention for such, and miscommunicated, the Holy Host being stuffed up her anus.* Christianity is seen, as apparently it first was in Rome, as a fanatical cult replete with bloody horror, the conception of "a leprous Jew who, born of a slut and a soldier in the world's meanest stews, dared fob himself off for the organ of him who, they say, created the universe!"

The passage is footnoted with an inference of sodomy between Christ and Peter (via the text "Thou art Peter and upon this Rock I will build my Church"); it concludes, "these atrocities are not what we want for our guidance; I should prefer to die a thousand deaths rather than believe them. When atheism will wish for martyrs, let it designate them; my blood is ready to be shed."†

De Sade's emancipation required energy, a true leap of the imagination. For, following the agnostic determinists, and witnessing in daily life the discrepancy between Christian profession and

---

* De Sade invented nothing here. Some such desecration of the Host, over which the magician sometimes ejaculated, was an essential ingredient of the Black Mass, as the *Grimoires* and the *Malleus Maleficarum* attest. The seventeenth-century Marquise de Montespan had the Host inserted up her cunt.

† In fact, de Sade was more of a gnostic than an agnostic, writing a frenzied gloss on Augustine's "Love [God] and do what you will." For the gnostics "the world was thoroughly evil and its accepted moral codes had been invented by the Archons to keep men in subjection . . . They said that good and evil are meaningless labels and that the way to perfection is to experience everything" (Richard Cavendish, *The Black Arts,* New York: Capricorn Books, 1967, p. 293).

practice, de Sade offers us a different secret to the mysteries of being—*sex*. Nature is what rules the world, not God. And nature is greedy, cruel, destructive. As in Balzac, the natural man mainly wants to screw, eat, and drink—on the side exploiting the weak in order to ensure that he does so in abundance.

Hobbes (cited by de Sade) had told us something of the same, and Swift put forward the resultant syllogism in satire: namely, that civilization is then presumably so much departure from nature. If that is the case, why may not bourgeois morality emanating from religion, and presuming to have abstract laws based on the human contract, legitimately require our obedience? Surely the Ten Commandments must exact our allegiance?

To some extent, de Sade was caught in the trap of this tautology, notably in his view of crime. In his perfect state, inasmuch as one can systematize such, there are virtually no crimes except those directly suborning the human organization itself (rape and murder). "For since Nature dictates to us equally vices and virtues . . . her inspiration would become a certain rule for what is good or bad." Murder deprives man "of the only gift he has received from Nature and the only one whose loss is irreparable." There is clearly an incompatibility here between the inequality of nature and, since all human inclinations are natural, the desiderated equality of society.

Just so. De Sade took a full look at the worst and seems generally to have concluded that man is still a part of nature (or, that nature still has a strong part in man). This being the case, we must unfortunately evolve some laws by which to protect the weaker among us. That is why Baudelaire wrote of him, "*Il faut toujours en revenir à de Sade, c'est-à-dire à l'homme naturel, pour expliquer le mal.*" Since Christian morality did not recognize natural man, it was inadequate to this task. Voltaire had said the same; in that Leibnitzian optimism Voltaire castigated in *Candide* evil was simply a deficiency in the general system—one hears the echo today in "He's sick" of some rapist—and was not recognized as a force in itself. Christianity simply bottled such forces up, in the manner of much Freudian repression (an effect largely shared by the Ten Commandments). Thus for de Sade the worst ills in society were religion, private property, family relationships, all class barriers and any form of censorship—approximately in that order. It will be noted that all these imply *a priori* relationships governing conduct. Such never satisfied de Sade who was an intense, if pessimistic, realist.

The epistolary novel *Aline et Valcour,* which Professor Jean Fabre finds remarkably close to Laclos, concludes with a long account of a man called Sainville who reaches his Utopia through a Dystopia: the latter is called Butua and was everything de Sade had seen, feared, and detested. Butua is ruled by an absolute monarchy dominated by male chauvinist pigs (in fact, by horny cannibals), with women as well-subdued sex objects. A priesthood is in charge of education.

Sainville then founders for a fortnight on an island called Tamoé whose Prince, Zamé, shows him what was surely, for de Sade, the ideal society. Tamoé is without prisons or death penalty; its men and women are completely equal, children being brought up outside the family. There is complete freedom of the press, with truth conquering error in an open arena, incest is harmless and sodomy regarded with indifference. Population is limited and murder, like rape, is considered more in the context of an undesirable and eventually eliminatable error—"it should never be punished by murder" (viz. capital punishment). There are no property rights and, indeed, the most ardent Women's Libber would approve of the education of women, who not only may choose men but are trained in pugilism ("*pugilat*"). In a word, "if you make them realize the necessity of virtue, because their own happiness depends upon it, they will be honest people by egoism." Some of the constitutions in the newly independent Caribbean islands are not far from this ethic: you don't kill people, or infringe on their rights, since it is in your own best interests not to.

Yet we should not take this as a mere Swiftian sneer or, in de Sade's case, an aristocratic shrug of disdain. It would be wrong to think in terms of a policy of crude egoism. De Sade's ideal society, swiftly glimpsed in Tamoé, would involve that domestication of the libido, of our deepest chthonic drives, which lay at the heart of so-called "savage" societies of the past. Lévi-Strauss has been showing us as much lately. Jung tried to do the same:

> . . . man, whose fundamental make-up discerns an absolutely indispensable meaning in the happiness he brings to his neighbor, can never win his life's optimum upon the line of egoism. An unbridled craving for individual pre-eminence is equally unfitted to achieve this optimum, since the collective element is so strongly rooted in man that his yearning for fellowship destroys all pleasure in naked egoism. The optimum of life can be gained only by obedience to the tidal laws of the libido . . . If the attainment of this way consisted in a mere surrender to instinct, which is what is really meant by the bewailer of "naturalism," the profoundest philosophical speculation and the whole history of the human mind would have no sort of *raison d'être*. Yet, as we study the Upanishad philosophy, the impression grows on us that the attainment of the path is not just the simplest of tasks. Our western air of superiority in the presence of Indian understanding is a part of our essential barbarism, for which any true perception of the quite extraordinary depth of those ideas and their amazing psychological accuracy is still but a remote possibility. In fact, we are still so uneducated that we actually need laws from without, and a task-master or Father above, to show us what is good and the right thing to do.

As with de Sade, postulation of divinity outside or above the self means a reduction of the potentiality of libido. For the Indian and Chinese cultures Jung so suggestively examines in *Psychological Types* the reverse obtained. There was no projection ("God, i.e. the highest intensity of life, then resides in the soul, in the unconscious"). The closest our civilized society gets to this feeling of inward wonder and love is in childhood when, for a moment, all seems allowed and everything streams from within.

Now children are often selfish and cruel. De Sade was not saying we should live *as* children, but a little more *like* children. When Baudelaire called genius "voluntarily recaptured infancy," he was advocating the same, an eventuation of certain childhood processes under control on the adult plane. For in infancy the so-called "soul," later to be "projected" by religion, is a glorious libidinal accumulation to be shared by all. De Sade was thus pro-

posing, in his ideal society, another form of egoism, in place of
egotistical aggression; this would involve a new recognition of our
inner processes. This recognition would spread outwards into the
environment and make for an increase in total happiness, since
love and veneration for others would automatically become guid-
ing principles.

De Sade was, as de Beauvoir reminds us, dealing only with
humans. In electing for a God man denies himself. Everything de
Sade wrote was calculated to make men *recognize* themselves. Thus
laws based on revenge, like torture or execution, were useless as
well as repellently barbaric since they tended to remove responsibility for the original behavior. They were themselves so much constitutional crime.

Furthermore, in this act of self-recognition, we come up against
what Georges Bataille well calls "a sovereign and indestructible
element of mankind, yet one that *evades conscious appraisal*"
(italics added). This is cardinal since it tests everything we call
civilization. How can violence (like that at My-lai) happen in our
advanced societies? It must be a sickness, an error . . . in short,
sadism. De Sade, however, asked us to recognize violence as we do
death for, as Bataille puts it, "the same peoples are alternately
barbarous and civilized in their attitudes . . . all civilized men are
capable of savagery. Lynch law belongs to men who rate themselves
as among the most highly civilized of our age." We have to become
aware of our needs in order to contain their consequences; and
violence is frequently the motor of sex.

Professor Morse Peckham would press the indictment even
closer home. In a difficult passage in his classic work on pornography he deals with violence in a democracy as follows:

> The current challenge to police violence is, then, a challenge to
> the culture's belief system, and suggests that in a society with a
> democratic belief system police violence is directly related to the
> self-policing and nonuniformed policing in the society as a whole;
> that is, from this point of view, a democratic society must be a
> violent society . . . The extension of a democratic belief system from
> an aristocracy to an entire society, as has happened in American
> society, means an extension of violence as a mode of self-policing.

Consequently the current liberal challenge to police violence is rightly though obscurely felt to be a challenge to American democratic ideals and values.

This is very nice. In de Sade's day, as to a minor extent in the England of our youth, you had policed violence. We tried to suggest in our chapter on milieu that, on the whole, the general populace concurred in what correction was administered by its elected constabulary.

But the "democratic" belief system of modern America makes the criminal into a kind of peer. An act of crime becomes something very vague under this system, where a Charles Manson is likely to be on the Johnnie Carson Show before long and even Sirhan Sirhan, who was seen by 40 million to have killed Robert Kennedy, must be referred to as an *alleged* murderer. Under these conditions, with wide dubiety in the courts, the police will certainly become violent just as will we ourselves when settling a score with a mugger on some lonely street. An anarchy, unlike the eighteenth-century French aristocracy, is scarcely self-policed.

Peckham's point separates de Sade completely from the would-be socialist Utopias of our own time, all explaining away violence or trying to eradicate it by perfecting new social forms. The trouble is, a relief institution (such as a social form) cannot resolve these great, lumbering, atavistic tensions inherent in humanity. Only love can do that. "To strike so deep into human nature," Peckham points out, "is to uncover what most people would rather not face, a behavioral aspect so deeply buried by cognition and socialization that it cannot be recognized. Hence the horror which sadomasochism arouses, deriving either from defenses against accepting what is in every human being, or from simple failure to recognize it."

It is extremely significant that as regards sex our socialist Utopias have in fact turned out to be highly puritanical. Despite bonuses for children born out of wedlock (i.e. for cannon fodder), the Nazi state was intensely prudish; raids on and closing of Berlin homosexual bars were a publicized feature of the party's early life. All Hirschfeld's works to date were incinerated in the party's book-burning holocaust of 1933. Mussolini's Italy followed suit (see the bathing incident in Thomas Mann's "Mario and the Magician"). The first thing Castro did in Cuba, as Allende in Chile, was to close the nightclubs. Libya has followed suit.

De Sade worked from the other end of the telescope. As Freud was to tell us, we are moved to pleasure. But pleasure is fringed by pain (as in somewhat analogous matters of temperature, or eating). "Pain is merely a sentiment of aversion which the soul conceives for some movements contrary to the construction of the body it animates" (de Sade through Noirceuil). The emotions are experienced in the same place. The sooner we recognize this instinctual animal heritage in ourselves, instead of simply erecting illogical barriers against its appearances, the better. Our collective happiness depends on as great an extension of sex as possible—in the Marcuse manner.

In his notes on Laclos' *Dangerous Liaisons* Baudelaire observed, "The revolution was made by voluptuous men. Licentious books therefore comment on and explain the Revolution." This is well seen. It is not simply that we have a long record of male political power standing in for sexual power, extending from Machiavelli's *Mandragola* to the admissions of Léon Blum, nor was it merely that the libertine was interested in, among other things, liberty. Baudelaire knew that in the French tradition of licentious or gallant writings important revolutionary ideas lay embedded. Scabrous as he was, de Sade was the first revolutionary novelist, just as he was the last aristocratic theoretician. As today reality overtakes our worst dreams, we come more and more to lean on the fantasist; it is a fact that it was creative writers in America who were among the first to sense the direction and implication of the Vietnam "commitment." As Jung put it: "What creative minds bring up out of the collective unconscious also actually exists, and sooner or later must make its appearance in collective psychology. Anarchy, regicide, the constant increase and splitting off of an anarchistic element upon the extreme socialist left, with an avowed program that is absolutely hostile to culture—these are phenomena of mass-psychology, which were long adumbrated by poets and creative thinkers."

Paradoxically, if we admit this, and concede de Sade's true

egoism, we are *less* not more likely to trample on the rights of others. We simply would not need to take it out on society. If Christian "virtues" don't give us happiness, they cannot be in touch with our unconscious. " 'Sex' is as important as eating or drinking and we ought to allow the one appetite to be satisfied with as little restraint or false modesty at the other" (*Juliette*). In *Justine* de Sade had said the same (through a monk):

> "Now, if we avow that the senses' joy is always dependent upon the imagination, always regulated by the imagination, one must not be amazed by the numerous variations the imagination is apt to suggest during the pleasurable episode, by the infinite multitude of different tastes and passions the imagination's various extravagances will bring to light. However luxurious these tastes, they ought not appear more remarkable than those of an ordinary species; there is no reason to find a meal-time eccentricity less extraordinary than a bedroom whim and in the one and the other, it is not more astonishing to idolize what the common run of mankind finds detestable than it is to love something generally recognized as good. Unanimity proves organic conformity, but demonstrates nothing in favor of the beloved object. Three-quarters of the universe may find the rose's scent delicious without that serving either as evidence upon which to condemn the remaining quarter which might find the smell offensive, or as proof that this odor is truly agreeable."

This is really to assume a responsibility we have only recently dared to approach. It is to admit what we all secretly avow, even crave, and to eventuate the erotic into social life. It is, in a very real sense, to become children again.

And children have to learn the reality of relationships, that other people with equal claims as their own exist. It was undeniable that in de Sade's day women were subordinate in position, though not always in influence—if it is objected that no women could get into the inbred politics of Versailles, no more might a number of men, including poor Army officers like Laclos.

De Sade proposed that we take a new look at women, for it was the humbug of bourgeois morality, grounded on a male-dominated religion, that had kept women in subservience so long. One wonders how many of the termagants of Women's Lib, enveighing against something called "sadism," know that in de Sade's ideal state there is *complete sexual equality in every department of life*. Indeed, Apollinaire even advanced the notion that this was the motive of de Sade's work and precisely why he wrote *Justine* and *Juliette*.

Enlightening sidelights get thrown on this, from time to time. At current writing a lot of feminist ink is being spilt about trying to stop prostitution—as degrading to women, insulting, and the like. Once again, de Sade approached the problem from the other end. We cannot negate our sexual drives. Some are always going to want immediate sexual enjoyment; this did not imply possession ("I have no right to the possession of the stream that I come to on my road, but I have to its enjoyment"—as with the comparison between meal-time oddities and bedroom whims, de Sade's analogies can be flawed by strict logic). Rather than proposing that men should not have access to prostitutes, de Sade said that women should have similar access, at any time, to desirable males, who would not be allowed to refuse their slightest sexual whims.* As de Beauvoir suggested, there is a strange fraternity between sadism and stoicism.

Moreover, in common with Laclos, de Sade predicated a greater intensity of sexual drive in women than in men. This is summarized in that moment in the third volume (1st Pauvert) of *Juliette* when Clairwil, who has known every possible vagary of erotic ecstasy, cuts out a boy's heart and stuffs it, still palpitating, into her cunt. She recommends the practice to Juliette who then remarks she once knew a man with similar tastes; he made a hole in an equally throbbing heart, shoved his prick through it, and discharged. But Clairwil corrects her: " '*Cela pouvait être charmant,' dit Clairwil, 'mais moins joli que ce je fais.'* " Juliette duly tries it but, her orifice proving too small, she has to slice the organ up for entry ("*une partie c'est tout ce qu'il faut*"). Evidently the cut-up heart (male again, we note, it could have been a girl's) produces

---

* Compare Manhattan's current The Golden Tongue Salon "For the Liberated Woman . . . on the fashionable East Side," offering "10 straight men" specializing in everything from "tingling tongue massage" to "toe sucking" ("Luncheon served—special group rates. Bring the entire mahjong group")—all under the rubric, "Be the first on your block to hire a cock."

even more exquisite sensations. De Sade is once more moralizing, of course. And the heart is that of Zagreus/Dionysos.

He is saying that we are in love with pleasure. Pleasure is produced by sensation, and ecstasy can cohabit with pain, which fringes pleasure. Here de Sade is making real contributions to our understanding, not only in the over-spill idea advanced by Ellis, but in other ways. Ellis cites "a woman who delighted in arousing anger for the pleasure it gave her, and who advised another woman to follow her example and excite her husband's anger, as nothing was so enjoyable as to see a man in a fury of rage." Yet the Reikian description, somewhat elaborate, of love's constant hunt for intensity also comes in here. Reik shows this to be highly ambivalent, with love Janus-faced and quickly converting to hatred when thwarted.

Thus de Sade was a true Enlightenment figure. Man was an animal, and therefore a machine. Agnostic La Mettrie had said the same and, as a result, had had to flee for refuge to the court of Frederick II. De Sade added the idea, on which much modern psychology rests, that the clockwork with which this man-machine is wound up is sex. The motto of his state might well have been Rabelais' for his Abbey of Thélème—"*Fay ce que vouldras*" (do as you like . . . or, if it feels good, do it). Nature does not forgive Justine for her obstinate objection to it (for which read Christian repression), striking her finally with a thunderbolt, in a parallel/parody of the taking of Semele by Zeus himself.

In real life de Sade had seen kings killed, destruction turn into an ecstasy, crime become the law of the land. It was Camus who claimed that the killing of the king in France was also the effective guillotining of transcendant values in society (he ignored the British regicides of 1649 who might have demonstrated his thesis even more clearly, Charles I refusing to stand trial since, he said, he had no human peer). The "Bloch"-Dühren biography of de Sade is replete with examples of how his work mirrored social events of the time; the satanic fatal man raped the persecuted maiden of old institutions, including Christianity. It was a very Gothic agony, indeed.

So man has no free will. Yet he has one gift that makes him

a god. This is his imagination, the built-in "conversion" device of our species. No animal has it. The sense of this aspiration in ourselves, the god within us, which Baudelaire was to seize on again and again, and call "the queen of the faculties," would alone be enough to give de Sade a place in the entomology of the man-machine. "The pleasure of the senses is always regulated in accordance with the imagination." Again, "Man can aspire to felicity only by serving all the whims of his imagination." It is this recognition of the role played by the intellect in sensation that makes de Sade speak to us today. It is truly prescient and, to someone interested in s-m, it is all-important.

For we are not all clods. Intelligence *is* a turning-on trait. Women notoriously find intellectuals exciting, and they do so in measure as their own is developed. No gatefold center-spread in *Playboy,* no one-night stand with throbbing stud or quivery teeny bopper, can really substitute for a relationship between minds. "You have given me your mud," Charles Baudelaire told the world, "and I have made gold of it." De Sade has his anti-monk say the same:

> "Objects have no value for us save that which our imagination imparts to them; it is therefore very possible, bearing the constant truth well in mind, that not only the most curious but even the vilest and most appalling things may affect us very appreciably. The human imagination is a faculty of man's mind whereupon, through the senses' agency, objects are painted, whereby they are modified, and wherein, next, ideas become formed, all in reason of the initial glimpsing of those external objects. But this imagination, itself resultative of the kind of organization man is endowed with, only adopts the received objects in such-and-such a manner and afterwards only creates ideas according to the effects produced by the perceived objects' impact . . . these fundamentals once grasped, it should not by any means be cause for astonishment that what distinctly pleases some is able to displease others, and, conversely, that the most extraordinary thing is able to find admirers. The dwarf also discovers certain mirrors in which he appears handsome."

This marvelous transforming mirror we may hold up to reality can, in love, create artists of us all. For an enchanted moment we can make the hideous world lovely. Throughout *The 120 Days* the ultimate in ugliness (chiefly, feces) is converted into sexual stimulation, as de Sade hectically, and not a little heroically, pushes on his thesis.

Thus de Sade stands on the threshold of that long romantic tradition of Our Lady of Pain, the figure in whom beauty and death are twinned, and which by implication rejects the "normal" world whose airline-hostess standards of good looks are seen as insipid. Beauty is as much a social norm as the manner in which we regard dwarves. De Sade opposed his society, and our own, when he wrote, "Many people prefer for their pleasure an old, ugly, even a stinking woman to a fresh and pretty girl."

The theme of cursed beauty was, of course, one that drew Baudelaire to Poe, as Nerval to several "fatal" visionaries, and both men in their own lives to disastrous erotic liaisons. Mario Praz furnished an entire litany of ladies of pain in the chapter of his best-known work called *La Belle Dame Sans Merci*, ranging from hunchbacks, dwarves, amputees, to lovely epileptics, seductive hags, sensuous consumptives, delectable idiots and, needless to say, that epitome of social deformation, the prostitute.

De Sade stands at the genesis of much of this. Kleist, Mérimée, Baudelaire, Hoffman, Poe, Gautier, Strindberg, D'Annunzio, even Ibsen (whose Rebecca West, after all, "kills" the man who loves her)—the list of contributors to the tradition could be continued to Proust and Joyce, for Leopold Bloom's masturbatory fantasy, Gerty McDowell, is, we notice, lame. Why? She does not have to be so. It is not her limp that turns Bloom on. No, this is what Erich Heller, when discussing Thomas Mann's physically sick yet sexually attractive Clavdia Chauchat, neatly called her "invalid love rising from the invalidity of life."

When reality is as deficient as it was for de Sade, it must be redeemed, transvalued. S-m can assist in this necessary esthetic transcendence, in which the lover's relation to his beloved is that of an artist to his work. The memoirs of Edith Cadivec, a flagellantine Viennese schoolmistress in the 1920's, are full of cries of admiration of the artistry of the dominant in this particular s-m situation. ("My adored Dominatrix . . . You great artist, you play upon my soul as upon an instrument. You know me better than I know my-self, only you have shown me where the primordial grounds of my being lie.") For, contrary to much popular assumption, such in-spired play can be nearer pure contemplation than blows and force. Indeed, de Sade comes oddly close to Schopenhauer at points, sen-sing how exposed the individual may be in his raptures and sorrows. The true servant of art and Eros aspires to an Apollonian illusion, a balance between hostile forces in the psyche, which can lead to the pinnacles of bliss. As de Beauvoir put it, "The image is the enchanted domain from which no power whatever can expel the solitary despot."

De Sade paid his price for grasping this great beauty, of daring to go beyond biology, to be both victim and executioner in one. In this sense Borel was right: de Sade was a "martyr," to new knowl-edge. De Beauvoir once more correctly describes the case:

> In demanding that his partner mistreat him, he tyrannizes over him; his humiliating exhibitions and the tortures he undergoes humiliate and torture the other as well. And, vice versa, by befoul-ing and hurting the other, the torturer befouls and hurts himself. He participates in the passivity which he discloses, and in wanting to apprehend himself as the cause of the torment he inflicts, it is as an instrument and therefore as an object that he perceives himself. We are thus justified in classing behavior of this kind under the name of sadomasochism.

Today de Sade's voice is calling to us more clearly than ever before, as we stand on the brink of annihilation of the human race. He is telling us to liberate the monsters in the sealed cells of our unconscious; unless we do so, we shall continue to have more wars— for peace. He saw the direction of our civilization in advance and he pulled it out into the open for us to have a good look at it.

As he put it of himself, a man whose worst crime was to have beaten the bottom of a whore was somewhat less destructive of society than a general (Hershey, Westmoreland . . . Lieutenant Calley?). What de Sade was saying is implicitly at the heart of the present book, namely that s-m is not cruelty. Gorer catches this admirably when he writes of de Sade's philosophy:

It will explain the horrible fact that whenever men get unrestrained power over their fellows—whether in revolution or counter-revolution, in prisons, through their living among races they are allowed to believe inferior or through position and wealth—they will practice on their victims the most revolting tortures, and tortures which receive a greater or lesser, and usually greater sexual tinge. And not only does it explain these horrors, it suggests a possible solution; if you can give to all people the education and opportunity for constructive sadism, you may perhaps do away with the unnecessary miseries that human beings now delight in inflicting on their fellows.

THE
ROLE
OF FANTASY

The German psychiatrist Schrenck-Notzing, from whom Havelock Ellis borrowed the term "algolagnia," was one of many of his time who felt that our whole sexual behavior was shaped by our environment. To an extent we have ourselves suggested such environmental causation, in the widest and most reciprocal sense, in the section above on America and masochism. Just as Schrenck-Notzing prescribed alcohol and a pretty prostitute as a "cure" for homosexuality, so he presumably might have tried to decondition the male masochist in the same way—two dry martinis, a supple rod, and an obligingly submissive female.

Behavioristic therapy of this type is usually backed up by lavish and pretentious correlations between animal and human behavior. Rats have been trained to go beyond mere resistance to electric shocks for a food reward into actual persistence towards pain itself—without such reward. Jack Sandler, in *Psychological Bulletin* (1964), makes typical analogies between such laboratory mammals and human masochists.

In some cases generalizations between animals and humans in locomotor learning have proved useful, but we are a civilization far too prone to accept a thesis via a kind of Gresham's Law of its lab content. Our advertisements attest as much, filled as they are with white-coated physicians and sterile-looking nurses ("Research has shown . . . "). The testing methods themselves are behavioristic, and evince the very nature of the environment, one paranoically technological.

For animals are not men, nor is fantasy a pragmatic factor. Humans are symbol-handling beings, and no one has better emphasized the *innate* qualities of learning in children, as against the input-output arithmetic of the behaviorists, than Noam Chomsky. In the case of s-m the original conditioning situation is invariably given as childhood beating on the buttocks. But the question is far deeper and more complex than this.

In a sense, then, our environment in America is its own self-conditioner. Technology tests the technology. After the last experiment is successfully concluded, everyone pats everyone else on the back and we really imagine we know more about sex. De Sade seems to have sensed, if not foreseen, this teleological arrogance in advance.

Sexually, America has lately given the appearance of climbing up a liberating ladder or, to better the metaphor, inventing new jigsaw puzzles of freedom. Antagonism to censorship has always been doctrinal in a republic that never countenanced those political suppressions, or reticences, which Europeans have accepted as facts of life for centuries. In the United States censorship has been regularly challenged wherever and whenever it raised its head, usually in the spirit of Milton's *Areopagatica,* that if you let truth and error into the same arena, the former will always win. Liberty of language, at least, seems presently about as close to absolute as it can be in America. Once more, something called sadism is here the last taboo.

Thus alongside British deference to the royal family, not to mention French repression of anti-Gallic documents (Kubrick's *Paths of Glory* has yet to be shown in France), we on our side can see a recent play that accused a President of the time of assassination. While French Ministry of Interior censorship was tightening, we could cite open advocacy of homosexuality, lesbianism, nudism, necrophily, and even bestiality on the American stage. What would de Sade have thought of the Formentor Award being given to a novel replete with pony-girl fantasies, a Guggenheim grant to one whose latest play contained "sodomy performed on stage," a Swedish movie showing a woman copulating with a dog, of the (remarkably realistic) extraction of a young boy's entrails at the American Place Theater, or the exhibition of sculptured excrement in a plush Manhattan art gallery, greeted merely by yawns from *The New York Times* ("These aggregations of colonic calligraphy contain many formal excellences . . . ")? In 1965 Supreme Court Justice Douglas decided, "I would put an end to all forms and types of censorship and give full literal meaning to the command of the First Amendment."

Yet the sliding-scale concept of our sexual liberty is disconcertingly deceptive. It may be that the Supreme Court has now conceded the right of every individual to possess pornography (*Robert Eli Stanley v. State of Georgia*, April 7, 1969), and thus by implication to purchase it. It is true that a Presidential commission saw no harm in porn, and that the "contemporary community standards" allowed as a test by the Supreme Court's *Roth* decision seem today very liberal indeed. The pursuit of happiness as an absolute right has by now almost wholly validated aphrodisiac, or turning-on, literature, if a few final freedoms have still—*pace* the s-m metaphor!—to be thrashed out in the iconic sphere. Such are the platitudes of our cultural scene. And the sad fact is that they may have little to do with the liberation of true fantasy in our lives.

For the point is that prurience, by a self-reflexive paradox, virtually runs the American economy. This stains sex and turns libido back on itself. The purpose of sexual arousal not invariably being dollars and cents, the culture becomes inordinately guilt-inclined—and guilt is the fuel of power pornography. The sexual prowess shown by protagonists in what we would like to call the *hornos* is not merely a surrogate of financial power, it is frequently clearly identified with it. Our advertising lives off anxiety about sex and fosters its maladjustments (as in obvious cathections like the narcissim of the *Vogue* syndrome or those increasingly successful attempts to organize a man's sexuality into a woman's, and vice versa, so that you can sell one product, e.g. a deodorant, to both sexes).

This is merely to unman ourselves in a new way. The damage that a capitalist economy has done by extending its biases into sexual behavior is probably incalculable, and almost certainly responsible for wars. It was the man who threw de Sade into prison, Napoleon Bonaparte, who once remarked, "We are a machine made to live . . . " The same man wrote, in a letter to his brother Lucien, "The greatest woman is she who has the largest family."

The vocabulary of our advertising, as of much of our popular culture in general, stipulates an almost wholly erotic role for women and this, by robbing her of stability and surrounding her with ever-increasing anxieties, pours back cash into the coffers of the economy. The late, and lamented, Judge Jerome Frank hit this particular nail on the head in a dissenting opinion in the U.S. Court of Appeals of 1955:

> Suppose we assume, *arguendo*, that sexual thoughts or feelings, stirred by the "obscene," probably will often issue into overt conduct. Still it does not at all follow that that conduct will be antisocial. For no sane person can believe it socially harmful if sexual desires lead to normal sexual behavior since without such behavior the human race would soon disappear . . . Suppose it argued that whatever excites sexual longings might *possibly* produce sexual misconduct. That cannot suffice: Notoriously, perfumes sometimes act as aphrodisiacs, yet no one will suggest that therefore Congress may constitutionally legislate punishment for mailing perfumes.

So the inexorable demands of the repetitive industrial system, with its "mandate" for unbridled competition, commercializes sex and does so by trading off the ambiguities introduced into love; to make a fetishistic ideal out of allure, or "glamor" (an old term for magic), is to introduce a sense of increasing inadequacy into intersexual relations. Meanwhile, the metaphoric vocabulary of sex is not only mechanomorphic (*turn on, score*) it is insistently associated with deception. In the Preface to his *Dictionary of American Slang* Stuart Berg Flexner writes, "As expressed in slang, sex is a trick somehow, a deception, a way to cheat and deceive us. To curse someone we can say *screw you,* which expresses a wish to deprive him of his good luck, his success, perhaps even his potency as a man." We note that it was this word that was chosen from the available repertoire for America's leading sex newspaper.*

Thus in both its freedom and its repression the teleology of American sex is exemplified. With its percentages of aphrodisiac assessments and regular Peter-Meter testings, *Screw* magazine epitomizes the "explosion" view of sex (exploded by Marcuse). The attitude is that so long as you have more, bigger, longer-lasting, and generally more dynamic orgasms (like the latest model Ford) you are succeeding sexually. *Screw* has, accordingly, never shown anything but the most patronizing attitude to s-m. For s-m is a "spread" pattern, streaming sex outwards from the psyche and diluting that anger and rage which the worst pornography lives off. In s-m, fantasy is conditioned by the entire relation to the unconscious, and is thus truly individual. We should like to suggest that for this reason alone it has been almost religiously extirpated by a technology, while the mindless hedonism of *Playboy* illides comfortably with the general pattern of consumerism.

On the other hand, we might well be asked: What of the blue-nosed sheriffs and police chiefs around the U.S. of A. forever seizing random samples of "filthy," "lewd," or "lascivious" items and hauling them into court? Apart from the obvious fact that they now do so less and less, knowing that they will almost certainly be clobbered from above if the case is pursued, they did indeed evolve a bizarre sort of *de facto* censorship which speaks richly for itself. It is, or was, a parallel by contagion of the attitude to sex that *Screw* espouses. Even if the two elements don't know it, or wouldn't admit it, they are kin.

Thus American small-town police chiefs seem to have shown primary sensitivity to sex. Political censorship has usually run second place, unlike what happens in Russia or China. The result was that a sheriff became empowered by local obscene-materials laws to be able to remove books and magazines from newsstands, thus conscientiously serving his "contemporary community standards." In common with the Post Office, the Interstate Commerce

---

* It is only quite recently that the sexual sense of *screw* has been imported into England, from America; a century ago *screwed* was sometimes used for being drunk (tight). In England a workman's weekly *screw* was his salary.

Commission has been notoriously hostile to sadomasochistic manifestations and materials.

But yet, as an erstwhile magazine publisher, James Lincoln
Collier, confesses, "even the cleverest of men cannot make a ruler
which measures itself." As regards books, that is, the Supreme
Court for a long period struck down nearly all such seizures on the
basis of semantics. What is "prurience"? Who is "normal"? What,
in any case, is a "community"? Even the liberal Brennan decision
came to be uncomfortable to the Court, since it allowed language
to criticize language. Supreme Court decisions consist of abstractions which have to be measured by other abstractions. The result
may have been to legitimatize ("legalize" is still too strong a term)
aphrodisiac fiction over the past decade or so, but it has scarcely
changed the idea of sex as a sort of feed-belt system, one closely
meshed into the economy.

Popkultch, fashion, movies, advertising are all American institutions accepting the premise that the arousing of prurient interest
is healthy when pecuniary. We are, in a word, the whore civilization *par excellence*. Was not the Victorian age in England the
same? To some extent it was. However, as Collier well puts it, at
that time "the general feeling was that it was not the act that
mattered so much, as the appearance of it."

The American obscenity laws, therefore, have usually been
so many contradictions in fact; this resulted in their breakdown,
more or less. Judge Frank was right: the huge subculture of
aphrodisia in this country, unequaled in extent anywhere before,
owes its inception to the moment when the publication of pornography became big business. Mass production is a feature of a financial culture and the glossy billion-dollar West Coast rubbishers of
erotica simply shared in the general stream of pleasure-capitalism.
They saw the bread-and-circuses crowds coming, and got in their
way. Nearly two hundred sex bookstores in New York City alone,
at present writing, with estimates of over two million copies of
porn "novels" going out each month from the rubbishers. "Pick
'em out, fellers, pick 'em out."

It but remains to interject that the great pornographers of the
past did not write for money. Cleland got a miserable £60 for his

masterpiece (plus, later, the backhanded compliment of a miniscule pension if he promised to write nothing more of the kind). Nerciat, exiled in Germany and proscribed by the Republic, got even less. The same with Apollinaire. William Burroughs, like Swinburne, possessed private means. All such authors were aware that they would be pirated instantly. The image of the writer of pornography as a sly, leering pander, out only for the quick buck, is a creation of *our* marketplace; in the past such people saw themselves as genuinely social beings. Even today we note that Mary Rexroth, daughter of poet Kenneth, when asked why she acted in hard-core pornographic movies, is quoted as replying, "Nobody's that hard up for money. That's *not* why *I'm* into porn." John Glassco well comments: "The best pornography has certainly not been written for profit, but was produced from a deep and compelling social sense, from the same impulse to communicate which is the mainspring of all art."*

So the small-town police chief might well have been working for *Screw*, instead of against it. Both used the same quantitative yardsticks by which to measure and define sex, and both saw sex as unilaterally physical and subversive. Qualitative mental activity, such as that intrinsic to s-m, is either queer, or funny, or both. Sex is a commodity. Thus, some years ago, unwritten local pornography laws only allowed magazines priced under fifty cents to show nipples of Asiatic and Negroid races; this in turn sent generations of American kids to the *National Geographic* to find out what the top deck of their sisters really looked like. Sex was then associated with the more steamy tropics and loinclothed ladies, a fact which at least one political commentator saw eventuated in adulthood as Congressional hesitancy to help such countries to industrialize. Pubic hair was disallowed, except in nudist publications. Any magazine with a net paid circulation of one million copies or more could reproduce illustrations of statues and paintings showing genitalia, provided these did not occupy more than ten percent of the picture, while works of art showing the actual sex could be used

* In *Art and Pornography* (New York: Basic Books, 1969) Morse Peckham gives further evidence of this and contrasts the pornographic writer with the painter to the latter's considerable financial advantage.

in any book printed on 80-pound stock, so long as the pages were twelve inches long and the book priced at $7.50 or more.

Only a few years ago, trying to handle topless dancing as a concept, the Alameda, California, County Board of Supervisors drafted and passed a law which contained the following provision:

> Violation would consist of a female who exposes any portion of either breast below a straight line so drawn that both nipples and all portions of both breasts which have a different pigmentation than that of the main portion of the breast are below such straight line.

The ruler and felt-tipped pen are enlisted as vice squad weaponry. (Laws against bigamy have been so easily applicable since they involve those of arithmetic.) Years ago, when writing her famous *Hollywood: The Dream Factory* (1950), Hortense Powdermaker detected the same illogic in the old Hays Code for movies, one in which "moral concepts are not distinguished from physical facts."

In short, statistics (price, size, format, binding, degree of rag content) were the elements that made an item pornographic. Sheriffs may have had to concoct these yardsticks simply in order to get some convictions under very vaguely phrased language. And the rules were broken with impunity on many occasions. But the impounding of a run could hurt minor girlie magazines, while repetition of the "offense" might result in conviction for a crime.

The entire attitude was American. As Collier reminds us, "Victorian sexual behavior, insofar as we know what it was, was not nearly so repressive as the intolerance of its display suggests." The Wilde trial showed tacit toleration of both homosexuality and mistresses, at least in the upper classes—*what was taboo was to mention it*. We are not saying that Victorian repression was anything other than an unhealthy situation, simply that it bore another shape than ours in certain particulars.

In America written pornography is not real, whereas photographs roughly are. The coining of our horn trade is: an illustration is worth a thousand words of text. No one prosecuted *Playboy* much after it had attained a $2 million newsstand circulation (on glossy stock), and, sure enough, that magazine joined meekly in the maximum exposure sweepstakes, finally showing pubic hair. On the other hand, *Screw* made its initial impact, and got its impetus, by deliberately flouting all the going guide rules, and showing enlarged close-ups of the female anus on *newsprint*. Moreover, it was mostly fact (some of its early issues could have doubled for gynecological texts). Fact is what we seek. Kinsey duly supplied it. Science is our god, not sex; and the winners are those who share in the profit motive built on this understanding.

We can only say that true s-m depends on a complete reversal of this attitude, and a restoration of fantasy to its proper role in life. The isolation of sex as a statistic has resulted in a false perspective in our society, one which has operated on a sort of normal/deviant fulcrum. Any variance of sexual practice is thereby seen as a mutilation, rather than enhancement, of sex. As Eustace Chesser puts it in *Strange Loves:*

> Thus the sex act is isolated from everything else. It is judged solely from *what* is done, not *how* it is done. In the example already given the fact that a man wanted to be caned would be regarded by many as a deviation bordering on perversion. From this traditional angle the most important question is taken to be whether such behavior is a deviation or not. But looked at from another angle this has no importance whatever. What matters is not what is done but whether it is mutually enjoyed.

Now, it would be absurd not to admit that fantasy has long been suspect in Western societies. We know the old Platonic charge. Poetry is fantastic, misleading, and therefore inimical to the formation of the good society. "We must remain firm in our conviction that hymns to the gods and praises of famous men are the only poetry which ought to be admitted into our State." It should perhaps be added that the celebratory intelligentsia proposed in this part of *The Republic* may have been, according to the reading of some scholars, a tongue-in-cheek satire—which is far from what is the actual case in Russia and China today. Love it or leave it, if you can.

This is to take a somatic attitude to fantasy. The imagination is valued for what it does, not what it is. Art should tell the literal truth, be morally edifying, or else get out. Maurice Hindus recounts the typical neo-Platonic position as given him in the Soviet Union by a then-prominent professor of philosophy:

> "Einstein," I said, "was one of the greatest scientists of all time, and so far as I know he never accepted the philosophy of dialectical materialism."
>
> "We have translated the book Einstein wrote with Enfield [Infeld]. We study the book because the authors are great scientists. But we reject their idealistic doctrines."
>
> "Suppose the student sees merit in these doctrines?"
>
> "We argue him out of it."
>
> "But suppose he remains unconvinced?"
>
> "Impossible. We have the question period and we hold seminars and in the end we defeat our ideological enemies."
>
> "But if the student persists in contradicting the professor?"
>
> "It doesn't happen. It cannot happen. Our arguments are incontrovertible."
>
> "And if it were to happen?"
>
> This time the professor replied solemnly: "Then the student would place himself outside our Soviet society."
>
> (*House Without a Roof*, 1961)

S-m does not tell the literal truth, is rich in imagination (even, as we have seen in de Sade, in the impossible), and so is classed as subversive by such minds, rather than therapy. It is represented as a mutilation, of mind, as of sex. The best way you can conceive of poetry here is to allow it a kind of irresponsible rhapsody, as in the *Ion* or *Phaedrus*, and as in Allen Ginsberg.

It was Aristotle, then, who first took the therapeutic view, rebutting Plato's suspicion of the senses in the famous "purgation" passage of his *Poetics*. Perhaps we are not all here just to be good citizens, but whole human beings as well. Perhaps we can experience a catharsis of emotions, allay and pacify the cruel forces of anger and hate by feeling fear and pity as we watch our instincts enacted on the stage. "A tragedy," writes Kenneth Burke, "is not profound unless the poet *imagines* the crime—and in thus imagining it, he symbolically commits it."

This intellectualizing of our instincts has always been deeply suspect, if in varying degrees, to our various societies. For vicarious participation in a crime (on stage, in a movie, or book) means the release of forbidden impulses which we have shunted out of sight and are now suddenly compelled to recognize as part of our nature. Naturally we want to see them punished for us. The infringement made by *Lolita* was (for many critics) that the crime, so-called, received no direct retribution; the criminal, Humbert Humbert, died of a heart-attack in jail.

So it is not only that the claims of the unconscious in something like s-m threaten to put at bay and actually overbalance us, it is rather that their existence makes us feel particularly puny since we have not, in our daily discourse, allowed them any existence. Of a Sadean scene in *The 120 Days* a London psychiatrist, Masud R. Khan, extremely antipathetic to de Sade, writes: "The very absurdity and unfeasibility of this event lends it a new power: it has transcended the innate physical limits of the human body to experience pain and excitement." This is to say that the scene has been located in a new terrain, that of the imagination, which knows no ethical allegiances or laws. Such is its true infringement.

Social demands have therefore always (and understandably) dogged the imaginative act. At the end of a Shakespearean tragedy we feel a sense of exhilaration despite the carnage and, often, torture, because the demands of fantasy have been fully met. We have become covert participants and for a while have overcome the "laws" of the real world (sex, age, time, etc.). As a result, we go away from such a tragedy relaxed. Even more integrated, rather than less.

Yet Sir Philip Sidney, penning his great defense of poetry in 1595, felt it incumbent on him to shore up a whole host of Renaissance arguments against the persistent Platonic view that fantasy literature was an immoral lie. The ancients did it, he argued; and, besides, crime, perversion, and madness were justifiable literary fables since they were so many social consequences. (Later, in the Romantic era, they came to be seen more as causes.) When the long novel entered as an attendant on the great capitalist civilizations, its extent of fantasy again aroused the Platonic policemen. Here is one at work in *Tom Jones:*

Sophia was in her chamber, reading, when her aunt came in. The moment she saw Mrs. Western, she shut the book with so much eagerness, that the good lady could not forbear asking her what book that was which she seemed so much afraid of showing? "Upon my word, madam," answered Sophia, "it is a book which I am neither ashamed nor afraid to own I have read. It is the production of a young lady of fashion, whose good understanding, I think, doth honor to her sex, and whose good heart is an honor to human nature." Mrs. Western then took up the book, and immediately after threw it down, saying—"Yes, the author is of a very good family; but she is not much among people one knows. I have never read it; for the best judges say, there is not much in it."

When the Platonic censor appears a century or so later, in the form of Pastor Manders in Ibsen's *Ghosts*, we find the fantasizer, here a married woman called Mrs. Alving, somewhat more confident concerning the illicit activity:

MANDERS: Do you read this sort of thing?

MRS. ALVING: Certainly I do.

MANDERS: Do you feel any the better or the happier for reading books of this kind?

MRS. ALVING: I think it makes me, as it were, more self-reliant.

MANDERS: That is remarkable. But why?

MRS. ALVING: Well, they give me an explanation or a confirmation of lots of different ideas that have come into my own mind . . . But what is the particular objection that you have to these books?

MANDERS: What objection? You surely don't suppose that I take any particular interest in such productions?

MRS. ALVING: In fact, you don't know anything about what you are denouncing?

MANDERS: I have read quite enough about these books to disapprove of them.

In puritan capitalism, novel reading involving the use of fantasy is, at best, so much moral slackness and, at worst, outright vice. In a world of busy-ness this evidently effortless yielding to fantasy was self-indulgence, mental masturbation. It paid small court to official morality and, above all, *it wasn't true*. Hazlitt took roughly this view of prose and it found a bizarre echo in Britain's House of Lords a few years ago when a group of noble Earls woke up to find that something called *Lady Chatterley's Lover* had been permitted to be printed integrally owing to a new Obscene Publications Act. "Let us get down to the realities and the origin of this deplorable book," thundered Lord Teviot. "It emanates from the warped mind of the author. The story he tells is pure invention; it never actually happened." This was in 1960!

So the moralistic tradition has been hardy. It survives the apparent freedoms of our market place in many guises, not simply in the licensed lunacy of the House of Lords (we have suggested a sort of inverted puritanism in *Screw*). Today *Lolita* scarcely seems a very subversive book. In the two decades since its publication it has not been shown to have stepped up that affliction which was a normal libidinal state in the Renaissance called *neanirosis*, love of young girls. When it came out, in fact, a bride of ten (to be a divorcee by twelve) was heard from in Columbia, Mo., while more recently another ten-year-old, Mirta Fontora ("Little Mom"), gave birth to a lusty boy in Buenos Aires. There was not a four-letter word in *Lolita* and it has not been shown to have led to a rash of Humbert Humberts.

When the novel came out, however, Gilbert Highet, Anthon Professor of Latin at Columbia University, fulminated against it as "a wicked book." It showed an evil practice in alluring guise. What's more, the criminal was not corrected. "The principal effect of *Lolita* is the enjoyment of wickedness." Highet then went on to ask us if, by analogy, we would want to allow the publication of a novel showing arson as attractive. "I am sorry it was ever written," he wrote of the book.

Now this is to suppose precisely that dissociation in our sentient processes which continues to rob our lives of quality. By implication, it is to suggest a reader so primitive that he will confuse the symbolic with the actual, like some aboriginal native in flight from the first movie screen he sees on which figures are shown advancing towards him. Frankly, it seems quite extraordinary to us that anything more than an embarrassed laugh ever greeted the work of someone who could so confuse Baudelaire's poetry with his private life that he could write of him: "From his youth he was psychically abnormal. His sexual life was decidedly abnormal. He had love-affairs with ugly, repulsive women—negresses, dwarfs, giantesses." Thus Richard von Krafft-Ebing on "the French writer C. P. Baudelaire, who died insane" [*sic*]. Passing over the arrant racialism in the above comment, it is by now fairly well established that C. P. Baudelaire had about as much sex with his mulatto housekeeper for so many years, Jeanne Duval, as he did with the giantess of his famous poem "*La Géante*."

Henry James, so many of whose fictions deal with sexual/moral deficiencies or the vulnerability of inadequate knowledge, answered for art, and for fantasy, in a celebrated essay called "The Art of Fiction" (a reply to the moral critic Sir Walter Besant). How could a picture be moral or immoral? James asked. It lived on another terrain altogether than that of morality. We were a civilization staked out by so many prohibitory signposts all based on "a traditional difference between that which people know and that which they agree to admit that they know." He went on (and for James' *art* we can legitimately substitute *fantasy*), "The province of art is all life, all feeling, all observation, all vision."

By the canons of this argument James would have insisted that we both could and should show desirable arson, if needs be. For unless we know arson from inside the mind of a convinced arsonist, we hardly know what it is. It may be argued that such confessions belong more to the clinics but literature, as de Sade's showed, seems to be our collective clinic in advance. Nor do you learn what s-m is from a Masud Khan.

The finer minds among us are today allowing fantasy full scope of this kind of art. Reviewing *Lolita* Lionel Trilling wrote, "It is one of the effects, perhaps one of the functions, of literature to arouse desire, and I can discover no ground for saying that sexual pleasure should not be among the objects of desire which literature presents to us, along with heroism, virtue, peace, death, food, wisdom, God, etc." This was almost to rephrase Sir Kenneth Clark's dictum on the nude in art:

No nude, however abstract, should fail to arouse in the spectator some vestige of erotic feeling, even though it be only the faintest shadow—and if it does not do so, it is bad art and false morals.

Such generosity deserves to be applied to the realm of sex. Human personality is integral and we cannot arbitrarily redistribute libidinal power, as advertising, the champion of the sexual explosion, would. "To accept animate life as good," writes John Wilson in his *Logic and Sexual Morality* of 1965, "is to accept the satisfaction of desire as good."

Modern secular technology has accepted the latter part of this premise without the former. It is in this way that the liberties we have allowed the imagination of late may be somewhat illusory. "Each new day," Jung wrote, "reality is created by the psyche. The only expression I can use for this activity is *fantasy*." In this respect, fantasy is a positive drive, a bridge built by the psyche between our inner and outer worlds—"the creative activity whence issue the solutions to all answerable questions." Yet, as Jung himself sadly conceded, "in the world of science fantasy is just as much taboo as is feeling."

For an empirical age is slowly ironing out all creative fantasy from life, substituting in its stead collective concretizations permitted by liberal "contemporary community standards." This philistinism of a pragmatic and pecuniary reality (incidentally pilloried in James' *Washington Square*) is in dire need of the fantastic element to qualify, moderate, and "place" it. For we have reached a stage in our civilization when a degree-bedecked professor can write about sixty million Americans killed, in an initial nuclear attack, as a necessary "defense," and still go to breakfast with equanimity. We watch battlefield bloodshed between the pantyhose ads; a bomber pilot describes the dispatch of his missiles on humans as resembling the scattering of Rice Krispies. So everything non-empirical gets regarded, with us, as fantasy. Religion no longer contains, as it did in the past, obscenity and we check out sex in laboratories, imagining we are thereby getting somewhere. "If psychology remains only a science," Jung added, "we do not reach life—we merely serve the absolute aim of science."

We must reach this life within ourselves. Which is another way of putting W. H. Auden's injunction that we must love one another or die.* Naturally, s-m is our last taboo since it is so signally rich in fantastic content. Again: we are not here advocating some simplistic notion that everyone should promptly indulge in s-m play, and the world's ills will be solved. But (once more borrowing Jung's formulations) creation is accomplished by the play-instinct out of inner needs—"The creative mind plays with the objects it loves." S-m will certainly allow hidden drives and desires to be handled as play, and so assist those who are not naturally creative to be more so.

Fantasy is not reality. "It is a mistake to seek in fantasies the key to concrete behavior," writes Simone de Beauvoir. "For fantasies are created and cherished as fantasies." "There is not a stealthy infamy that I have not committed in my dreams," equally suggestively wrote Marie Le Hardouin. The nature of science is to erode this abstraction. With its pretensions to objectivity science is today drying up and denying all ideals, all mystery, just as it invaded and eroded religion in the past. Our lovers become copulating mammals celebrating so many equal rights. And s-m seems at first sight the ultimate heresy.

Moreover, pornography has to be seen in a whole context. One specimen will surely shock. In his *Art and Pornography* Morse Peckham puts this best:

> When one examines the full range of European and American pornography from the late fourteenth century to the present, one is struck by an irresistible fact: it has been as steadily innovative as science itself, the great instrument by which the West has terrifyingly unleashed the deadly and transforming powers of innovation, which may, after all, be our salvation.
>
> "Creativity" is our supreme accolade; innovation, then, is at the center of our culture and what we are proudest of. It is another

---

Cp. "When devils drive the reasonable wild,
    They strip their adult century so bare,
  Love must be regrown from the sensual child:"
                    —W. H. Auden, "Montaigne"

name for sin . . . Pornography may very well be the great key which
has freed the energy locked into the trivial by social management.

We, all of us, have at some time to adapt to an external reality.
Instead of hindering us from doing this (as is often popularly supposed) imagination will help us on our way—help, if needs be, by
rejecting transition when the reality is detestable. In his insistence
on the primacy of the imagination, and his identification of it as
something considerably more than so much Platonic rhapsody, de
Sade would (virtually did) go to block and rack for the following
statement of faith by the great Zürich investigator:

> every good idea and all creative work is the offspring of the imagi-
> nation, and has its source in what one is pleased to term infantile
> fantasy. It is not the artist alone, but every creative individual
> whatsoever who owes all that is greatest in his life to fantasy. The
> dynamic principle of fantasy is "play," which belongs also to the
> child, and as such it appears to be inconsistent with the principle of
> serious work. But without this playing with fantasy no creative
> work has ever yet come to birth. The debt we owe to the play of
> imagination is incalculable. It is therefore shortsighted to treat
> fantasy, on account of its daring or inacceptable character, as of
> small account. It must not be forgotten that it is just in the imagina-
> tion that the most valuable promise of a man may lie.

So the point about s-m is that it can, when necessary, help in
individuation in the largest sense. For a moment of controlled self-
divestiture the past can become vocal, atavistic urges be recognized
and assimilated. This is surely what James meant when he wrote
that "The essence of moral energy is to survey the whole field."

We can only be socially and psychologically at full energy with
the complete participation of all of ourselves; Ellis' "Florrie,"
whom we shall describe in the following section, was an example
of this. S-m is not a mechanism for defense against, but rather of
release for, culturally repressed tendencies. As Anthony Storr puts
it in *Human Aggression*, "to forbid a child to watch television or
read stories in which violence occurs is a fruitless prohibition more
likely to cause anger than to prevent it. It is the crudity and vulgarity of horror comics, television serials, and some pornography

which should invoke our condemnation rather than their contents. If we study the content of fairy tales or myths, we shall discover all kinds of horrors from castration to boiling in oil."

America may be the greatest technology the world has ever seen, but the dissociation of consciousness it has effected in its citizenry has been a crippling one, a high price to pay for political power. Primitive claims rumbled even more disastrously unheard in the underworld of the German *Geist* of this century. Yeats' question haunts us still:

And what rough beast, its hour come round at last,
Slouches towards Bethlehem to be born?

THE
ROLE
OF WOMAN

For the so-called "passive" partner in the assigned love code of the West particular difficulties inhere. We do not presume in this book to be able to make some sudden about-face in our received human relationships, but rather hope to be of assistance in suggesting new, perhaps hidden, perspectives. For, to start with: if an American woman wants to be a dominant in s-m play, she is not so much getting fantasy relief as extending reality into her dreams. This does not invalidate either. We are not knocking the dominatrix. We do feel, however, that in a paternalistic society (Germany, England) punishment was effected for children by males (father, schoolmaster—for girls it was admittedly less structured); in America it is Mom who wields paddle, hairbrush, or slipper, more often than not.

So, as we tentatively suggested in our section on milieu, America has a certain built-in s-m polarization. Covering a two-day male/female symposium sponsored in 1972 by impressive psychological and psychiatric associations, a *Village Voice* reporter summarizes the findings as follows: "It also seemed generally agreed that [American] men aren't as manly as they once were, but nobody explained how or why. It seemed further agreed that most [American] males felt inferior to women."

It scarcely needed the success of a new and furious wave of

feminism to tell us this. The country's sexual psychodrama was pointing out the same, in all directions. Anyone watching even the developments in American dolls would have deduced the patterns. For European dolls generally conjoined young girls into practicing motherhood. In the 1950's American dolls carried the verisimilitude of this to fantastic extremes, burping, farting, "wetting" (even giving birth) far more than might their human originals. Still and all, they remained so many preparations for motherhood.

They ceased to be so when, well before the advent of Ms. Steinem and Greer, a company put a million-dollar budget behind their Barbie doll and the ideal of the mother caring for her child came to seem extremely tame. The world of Barbie, Dawn, Trudy and other such (subsequent) dolls was a constant round of aggressive dates, parties, popularity. The life being pushed on to countless little American girls was one of cretinous hedonism, continual glamor, and endless interchangeable boyfriends, slavering semimale* digits who were easily dominated by allure.

In one of his neatest satirical columns Art Buchwald saw the psychic substrate on which this industry was so ardently founded and proposed that what was really going on was that these dolls were getting Miss America ready for her chain of divorces. He wasn't kidding. The California rate went up 40% in the year in which the term *dissolution of marriage* was officially substituted for divorce. In 1969 there were 81,670 such "dissolutions" out of 162,303 Californian marriages, a going rate of over 50% that has led one counselor to suggest replacing marriage by the term *serial monogamy*. This is the end result of the physical rather than fantastic union. The end, in truth, of the true relationship. S-m bonds would seem solid by comparison.

Until recently Europe enjoyed a rich period of genuine adolescence, a subsoil for creativity, as Proust showed. England did. Its strong stock of women novelists throughout the last century evinces as much. Amid the rest of the accompanying flim-flam and brouhaha, it was interesting to learn that the new American Crissy doll is, for sundry licensing and tax-saving purposes, manufactured

---

* Since neither male nor female dolls have (as yet) genitalia, the denuded boy doll looked singularly more silly than his feminine friend.

in Hong Kong. Flown to France, where there is a last lingering adolescence still, the idiot regularity of her pre-airline hostess face was too much; the French stuck on a new head. This says a lot.

Equality doesn't mean sameness. Writes Susan Lydon, a contributing editor of *Ramparts* magazine, "female sexuality is subtle and delicate, conditioned as much by the emotions as by physiology and sociology . . . A difference remains in the *subjective* experience of orgasm during intercourse and orgasm apart from intercourse. In the complex of emotional factors affecting feminine sexuality, there is a whole panoply of pleasures."

We hope we have made it plain that writers of the eighteenth century, like Laclos and Diderot and Richardson and de Sade, were concerned to show woman's sexuality as immensely varied and delicate, as well as powerful, with the result that literature, even some pornographic literature, may be a better guide to it, and to feminine response levels, than the clinics. We have suggested this in the matter of clitoral response. Nerciat and de Sade indubitably enjoyed women, and closely watched their reactions. They were not in need of electrodes for their "findings." They let us know, once and for all, of the Casanovian check—you can tell if a woman has come by a slight finger on one of her pulses.

Ms. Lydon puts it well:

> Certainly the sexual problems of our society will never be solved until there is real and unfeigned equality between men and women. This idea is usually misconstrued: sexual liberation for women is wrongly understood to mean that women will adopt all the forms of masculine sexuality. As in the whole issue of women's liberation, that's really not the point. Women don't aspire to imitate the mistakes of men in sexual matters, to view sexual experiences as conquest and ego-enhancement, to use other people to serve their own ends.

So let us simply say here that in the socially "appropriate" role for the sexes, in this America of ours, the dominatrix does not seem so far out. Monique von Cleef was evidently able to find a male masochistic clientele ranging from truck drivers to college presidents.

What, then, of the female masochist? Of the American woman

who yearns to be dominated? Here we merely hope to show that the female sexual masochist is frequently an extremely strong, if not dominating, social personality. In doing so we should at once admit the considerable difficulties of sampling involved. The meek and mild do not hasten forward to give statistics. A. H. Maslow admits this frankly:

> Any study in which data are obtained from volunteers will always have a preponderance of high-dominance people and therefore will show a falsely high percentage of non-virginity, masturbation, promiscuity, homosexuality, etc. in the population. This criticism must be directed to some extent against [Robert L.] Dickinson, for we know that the low-dominance woman shuns pelvic examination whenever possible, and will not volunteer comments about her sexual history.

In s-m imagination is at stake. The masochist, either male or female, is *not* a doormat. It is a singularly high self-esteem person who seeks his kind, another high self-esteem person. Mirror and image. This is absolutely operative for the woman in the relationship and should be recognized as such from the start.

Maslow seems to define dominance-feeling as somewhat synonymous with self-esteem, both side-products of sexual drive. By odd implication (which we will return to below) this is to posit that the masochist *is* a dominant. This is no mere philosophical hair-splitting but, rather, sexological fact. One of Maslow's subjects was a nymphomane who could induce orgasms simply by looking at a man, yet who reported, in the cases of two men with whom she could not gain orgasm, "I just couldn't give in to them. They were too weak." Simone de Beauvoir puts the essential democracy of this innate relationship (one which Baudelaire recognized in his poem "*L'Héautontimorouménos*") into allusive terms:

> What the torturer demands is that, alternating between refusal and submission, whether rebelling or consenting, the victim recognize, in any case, that his destiny is the freedom of the tyrant. He is then united to his tyrant by the closest of bonds. They form a genuine couple.

Now, in a society which relies on insecurity in order to sell products, the good citizenry might well be excused from feeling insecure themselves. Indeed, secure individuals will tend to give off a (turning-on) aura of strength and power. In the 1940's Maslow found no resentment to the prone sexual position on the part of secure women, who failed to see any submissiveness therein. Like homosexuality, or skin color, such matters seem to be heavily culturally coded.

At the same time, where the dominatrix extended her presence not only into the fantasy but, rather, into the reality, dangers might ensue:

> In terms of status this means that marriages with equality status or "split-dominance" status, or the husband in dominant status (but not markedly so) are most conducive to happiness and good adjustment for both husband and wife. In those marriages in which the wife is definitely dominant over her husband, trouble is very likely to ensue in the form of both social and sexual maladjustment unless they are both very secure individuals. This seems to be true also, but to a lesser extent, in those marriages in which the husband is *very* markedly dominant over the wife.

We further learn from Maslow (as if it had to be told) that:

> For the woman who is high in dominance-feeling only a high-dominance man will be attractive. He must be highly masculine (psychologically at least), he must be self-confident, fairly aggressive, and even "cocky," sure of what he wants and able to get it, generally superior in most things. Strength and forcefulness of personality are stressed.

It is as we descend the Maslowian scale of "dominance" (sex drive) that the estimates of sympathy, consideration, fidelity, and the rest of the romantic love absolutes occur, while ideals of conquest weaken. The "dominance" here defined thus seems akin to what used to be called sex-appeal. Subjects low in it are repelled by those high in it, as vice versa.

The lower you travel on this scale the less importance is attached to being a good lover, and the more to being a socially provident spouse. "Also, we find in men and women at various levels of dominance-feeling almost perfectly complemental characteristics. The high-dominance woman demands only a high-dominance man, but also the high-dominance man prefers the high-dominance woman." The imaginative mate seeks out his or her kind.

There is no fear of sex in such people. They are the sexual aristocrats of the race who have allowed the libido access to their fantasies—indeed, "the high-dominance woman unconsciously wishes to be raped." Provocatively enough, Maslow finds that in the highest brackets of his scale deception in wedlock, the celebrated "double standard" forever pilloried in *Madame Bovary,* is almost nonexistent. To us this is an understandable paradox. Far from inclining to infidelity, the high-dominant union works for the reverse, a cementing of relationships, since it is based on the common imaginative faculty rather than the physical (we will touch on the enrichment of sex in old age in this respect below).

The high-dominance woman, with a strong sex drive, is, then, the one more likely to want to be taken than asked. She will typically enjoy cunnilingus and find the male penis "a very beautiful object in a truly esthetic sense." Nor will she draw back from "practically every form of sexual behavior known to the psychopathologists as well as the sexologist," since "the dynamic meaning of the act is far more important than the act itself." Masturbation, involving the whole body, is likely to be lifelong. Rape dreams are reported. Joseph Kessel's *Belle de Jour* comes obviously to mind.

> High-dominance people (if not too insecure) have little or no fear of the body or of any of its functions. Thus the sexual organs are not feared, are even especially attractive . . . Generally the sexual act is apt to be taken not as a serious rite with fearful aspects and differing in fundamental quality from all other acts, but as a game, as fun, as a highly pleasurable animal act. Such couples speak about it freely to each other, smacking their lips over anticipated or remembered pleasures, and becoming excited all over again in the process . . . it is just those few women who show no signs of this culturally expected attitude of deference to men in whom we find what seems to be a much more truly masochistic attitude (in a psychological rather than a cultural-conventional sense).

Those women of great external political dynamism seeking out figures stronger than themselves in their fantasy lives, almost as a mark of self-esteem, seem to have been legion in our time. One thinks of Florence Nightingale if not of de Beauvoir herself. Princess Marie Bonaparte, active in the defense of Dreyfus as a girl, helping Freud escape in her middle years, then flying to see and intercede for Caryl Chessman in her old age, felt that a woman needs "more than a pinch of masochism to add to her erotic brew." Rosa Luxemburg contained something of the same. Shaw's heroines often exhibit a knowing play on the identical ambivalence. Queen Victoria "surrendered her whole soul to her husband" (one who had a considerable homosexual quotient within him) while being herself manifestly masculine on the political level. Lytton Strachey gives the now famous, if ill-authenticated, anecdote to the point:

> When, in wrath, the Prince one day had locked himself into his room, Victoria, no less furious, knocked on the door to be admitted. "Who is there?" he asked. "The Queen of England" was the answer. He did not move, and again there was a hail of knocks. The question and the answer were repeated many times; but at last there was a pause, and then a gentler knocking. "Who is there?" came once more the relentless question. "Your wife, Albert." And the door was immediately opened.

As briefly mentioned in an earlier section, Freud seems to have been dissatisfied with his own inability to clarify masochism in women; endless case histories merely added to, rather than resolved, the mystery. (To date the best "correction" of Freud's theories about masochism seems to be Gilles Deleuze's book mentioned.) Returning to the subject in *The Economic Problem in Masochism* of 1924, Freud divided masochism into categories; in the main, there were two— (a) sexual or erotogenic, and (b) moral. S-m, we should make clear, is the former. It may involve being an object, but yet *an object of fascination* to the partner. In moral masochism, from which sex has been drained, the object is of no interest, merely a doormat (e.g. the martyred wife or mother). Thus for an s-m woman masochism is far from so much passive submission. De Sade saw this and de Beauvoir, in her great feminist tract, *The Second Sex,* saw that he saw it. Torment can give pleasure, but "Pain, in fact, is of masochistic significance only when it is accepted and wanted as proof of servitude."

This servitude is only possible with a worthwhile love partner since it involves one's esteem of oneself. S-m or erotogenic masochism is thus not being a thing, but *playing* at being a thing. As Sartre put it a trifle more complexly, "Masochism is an attempt not to fascinate the other by my objectivity, but to be myself fascinated by my objectivity in the eyes of the other."

Moral masochism is more that form of self-punishment (basically, perhaps, auto-erotic) that comes out in certain obvious social roles—put-upon relatives, various forms of local martyrs. It is the ego's uncomfortable adjustment to social and economic situations which have for so long frustrated women. Masochism in s-m, however, can be completely healthy; it permits woman to help solve the social problem, to set new political boundaries for herself since she has been able to tap new energy from whole hidden regions within her, previously unoccupied or repressed.

This liberation of the erotic sphere means an unmanacling of woman's possibilities, and it is interesting to note how vividly and poetically the feminist de Beauvoir responds to it:

> Woman can gloriously accept her sexuality because she transcends it; excitement, pleasure, desire are no longer a state, but a benefaction; her body is no longer an object: it is a hymn, a flame . . . in responding to her lover's demands, a woman will feel that she is necessary; she will be integrated with his existence, she will share his worth, she will be justified . . .
>
> The woman who finds pleasure in submitting to male caprices also admires the evident action of a sovereign free being in the tyranny practiced on her. It must be noted that if for some reason the lover's prestige is destroyed, his blows and demands become odious; they are precious only if they manifest the divinity of the loved one. But if they do, it is intoxicating joy to feel herself the prey of another's free action. An existent finds it a most amazing adventure to be justified through the varying and imperious will of another; one wearies of living always in the same skin, and blind obedience is the only chance for radical transformation known to a human being.

In all that long litany of pain, handed down to us until the last world war as catalogues of "deviation" by the diligent Austrian clinicians, no case is more touching and, in this respect, telling than that of Havelock Ellis' "Florrie." She makes a pertinent summary of this section.

Ellis first published this case in *The Psychoanalytic Review* of 1919. In 1925 Stekel commented on it, and Ellis then bound both his original hundred-odd pages and a surrejoinder to Stekel into his subsequent volume on *Eonism*. If somewhat inaccessible, it has now become famous for it is indeed a textbook example of feminine repression in our times. One point about it is that, unlike the repetitious and self-indulgent Cadivec memoirs, every line of "Florrie"'s many "written communications" seem to glow with sincerity.

In common, perhaps, with her analyst, "Florrie" was a urolagnic. She had a standard, reasonably happy, upper-class childhood of any English girl of the time (evidently the latter half of the nineteenth century). One governess used to send her to be chastised by her father (in modern America the punishing agent would be Mom), not so very uncommon then. "Florrie" describes the typical ritual of preparation and then the whipping, across tightly stretched drawers, with a lean ladies' riding switch. It was never frequent nor overly severe, and was always accompanied by love; as a matter of fact, one ought to take into account, in these Victorian histories, that a whipping over the skirts and chemises worn by the feminine sex in those days would scarcely have been felt! The admixture of shame and adoration "Florrie" knew when her father subsequently kissed her, in forgiveness, filled the girl with an overwhelming intensity of emotion. In her later life she was to write to Ellis of her requirements for a dominant, "It must be someone I know, like, and respect, and secretly adore."

Another governess spanked "Florrie" on the bare buttocks when she asked to relieve herself, and could not. Urinating soon became a passionate subject of her daydreams, and more; for she began to practice clandestine urination, for example standing up in a conservatory or even, once, by the side of the road. She wore the long skirts of the time, of course, and so managed to relieve herself standing. If she stained herself, she said she had been caught in a shower of rain. As indeed she had.

Urination of this nature clearly satisfied one side of "Florrie." She felt it degrading that, unlike a man, a woman always had to crouch to pee; she envied her brother his abilities in the upright posture, remarking rather charmingly of herself, "No teapot without a spout felt so forlorn." When a girlfriend then told her of WC's where women stood erect (as in France), she was thoroughly delighted and so indulged herself repeatedly. Particularly did she enjoy urinating out of doors, in the depths of some wood, the sound of her piss hissing down on brittle leaves being especially satisfying.

By her late teens "Florrie" was a painter, an ardent suffragette, and enjoying s-m and urinary fantasies. She had never known an orgasm. Her feminism continued strongly into adulthood. She actually published articles attacking the language of the marriage service (criticizing, in particular, the word *obey*), as also militarism. But her own daydreams were of wives whipped by husbands, and they intensified considerably. She appears to have developed a gluteal obsession at this time, to have experimented with an enema nozzle, and taken elementary photographs of her own buttocks. In 1919 Ellis' prose had to be relatively reticent.

She then married a doctor twice her age. Throughout all their years together this man treated Florrie with constant tenderness and solicitude, if never passion. On the wedding night, indeed, he seems to have been reluctant to infringe on "Florrie" 's total ignorance of sex. For she was one of those numerous Victorian maidens who were sent off by their mothers at the church door with their only sexual instruction, "Goodbye, and remember that whatever you have to go through your mother had to go through the same."

The pattern must have been that shared by so many of the time—of both sexes. "Florrie" developed what she termed a "whipping craze." She thrashed her own buttocks with a riding switch and lay panting, face down, on a sofa after. She became obsessed by the subject and more and more guilty of keeping it from her husband, who would have felt too much affection for her, she later told Ellis, to ever want to hurt her.

Coming upon a cheap paper full of spanking letters, she joined in the correspondence under "A Contented Wife." Skillful with pen, she was able to draw out other letters on her favorite topic. Her own advocated the corporal chastisement of wives—and she even once corrected her real self in the matter of the wife's marriage semantic!

So while "Florrie" was pursuing feminism in her public life her pseudonyms were counseling the chastisement of suffragettes. Finally, she hoaxed a letter from a supposedly spanked suffragette which seemed so genuine it even attracted the attention of the police (who soon found it to be fake). "Florrie" was now regularly beating herself after breakfast, as soon as her husband had gone off to work; she used a ladies' riding switch, whalebone covered with gut, and still she had never known orgasm. She was, in a word, in a state of dangerously perpetual erithism.

At this point she corresponded with a man called "N". After exchanging spanking letters with "N" "Florrie" consented to meet him in an hotel in a nearby town. Between the lines we can assess the pressure of her "craze" since it required considerable courage for a refined and sedate physician's wife of her class and day to expose herself in this way. Even in the 1920's the same action (of a sort) by the heroine of *Belle de Jour* represented an alarming infringement.

"N" turned out to be intelligent and of her own age, though not class—"a fascinating barbarian," "Florrie" termed him. The couple were solely united by flagellomania and, though "Florrie" stripped buttocks for her increasingly demanding dominant, she never enjoyed sex with him. They met several times and he appears to have thrashed her soundly and skillfully, usually with a riding crop or birch. Her comment to Ellis was characteristically direct and to the point: "I wanted it, I craved it, and I got it!"

The woman was now so driven by her taboo desires that she was on the threshold of considerable psychic danger, as Ellis realized when she presented herself to him, having stumbled on a copy of his "Love and Pain" monograph. She was then aged 37 and evidently big, being 5′ 6″ tall and weighing 178 pounds (though the weight, we notice, was taken clothed and clothes were heavy then). "Florrie" confessed to being highly stimulated yet deeply ashamed . . . alarmed with and disgusted by herself, and at all the social secrecy involved. Above all, she admitted never having known orgasm. It is our guess that if "Florrie" had gone to a lesser analyst, she might well have killed herself. Ellis himself mentions madness.

Talking with someone as sympathetic as Ellis, however, made all the difference. She began to realize that she had not been guilty of some crime, nor were her "simply luscious" dreams so very sinful. In short, Ellis de-fused and diffused her fantasy. "Florrie" 's unlearned description of her first orgasm thereafter, following a bout of whipping herself, must surely rank as one of the most moving in the annals of sexology.

After three or four years she passed out of Ellis' ken, considerably soothed. He later heard from her after he had published her case (with the presentation of which she wholly concurred). Her first husband died and since she married twice more, it is likely she could now handle a sexual relationship. As Ellis put it of her:

> Florrie is not, and never will be, completely what we are pleased to term "normal." She is reconciled to "normal" sex relationships, but they do not afford her any intense gratification. Her disposition, and the ideals based on that disposition, remain essentially what they always have been. *But now she understands.* She is no longer obsessed and tortured. She is content and at peace.

This was in reply to Stekel's ponderous and obtuse pawing-over of the case in his 1925 work on sadism and masochism. Ellis shows us Stekel entirely misjudging reticent English girlhood of the time by foreign norms and again failing to account for the innate nature of the imagination.

Of course "Florrie" was born into a "child-whipping milieu." Of course her adult s-m fantasies were based on the imagery of her childhood chastisements by her father. We have indeed stated that we are against the corporal correction of children which can so easily turn a tendency into a compulsion. And of course there are likely to be considerable urolagnic associations for such a girl since, unlike a boy, she must bare her nates to pee.

But to stand sternly at the side with a slide-rule of "deviance," as does Stekel (and as does *Screw*), is wholly to miss the point. The collective unconscious, the social past, rather, finds an early surfacing in such physical punishments, to which the child vividly responds; Edith Cadivec also groped for this understanding, "As the years went by only I [among her siblings] was consumed by the erotic power of birching! Why? This question has often occupied my thoughts. Is it an accident or did I possess this tendency from birth?"

To try to prune the tree back, so that its branches will make socially acceptable patterns, can lead to disaster. Ellis beautifully understood this in "Florrie" 's case and his comment on her final development is truly moving:

> She walks in light where formerly she stumbled in a darkness full of awful specters. For years a mysteriously cloaked terrible figure had seized her from behind in an iron clutch she could not shake off, threatening her with insanity and all sorts of dreadful fates. Now she is able to turn around and face it, to observe, with calm critical eyes, and that quiet shrewd humor native to her, what it is made of, and the iron clutch loosens and the monster dissolves into mist, a mist that even seems beautiful.

WHAT
IS
S-M?

It may be that the nomenclature adopted for the sexual mode described in this book has its limitations. Yet some breach needed to be made with what is generally considered as "sadism." It was necessary to clear the air and come out with it: s-m is not sadism. Our new terminology is unimportant. Rejection of the old seems essential, however.

We have outlined basic study into the subject and suggested that it is today possibly taking a new course, thanks to more enlightened attitudes to "deviance" in general. This is a healthy sign. The widening of sexual affects in our society of late has been in complete consonance with what s-m is, and what de Sade himself proposed, despite much slander to the contrary.

Before the last world war there flourished, in England, an illustrated magazine called *London Life*. With a change of format, and editorial policy, in the late 1930's this periodical (which carried no advertisements) turned into a compendium of the s-m situation. A glance through its pages today would show how wide the libidinal range here may be and how little associated with cruelty (if usually, however, with some form of restraint or punishment). Letters, articles, photographs, often of a most affecting and clearly genuine nature, poured in about high heels, boots, leather garments, corsets, stockings, knickers, bloomers, bondage, enemas, raincoats, satin, velvet, rubber, hair, braids, toes, gloves, horse-training, hydrophilia, etc. The range seemed virtually inexhaustible, if somewhat exhausting. The readership in fact awaited what new area could be charged with libido. It was a testimony to the imaginative act.

Unfortunately, such a glance is rare today. The British Museum file of this periodical, highly estimated by the s-m underground, was badly mutilated at last inspection, and any owner of a mint set has a collector's item indeed. Loosely associated with this latter *London Life* was one who called himself "John Willie." He was, in fact, a member of a prominent British family called Coutts (to rhyme with boots, as he used to say). Most correspondents, however, would seem to have come from the middle- and lower-middle classes (clerks, typists, small shopkeepers, etc.). Creator of a widely plagiarized s-m comic strip about a persecuted maiden called "Sweet Gwendolyn," insistently and fairly unavailingly menaced by a lecher named "D'Arcy" (a satiric self-portrait), Coutts-"Willie" crossed the Atlantic after the war and continued *London Life* in *Bizarre,* until repeated piracy turned him off. He died some years ago. What may sometimes be seen on the stands today as *Bizarre* is usually a repulsive travesty.

For the *London Life/Bizarre* pages, almost soporifically mild by present standards of aphrodisia, were generally charming and tasteful and, above all, they nearly always testified to the wide net spread by the s-m pattern. Whipping letters were often in a minority. What unified the whole was the *spirit of play.* Indeed, nearly every issue would have some correspondence in it concerning the punishment of an adult, male or female (usually the latter— "Willie" was a straight), by being made to wear a young girl's garments, i.e. those of that European era, short-skirted frock, prominent knickers, fluffy socks, buckle shoes. It is fascinating to anyone acquainted with this magazine to see on the streets of New York today women wearing outfits which carry out, even far surpass, the fetishist motifs surreptitiously shown by "Willie"—short tight skirts, high heels (chunky or stiletto), boots, leather, feathers, fur. The Picadilly prostitute of the postwar London period would strut unnoticed now in New York, where every second boutique could outdo the kinkiness of her attire; as a matter of fact, Times Square hookers are said to be considerably bothered by the difficulty of attracting male attention by mere fashion (or lack of it).

"The person who allows himself to have infantile moments of loving is going to find it easier to strike out into the world the next day," claims Desmond Morris, noted zoologist and author of *The Naked Ape*. "He will have an inner strength and sense of security." *The New York Times* interview from which this quotation was drawn (February 19, 1972) was placed above a fashion story headlined "The 4-Inch Heel Returns—But This Time It's for Men." "John Willie" would have smiled.

In a 1971 *Screw* magazine interview, presumably authentic, with three masochists, all of them Americans (two males, one female), the width of reference we are portraying here is extremely evident. For one, indeed, "masochism is just a form of achieving ecstasy." Another, called "Bob," resented being pushed back into specific definitions at all:

> Masochism is a term. For me, the term is placed on the realization that I like certain parts of my body touched, played with, manipulated. I had no idea that was called masochism. Because I like hands on my body, I don't want to be called a homosexual. What is called the simple homosexual act was not enough for me. I wanted other parts of my body touched, played with and the playing had to take on stronger points that were hitting—and what you would term punishment. My fellow member talked about suffering, misery, and I don't really find masochism leading to suffering and misery, but joy. So we're working in a stupid framework where things are labeled. And as I said earlier, there are thousands of people who do the same activities as we do—in their marriage beds, in God knows where—and they are not labeled masochists. We got hung-up somewhere.

To recapitulate: s-m basically links sex with the imagination rather than uniquely with biology. It does not demand to be insistently genital, though it may be so at will. Far from being aberrant, such polymorphous love play is likely to let us see our unconscious in manipulatable quantities, and so perhaps defuse something of our societal aggression.

Some two years before these words were written a case came into the London courts reminiscent of the park plait (braid)-clippers of the past (echoed, inevitably, in Joyce's *Ulysses*). It received enormous publicity, notably in the Sunday *News of the World*. It seemed that a middle-aged bank clerk, a shy and retiring suburban bachelor of impeccable reputation, had been photographing women from beneath. A devotee of feminine underwear (like Joyce), this individual had contrived to affix a small camera to the toe of his right shoe and, moving up behind his victim in department store or at bus stop, would get a shot of her *dessous*. These cannot, in contemporary London of a summer season, have been considerable but the manner in which the offense was prosecuted at Bow Street was extraordinary. The man might have committed the most heinous of crimes, instead of a pathetic infringement of privacy. And though he eventually did get off with caution and a fine (he had "molested" nobody), the hearings were clearly punitive: as the evidence was read out, to jeers and titters from the public, the man hid his face in his hands, broke down, and wept.

We feel that this day should be long past. Hopefully in America it is. We are more than mere animals, and by now carry a considerable cargo of historical development as a species. Scarred by past legends, bruised by contemporary complexes and frustrations, modern man yearns for some erotic transcendence, something rather more lofty than that imminent explosion proffered as the be-all and end-all by the *Screws* and *Playboys* of this world. S-m is a mechanism of infinite resilience for positive release of much more than mere flesh.

It is for this reason, perhaps, that, aristocrats of the instinct, s-m people have shunned the barricades. For theirs is truly a last romanticism, the ultimate Venusberg of our senses. In the forest darknesses they have heard the music of the gods rippling on and on ". . . This sorrow's heavenly . . . It strikes where it doth love." They know which dreams stalk out between the gates of horn and those other gates of ivory.

In a world of ceremony and distance, of play and counterplay of the most vivid lightning within us, the thudding of the blood has been the only brave sun to stretch out its rays and master those black enemies pouring out of our ancestral urns. In the dusky smoke they have gazed into the deep waters and have seen a crown of pearls. Should we deny it them any longer?

S-M
IN DAILY
LIFE

U p to this point we have tried to lock horns with some of
the major sexual prejudices of our time inhibiting sadomasochism,
with those Dr. Alex Comfort has so aptly defined as "professional
manufacturers of sexual anxiety." Directly some clear focus is
achieved, and a little of that green lighting around the subject
alleviated, it begins to relate usefully to life. Inevitably, in attempt-
ing to lift something of the stigma that makes this potential for
joy so unacceptable to our society, we were compelled, a little
reluctantly, to grapple also with contemporary repression of sexuality *in general.*

Basically, however, it is still s-m that sets off our censorial zeals.
When the Victoria and Albert Museum mounted its magnificent
exhibition of Beardsleyiana a few years ago, in the heart of *le vice
anglais,* as it were, those pictures which might only be seen by
special application were uniquely flagellantine (the celebrated
illustration of a Victorian whipping club for John Davidson's
Earl Lavender was wholly omitted when the show traveled to the
Gallery of Modern Art in New York).

At first glance we do seem in modern America to be dealing
with a truly phallophilic (or pro-sex) society, one determined to
pay new tribute to the Dionysiac experience. Here sex is visibly
the opposite of that dirty secret it was for the Victorians, and those

neo-Victorian henchmen, the Austrian clinicians. The fetishisms of "John Willie" and his kind are perhaps greeted with a snort of derisive laughter, by the squares; but in a sense the fetishists have the last laugh, when you consider contemporary fashion. Just as the walls of prison cells are today papered with the kind of photographs people were being sent to prison for publishing a few years ago, so Krafft-Ebing has taken to our city streets. Most of the fabric of fetishisms, held up in trembling fingers for our inspection in the 1920's and 1930's, have by now been thoroughly domesticated by usage.

Such are no longer actively impeded from issuance, and their devotees may have their say among us as equally as may those of almost any minority interest in America, from hamster-raising to the activities of vintage motor buffs. There was, until lately at any rate, a U.S. photographic magazine devoted to toes, and a Boswell of the trend, a West Coast photographer of note, who advertised a touching repertoire of toe movies. In the New York area a "Foot Erotica Club" announced brisk business—"Join unique club devoted exclusively to sexual stimulation of beautiful feet." If we are to call foot fetishism kinky, what are we to do about a principal element in a long Chinese civilization of enormous grace and intelligence?

Alas, preoccupation does not guarantee understanding; and the frenetic interest in sex on the part of a modern Western technology is in many ways antithetical to that spirit of sex worship seen in the ancient Near East—Phoenicia, Phrygia, Mesopotamia, and (later) Egypt.

Thanks to a long and fervent history of phallophobia (antagonism to sex), in the dispersion of Jewish wisdom and subsequent non-Jewish puritanism (shown in Rome by Livy), we modern Americans stand at the end of a tradition rather than, beside the true ancients, at the happy birth of pan-sexual understandings. It would require a great deal of temerity as well as time to cover this development in any detail here. Dozens of specialist works do so admirably. Gordon Rattray Taylor's *Sex in History* is a well-known popularization that is unusually reliable as well as readable. A survey of our kind would fail of office if it did not at least try to throw out tentative and opinionative ideas, hints, suggestions, reservations, all designed toward eventuating the s-m experience today, in that fundamentally phallophobic society which modern America has inherited (principally from Europe). We do not presume to be able to turn back that destruction wrought on the human psyche by centuries of repression in a day. Cybele worship in Phrygia must have meant immeasurably more than it did for Gérard de Nerval interested in it in nineteenth-century Paris, while being even less akin to what might possibly be practiced under the same name on the Coast today. Ugarit . . . Ishtar . . . Isis—the names stream glibly off the well-publicized tongues of our new urban occultists, but today there seems to be a mite of cant in such incantations. Our cults are strictly such, reactions rather actions.

This is sad. We ourselves are far from decrying such inner yearnings on the part of anyone in need of self-fulfillment. Why ridicule Zen in Oshkosh? You can sneer, if you wish, at earnest groups of middle-aged women collecting in some suburb to hear a course of lectures on Adonis and Aphrodite, but these are probably hopeful signs.

It behooves us to recognize and identify the social soil within which such are embedded. The practice of s-m in an ancient society —in even the relatively recent Roman era when (as evinced by those glowing frescoes in Pompeii's Villa dei Mysteri) the female sexual initiate was soundly thrashed—is entirely different from our own, wherein the same desires may have to be accommodated in a sedate office worker, a telephone lineman, a gas station attendant. It is probably far more different than is realized from the same practice in upper-class Victorian England. Again, we would speculate that the new porn movies may not have done so much damage in this respect. The protagonists of such, of both sexes, are sedulously shown as average Americans; someone like a shoe salesman, for instance, long a stock joke on the burlesque circuits, is shown to have considerable imagination as well as potency. Still and all, however well-intentioned, a lot of our sexual liberation may turn out to be somewhat spurious unless we are careful with it. Grieving as it may be to have to admit as much, our furious franknesses often betray their ostensible errands.

Thus while there was never a more important moment, with human annihilation possible, for eventuation of s-m Dionysia, there was also never a more difficult time for such in our civilization. Let us not play with paradoxes any more: modern man finds himself hemmed inside psychologically crippling environments, digitary tenements, small flats, rectangular rooms, crowded apartment houses, what Dostoevsky forever foresaw, in *Notes from the Underground,* as so many hen-coops, chicken-runs, ant-heaps, idiot replicas of the Crystal Palace, and all inducive of anxiety. As his celebrated protagonist put it: "Good Heavens, gentlemen, what sort of free will is left when we come to tabulation and arithmetic, when it will all be a case of twice two makes four? Twice two makes four without my will. As if free will meant that!"

It is in this context, against this metronomically arithmetical backdrop, that Kinsey, Masters, Johnson *et al.* perform. The ideal comes to be a sort of Fourier-like paradise or Wellsian utopia in which improvement of man's material substance will automatically improve his moral. This heresy is long-standing. Our recent sexual investigators are, in a word, almost touchingly nineteenth century. Theirs is the determinism de Sade ridiculed in advance, the optimism of the first French physiologists, of later Italian *verismo,* of the Russian Chernyshevsky's *What is to be Done?* that so worried Dostoevsky.

Since it is contra-cultural, s-m has clearly benefited by the new liberalism. It would be ungrateful not to admit as much. Yet it would be simply playing into the hands of the dominant technology to imagine that, given a handful of statistics about something called sex, we can suddenly free man from the Procrustean bed of his cultural prejudices, his sexual hang-ups, and be whole.

Before anything else, then, we should proceed carefully from the admission that s-m is the most proscribed of all our sexual proclivities; it is the hardest of all to intercalate into contemporary existence since it is antithetical to it. It is "other." Jung had told us as much a half century ago. No one need feel odd for not being able to find an outlet for s-m desires in our society, constituted as it is. Far from it.

S-m people know they are "outside" society. As all exiles and outcasts realize—all those who are sick, allegedly "perverted," deprived, maimed, distorted, of the wrong color of skin or sex for the ruling society—alienation awakens longings. In physical terms the starving man (as Knut Hamsun showed us), the terminal cancer patient, the blind or amputated know what it is to be human. Seeing life from beneath (in a deprived state) they are gifted with a vision of wholeness which we—the so-called "healthy" —so often miss. In *The Metamorphosis* Franz Kafka has a man wake up one morning as a beetle, or cockroach, and be subsequently treated by his family, and employer, with that fear and revulsion shown to the mental, as well as physical, aberrant.

It is true that the two states are different in their impact on the personality. Nevertheless, the yearnings of Kafka's mutilated protagonist are suddenly what Jung termed "antithetical." They directly refute the empirical world, the cash registers of the bank his father works for, as of his own former activities as a traveling salesman. In the guise of so much sensual magic s-m is a positive and tension-solving renunciation of what our world of commerce stands for. In the room of Kafka's transmogrified commercial traveler hangs a picture of "a lady, with a fur cap on and a fur stole, sitting upright and holding out to the spectator a huge fur muff into which the whole of her forearm had vanished." In all the ardent commentary on this text it does not seem to have been observed that this amputee is directly imported from Sacher-Masoch's *Venus in Furs*; Kafka's beetle (to lose a leg himself later in the tale) at one point sprawls over her and has an evident orgasm.

It might finally be objected that all the difficulties of cultural conditioning we have touched on so far have to an extent been met by the homosexual, of both sexes. This is partly true and perhaps one of the reasons, certainly in modern America, why s-m contains so many homosexuals within its loosely staked-out frontiers; the homosexual has already admitted deviance, and thereby unlocked the door of the imagination. He, or she, is already at grips with symbolic sexual living.

Furthermore, homosexuality can certainly involve deep love, which is operative to the true s-m relationship. S-m is a form of love. If it is sought out simply for selfish sexual gratification, glandular relief, it is no longer a relationship and it is open to all the abuses laid on other forms by self-indulgers. It is particularly important, of course, to the passive partner that a human relationship be established first.

S-m is thus that fraternity or pair-bond in which you lose your sex to gain it. It can be indulged in by two women or two men, alternatively by a man and woman reversing societal roles. In s-m you are initially a dominant or submissive, of either sex. This transexuality makes it so plural, and Protean, that s-m is unlikely to become a cult, with strutting packs of self-elected publicists heading for some pantheon in *Time* magazine, and that final march up Madison Avenue.

As we have endeavored to suggest above, s-m is strangely international. In various forms it has thrived even in Russia and China. But we are unlikely to see a movement of s-m lib. If of great psychosocial concern, it is still a very private matter, and a truly personal relationship. It virtually has to be so in order to reverberate as it does. Something like s-m suddenly reveals to us how emotionally immature we are, in many ways. Piling up totally disproportionate amounts of wealth or (often useless) personal possessions is a monomania parodied in those who collect ladies' handkerchiefs, or locks of hair.

THE
PROBLEM OF
ENCOUNTER

A few years ago a large sign used to flash its alternating neon outside a certain Toronto bar: SPAGHETTI—MACARONI. There was no one of Italian origin within miles of the place and in fact, as time went by, an order for a dish of either would be met with a blank look. The terms were local code for sadists—masochists.

In the same way there used to be a bar in New York's Greenwich Village, frequented almost exclusively by male homosexuals, where a parallel transfer system had been set up. If you went in with a glove under the left epaulette of your leather poncho, you were presumed to be *m* or masochistic; if worn on the right, the glove betokened *s* or a sadist. One was reminded of that moment in *Madame Bovary* when Emma wonders whether she should put her gloves in her glass at an aristocratic dinner table, in order to designate, according to local lore, that she didn't want champagne.

Duplicities of this nature are nearly always the result of some artificial social situation. Today Emma would be able to tell the wine waiters her wishes verbally, instead of being inhibited from doing so by social convention. Tomorrow, no doubt, the youths swaggering into that Greenwich Village bar will be less ashamed of or impeded by social judgments of their sexual tastes; they will not have to resort to a bizarre form of object language in order to announce their desires.

Until that day dawns, however, s-m people are forced to be more furtive, and thus by implication dirtier, than any other minority sexual group in America. At the height of the computer dating craze no application brochure we personally perused allowed for s-m as even an idea. In any case, the dating-bureau meeting place was, unlike that of a lot of small ads in the schlock magazines, far more human and whole since you entered it with a variety of interests, not only those of sex.

So the problem of meeting a partner in s-m is, as Ellis' "Florrie" found out, a burning one. Many have singed their fingers on it. The long lists, usually under "Personal Ads," of lonely people groping towards each other for some outlet of this sort, in this or that cheap magazine, attest to the intensity of the hunger; usually a code number is provided, the answer is then sent in a sealed self-stamped envelope with the number on it, and a forwarding fee of $1 or more is enclosed to the magazine for "handling." As we have already suggested, what happens to your letter after that is anybody's guess. The dollar bill agreeably swells the petty cash. The writer obviously has no recourse.

California's *Berkeley Barb*, the *San Francisco Ball* and some issues of *Free Press* (both L.A. and S.F.) actually ran sections of their smalls under an s-m heading, and were demonstrably reliable in forwarding. Toronto's *Justice Weekly*, a flimsy little newspaper, enjoyed a high reputation in this respect with s-m people for long, but there is reason to suspect their ads now.

Most Times Squares magazines, with their tempting titles (*Corporal, Obedience, Submission*), exacerbate rather than satisfy such needs, and in all probability a large proportion of people placing (or answering) ads in such are entirely unaware of the very strong teeth still left in U.S. Post Office laws governing "pandering advertisements" (*POD Pub. 123, Rev.*). Ralph Ginzburg received an object lesson in such. Section 124.4 of the *Post Office Manual*, dealing with "Obscene and Indecent Matter," quite explicitly equates sexual literature and writings about sex with crimes of violence (the correlation between alcohol and violence has not closed down our bars and liquor stores, however). There was a time when you could send pornography through the mail with impunity, but would have been open to prosecution if the same writing had begun "Dear Joan" and ended "Cordially, Jim." To its everlasting honor *Playboy* helped to expose this particular hypocrisy of our censorship code. As the saying goes, it's better to be safe than sorry.

Yet the needs exist. They certainly bothered "Florrie" and provoked her into her correspondence with "N". We propose here to deal first with those isolates who yearn to meet such partners rather than with people who have already established more or less heavy sexual relationships, including marriage (or "serial monogamy"). We will come to them in our next section. As regards auto-erotic interests, well, we prefer to fall back on John Stuart Mill: "The only part of the conduct of anyone, for which he is amenable to society, is that which concerns others. In the part which merely concerns himself, his independence is, of right, absolute."

But it would be burying one's head in the sand to deny that such lonely people will be attracted, in numbers, by ephemeral publications in the s-m field. Thanks to their illicit nature alone they will prove unusually tempting to some. Two such in front of us as we write, *The Capricians* magazine and *The Whipping Post,* emanating from California and Colorado respectively, are almost wholly composed of s-m ads (male slaves, female dominants predominating); the former has close to a hundred pages of them and the latter thirty-four. That both may be out of business by the time these words appear in print is beside the point; they are typical of a field. The jargon (plus spelling errors) is common to large numbers of these ads we have examined and, when a photo of the same model is used to cover more than one code number, the whole enterprise can only be viewed with the gravest suspicion.

For this is not service to s-m. It is, rather, so much accountancy. And the cart is put before the horse. Supposedly thousands of young, and often not so young, people (all ardent "swingers," of course) expect to come, through these ads, to know the most intimate and secret sexual preferences of another before the color of the eyes, the sound of the voice, the other's other needs and views and looks.

So prolific have these so-called sex ads become by now, so carefully couched in a specialized semantic (*mature* for permissive, *water sports* for enematic sex, *Greek love* for sodomy . . . *English* being automatically s-m), that we have even come across a compendium which purports to be, indeed is, no less than a little lexicon of what such language really means. "Puzzled by swinging terms?" asks the ad. All right already, *Swingers Book of Terms* (Pepperbear Press) announces itself as "a comprehensive book defining those *Special* terms plus vital *do's & don'ts,* abbreviations, how to write, interpret, and answer an ad for *Maximum results.*"

A degree of imposed secretiveness, plus punitive postal entrapment techniques, presumably made all this necessary. Added to which there may also be a certain facility, on the part of masochists at least, to internalize society's image of them. Having admitted as much, one must see how dehumanizing it is to have to fumble through the dark for one's likely love partner like this, one who (it is presumed) will share the most tender and vulnerable part of one's psyche. In a very real sense it is surely submitting such to a sort of prostitution, even though money may not be at stake. After all, the contact is sought out *primarily* for sexual release and to that degree is meretricious. It is already a matter of fact that the dating agencies which purported to match the *uniquely* sexual inclinations of total strangers have begun to die of self-suffocation. Even the wildest "swingers," it was found, wanted to have some depth relationship with the one they were going to "swing" with.

The first thing to realize, then, is that we are prisoners of semantic, and of what is called the self-fulfilling prophecy. There are perils in labeling, as anyone who has named a child well knows. The relationship between vocabulary and reality is complex and reciprocal. There are many Greeks who feel they have special rights over inception of democracy since the word is Greek by origin and therefore definition (like *tyranny,* too). Call someone a *hippie* or a *Madison Avenue executive* and you start self-reflexive patterns of evaluation. "If you spell it backwards," ran one of the most successful ads ever, "it spells Nature's." What we want to know is if it's any good as a laxative.

This false reckoning between words and what words represent

becomes acute in any taboo-ed area. Johnny Cash's famous song "*A Boy Named Sue*" played on this form of language playback. A boy repeatedly called Sue (or "chicken" or "freaky") is likely to develop compensatory behavior that may take him, not to mention the playmates he roughs up in his adopted role of tough guy, into the hospital for a while. Unfortunately, we do not have clinics for nations.

If you tell someone he or she is deviant and/or freaky it is highly likely the role will be enacted. It is a result of empirical testing that elementary school children will grow up "dull" if their teachers expect them to be "dull." No one has ever called his son Idiot Jones (Zero Mostel is a comedian yet). The way in which men and women have been labeled for life as criminals is annually brought out by cases of wholly innocent people who get embroiled in a crime. A few years ago a girl gave a ride to two men who then asked her to stop at a store so that they might buy cigarettes. When they came back out she resumed riding them to their destination. Unknown to her, however, they had stuck up the store. She was later convicted as an accomplice of the crime, her car dubbed "the escape vehicle." She was labeled a criminal and eventually became a criminal. As the underworld saying has it, criminals are those who get caught.

Now we must confess that the whole s-m field depends on these pigeonholes of classification—and the sooner you can escape them, the better. In this area of sex any discussion is difficult since individual human beings are thought of as social stereotypes. We would hope that in five or ten years' time the whole category of *sadist* and *masochist* for a person will have been abolished, or be totally redundant. To bring it down to a more literal level, a girl, instead of thinking "I am a masochist, I want to meet a sadist," might rephrase this to herself in a new society, "I want to screw with someone who will thoroughly dominate me . . . or do such-and-such. . . ." She ceases to be a social stereotype of the underground and turns into someone with special tastes (similar, as de Sade said, to those of the gastronomical table). If your society tells you that you are peculiar, deviant, then you will be driven to the correspondence columns, and their like, for release. But already new liberties are enlarging our sexual semantic. Do all men who want to fuck (willing) women up the arse *first* think of themselves as sodomites—once subject to no less than the death penalty? Are they all "Greek"?

There are several sides to the coin of this commerce. The step to meet any man on the part of any reasonably shy girl is invariably going to be fraught with all sorts of unknowns. Compound with this the fact that a masochistic girl may frequently be very shy (though not always). She has read of Charles Manson and heard him repeatedly referred to as a sadist; she may even have come across the eminent Lady Snow's authoritative-sounding attribution of the British Moors murders to the reading of de Sade. She herself, when all is said and done, is going to be on the receiving end in the relationship and so can legitimately wonder: What am I getting into?

Here we must fall back on our basic principles: (1) wherever possible don't think of yourself as deviant; you'd be surprised at the number of people sitting around you in a bus or train who surreptitiously share your tastes; (2) the more the matter can be aired, the better; (3) the further a *relationship* can be established, the less likelihood there will be of trouble.

Rape is never a relationship. In 1959 a Peeping Tom, or prowler as we would call him now, an Irish laborer employed on a British building site, panicked after indulging in some quiet voyeurism on a girls' hostel when he was returning from work one day. He entered the room and, when the girl there screamed, cut off her head with a kitchen knife. Interestingly enough, it was revealed at the man's trial that he had previously played the voyeur outside the same hostel and had also, on one occasion, entered an undressing girl's room. In that instance, however, the girl had kept her head, invited him to sit on the bed and talk with her. He left without incident. The reality of a relationship had been established, and it had anesthetized his violence.

We would further observe that a crime of this nature might not have been automatically reported by the national press as *sadistic* in other countries than England. In what did its sadism consist? It was more a case of voyeurism plus alcoholism. England, however, as we have tried to explain, is frightened of sadism on the social level since it has admitted it on the psychological. It has achieved in this respect what Ashley Montagu (in *Touching*) says happened in Japan with tactuality: a sexual mode was allowed, encouraged, dramatized, in childhood, only to be vetoed in adult life. Naturally it has to take to the underground. British reporters tend to refer to almost any pathological crime as sadist: Patrick Joseph Byrne, prying into the windows of girls' hostels, was thus another de Sade. In France he would have been referred to as an *obsédé*, an obsessed or haunted person.

Another case also held up as sadistic in England recently was that of John Haigh already mentioned, tapping blood from the jugulars of his several victims. Our nearest equivalent, the Boston Strangler, was far less frequently referred to as sadistic. But since the last war the two real bugbear examples of that brutality which will supposedly result if you play with s-m fire have been, in England, Neville George Clevely Heath (1917–1946) and Ian Brady. The latter killed children and buried them on the Yorkshire Moors. One at once notices that both were also alcoholics (Byrne, too, was ordered home by his foreman for drinking the day of his first murder). Towards the end of his life Heath was stupefying himself with liquor; his last request before facing the noose was for a double Scotch. All these people had mutilated upbringings, both Brady and Heath were Borstal or reform school children, and all were assuredly psychopathic before they were sadistic, on the basis of Eustace Chesser's useful definition: "A sadist is a psychopath if his behavior is anti-social—e.g. if he commits rape or violent assault. He is not classed as a psychopath if his behavior requires the free consent of his partner."

By the end of his life Heath, at least, seems to have been thoroughly certifiable. Introduced in expert medical testimony on his behalf, Dr. William Henry Hubert, a Wormwood Scrubs prison psychotherapist, stated: "He is not an ordinary sexual pervert . . . he's suffering from moral insanity and at times is quite unaware that he is doing wrong." The following exchange then took place in the courtroom:

MR. HAWKE: Are you saying the definition of sadism does not apply to Heath?

DR. HUBERT: It is sadism plus criminality in other fields.

Heath's actual grasp on reality, raised in the trial yet lamentably ignored outside it, was so entirely recidivist that in 1937 he was convicted of posing as an Earl, and six years later was court-martialled for sporting decorations to which he had no entitlement. Unabashed, he was fined the following year for wearing the uniform of a colonel. Here pathetic make-believe clearly illided with pathic delusion.

A child's first steps in learning involve relating to the world and to other human beings about it. In this way it learns to be social, and respect the rights of others. Nearly all the sexual psychopaths, held up in press and legend, those who have over the years furnished so much palpitating copy for *The National Enquirer* and *News of the World*, seem to have been pretty close to morons as regards any form of intellectual development. Heath was a compulsive liar of lower middle-class or trade background, who was thrice discharged from the services (the British Army and then the South African Air Force), mainly for fraud—even during his trial he sported a Hawks tie, that of a select Cambridge University club, to which he was not entitled but would have liked to have been. On June 21, 1946, he abducted a not unwilling married woman to a Notting Hill hotel, slept with her, tied her up and thrashed her with a riding crop. The weals may be seen on her naked back in the police photo published in that volume of the Famous British Trials series devoted to Heath's subsequent murder of this woman and, in Bournemouth later, of another.

Heath seems to have been totally out of his mind on these occasions and after them, not only mutilating the corpses with his teeth but gleefully sending the police clues as to the killer; he also pointed out to his second victim, a single girl, how like himself seemed to be the picture being built up of the wanted man. A handkerchief-filcher like Krafft-Ebing's trembling baker's assistant, Heath showed the customary over-spill of rage into sexual aggression. Albert DeSalvo, the celebrated Boston Strangler, also victim of a broken childhood, stuffed a broom handle into the vagina of one woman he killed; Heàth thrust a poker into Doreen Marshall's cunt, though apparently after she was dead.

The Moors murderers were even more sensational, and even more clearly psychopathic in origin. Copies of de Sade were, however, found in the room where Ian Brady, with his henchwoman Myra Hindley, tied up and tortured children, carefully recording their screams on tape for evidently delectable playback. Were any of these awful warnings conscious human beings? Brady used to starve cats for fun and, after they had died, bury them with ceremony. De Salvo could masturbate over the face of a female victim he had just killed and then leave a greeting card on the body ("Happy New Year"). Jack the Ripper is supposed to have sent a victim's kidney to the police with a note to the effect he had eaten the other. He has come down to us in British reports as a prime example of a sadist.

"If Brady had not found de Sade," writes Elizabeth Gunn, "he would have found something else." He might even have found Stekel or Krafft-Ebing. By this logic we ought to indict all the inter-war cataloguers of sexual pathology as sponsors of subsequent Nazi crimes. In fact, Brady did discover something else—in a sense. The celebrated tape recording he and his accomplice made on Boxing Day, 1964, of a ten-year-old girl screaming was almost certainly stimulated by reading about flagellatory tapes available in Germany (as later exposed in *The People*). Stephen Barlay reports hearing from a man "well-known in German film and television circles" at this time that "such tapes were certainly the thing today." He himself listened to this young man's collection:

> Among the later ones was a recording which started with a conversation among two men and an unmistakably frightened woman about some flagellation and torture . . . The actual "action" on one tape was definitely spine-chilling. The screams, the painful rattle in her throat and the occasional, hopelessly weak "no" were altogether much worse than anything you could actually see.

If Brady represented any more than about .001% of the British nation, the latter could scarcely have functioned for so long as a viable society.

Late one night a short while ago a girl lay screaming under a
rapist in Manhattan's Central Park. A youth came to her assistance,
tore the rapist off her, knifed and killed him and then, with the
bloody corpse in the bushes beside them, he proceeded to re-ravish
the girl himself, as if enacting a famous scene in *Candide*. It was
an American crime and he was not called a sadist. He probably
would have been in England. Such people seem truly to have
dropped out of the human race. In the light of these horror visions
of something referred to as "pathological sadism" how can we dare
to advance the paradox that the true sadist is likely to be a safe
partner? Yet we can and do.

At the same time, in writing a book like this, we must refuse
the snare of being driven to defend sub-people like Heath and the
Moors murderers, on the basis of warped upbringings and the like.
It is likely that at such moments of bestiality all humanity in the
strict sense seems to have departed from these perpetrators of evil.
Alcohol certainly helped on the numbing process in a number, if
not most, of such cases. An alcoholic is obviously someone to stay
away from, whether his hang-up is foot fetishism or the love of
ladies' gloves. Or even obsessive screwing, as in the case of De Salvo
who seems to have thought of little else. All the more reason, therefore, to have a relationship with a love partner *first* and find out
these potential Achilles' heels.

Obsessive collecting of, or concentration upon, almost anything
can, of course, become a mania, since it disturbs our natural ratio
with reality. As Lionel Trilling put it, though in another context,
"The obsessive contemplation of the objectivity of objects, the
thingishness of things, is a step toward surrealism, perhaps toward
madness." Krafft-Ebing seems generally to have assumed, in consonance with the popular mind, that the mania came first and the
murder second: thus his "P." was found with sixty-five switches
and tresses of hair in his home and, examined after several arrests
for cutting off girls' hair publicly, revealed that "When he touched
the hair with the scissors he had an erection, and, at the instant of
cutting it off, ejaculation" (Case 100). Another collected women's
pubic hair and ejaculated biting on it. Both were sent to insane
asylums. The celebrated British bus-driver Christie, who confessed

to having killed eleven women in 1953, had evidently made collections of their pubic hair in an old tobacco tin.

But has Krafft-Ebing got this the right way around? His "P." seems to have been a febrile and terrified individual from the first, "early affected with tics and delusions." When he found himself helplessly snipping locks he seems to have been deeply ashamed "and could not trust himself to go out for several days." At least he tried, one might say. Had he been a king, he would not have had to worry. It is said that Charles II owned a wig made entirely from his mistresses' pubic hairs. It is Krafft-Ebing who calls people like "P." sadists and sets them on the steps to Hell; Havelock Ellis entirely disagrees—"the hair despoiler is a pure fetishist, no element of sadistic pleasure entering into his feelings."

It is significant that large areas of even Heath's life were left out during his trial, when we sense that he was successfully hiding his s-m. One of his girlfriends, with whom he indulged it in London, is alive today, married and with children. Starved of such contacts in Egypt in the war, Heath went to brothels to indulge—again, the *relationship* was lacking and alcohol brought to the rescue. We note that the Moors murderers, Brady and Hindley, did not have an s-m relationship with themselves.

For such people, therefore, s-m was never couched in love, only in hate, a rage through which alcohol released hidden terrors until they went berserk and wielded axes or pokers. Both Heath and Brady seem to have been subject to states of sexual hysteria and panic which turned into their psychic "conversion" reaction rather than, as it should have been, love. The Boston Strangler may not have drunk to excess, but he indulged in such satyriasis with his wife that she turned from him. This loveless frenzy was quite clearly, as the psychiatrist perceived, a duplicate of his youth when his father would knock his own wife's teeth out or deliberately break the bones of her hand ("He took my younger brother and smashed him against the wall. My sisters always had black eyes"). Albert De Salvo had no relationship other than that of violent sexual assault with any of the thirteen Boston women he murdered between 1962 and 1964.

Once again, it is as well to face the worst in such matters, in order to see the importance of consent, relationship, proportion . . . and love, in this context. If de Sade ranks in the martyrology of sex, as Borel believed, then Heath and Brady and Byrne and De Salvo and the rest are its devil figures, streaming with blood as they gibber on the edges of public nightmares about the subject. They horrify s-m people more than any.

The fact is that since society has made s-m so intensely taboo, those in whom sadomasochistic traces have surfaced have to make considerable psychic efforts in order to achieve balance. It is an admittedly vulnerable personality, but in the psychic sense an energetic one. Anti-inhibitors like alcohol or drugs may well undo the dams of hidden control. The former is famous for its ability to release violence. It was an alcoholic who killed on the Yorkshire Moors, not a sadist.

How then, since we admit his fragility, may we say that the sadist is a safe sexual partner? The two positions are complementary rather than contradictory or antithetical. As a matter of fact, in their *Patterns of Behavior,* Ford and Beach list several eminently healthy tribes—Trobriands, Sirione, Apinage—who pattern pain as a direct coital preliminary. We would be willing to bet they have known few Neville Heaths.

The s-m person has defined the world . . . has had to. The heterosexual clod has scarcely got to know his world. The s-m person has not only confronted the dark and violent side of consciousness, digging into the forbidden, he has also seen the true pain of a universe ridden with wars and torture—and is horrified by the vision. Hence, his role-playing has made him singularly aware. Dostoevsky's understanding of the bond between suffering and consciousness (in the Russian for which *conscience* also lies) makes understandable his underground man's derisive jeer, "Reactionary as it is, corporal punishment is better than nothing." Anthony Storr has even gone so far as to suggest that the sadist is almost too safe a sexual partner: "Psychopathic or psychotic persons may act out sadistic fantasies without regard to the feelings of their partners; but most men who are possessed by such thoughts are actually over-considerate, less demanding, and less aggressive than is generally expected of the male."

We have said that neither Heath nor Brady were intelligent people. On the other hand, Swinburne was known to have been an extremely heavy drinker and to have had one of the most intense "whipping crazes" on record. *Lesbia Brandon* records his frustrated struggle with this obsession. Yet, so far as we know, Swinburne never harmed the hair on anyone's head. Fortunately for him, he was intelligent, and able to communicate. In sum: A psychotic may be a sadist, but a sadist is not a psychotic.

We thus tend to see the problem of discovery and encounter from two ends. The first is straightforward enough. It involves changing categories and classifications, as mentioned. Assume that you are not "deviant." Be honest from the start with your intended love partner. Take it as a life principle always to communicate with those closest to you. Without this communicative bridge you are likely to remain locked in a separate world. Remind yourself that all the great manuals of sexual technique, from the *Kama Sutra* to the *Ananga-Ranga*, admit as axiomatic that any lover slaps, thumps, scratches, and bites a beloved.

So long as, in Mill's formulation, you are not infringing on the liberty of another, so long as there is consent, there is nothing unnatural in what you want to do. According to the Kinsey report on American women:

> Towards the peak of sexual arousal there may be considerable slapping and heavier blows, biting, and scratching, and other activities . . . If the blows begin mildly and do not become severe until there is definite erotic response, the recipient in flagellation or other types of sado-masochistic behavior may receive extreme punishment without being aware that he is being subjected to more than mild tactile stimulation.
>
> (*Sexual Behavior in the Human Female:* note the gender of the recipient)

If your partner is in love with you, he/she will make the effort to understand any such revelations. It is part of the human bargain. Ellis' "Florrie" was too inhibited to do so, with her husband. And even if the love partner is *not* directly turned on by the s-m pattern, there is likely to be some form of symbolic cooperation—provided there is love. After all, it isn't such a big deal to accept (or give) a hand spanking as erotic arousal or mild pantomime of dominance-submission. In many cases it will prove surprisingly enriching.

Thus, by *communicating* with a partner, you have already ceased to be a total deviate. Suddenly, in finding someone else with whom to share these urges, you learn that you are human. There is one more like you in the world. It can be a considerable relief. Why, society had assured you prior to this that the only way back to the fold was by the "cure" of analysis. Instead of such you rejoin the species while retaining that uniquely liberating power of archetypal sexual imagination. In truth, the s-m person may perhaps be forgiven certain feelings of superiority . . . as the true artist of sex.

Delayed revelation to a partner, as we will mention below, makes it more difficult to adjust. Frankness may be hard but it is the only way to come to any understanding of s-m in yourself as in others. Fortunately, such openness is likely to become easier in our society than more difficult. One day s-m will cease to be a social brand. As D. H. Lawrence never wearied of observing, the one way to make sex dirty is to segregate it from the rest of life, to stop it up, and only allow the copulation of so much flesh with flesh.

For the time being it is best to bear in mind that, despite the minions of *Screw, Pleasure, Kiss,* and their ilk, sex is a very sensitive plant. For most of us it is a deeply personal and intimate and therefore creative thing, with the result that it should be shared first and foremost with those closest in the best sense.

In all the lava of legend of the many materials we scrutinized in this field the attitude to s-m by T. C. Mits was pinpointed in an article purporting to be factual, and sounding somewhat so, in a popular magazine called *Pix* (Knight Pub. Corp., vol. IV, no. 8, *viz.* May, 1972). Here a story called "My Excursion Into Sado-Masochism" by Elaine Stanton describes a girl's experiences into s-m with some honesty. She describes meeting various males with the proclivity and admits "the whole thing was with my own willing agreement." All of her partners of the ilk but for the last (was he added by the editor? one wonders) seem to have acted with complete control—if also with the stereotypical impotence. She confesses, "thinking about it beforehand had given me a far greater sensation of sexual thrill than the act." Finally, she met "Dan," went to the San Diego waterfront to pick up sailors for a "gang-bang." In the alcoholic encounter which ensued she got slugged in the face. Result: her "excursion" was subtitled *It Started Innocently Enough but Before She Knew it, She was Strapped against a Wall Facing a Guy With a Mean-Looking Belt!* As no "guy with a belt" appears in the story, one assumes that such is the characteristic cliché of s-m in such media.

Secret longings and languages are not only potential psychic release mechanisms, they are binding social elements. Special slangs, intimate love vocabularies, these are so many ways of saying: If this person speaks like me, he/she thinks like me, is one with me. Though s-m springs from the deepest wells of the human psyche, it can be established on this basis: To squander it in random encounters rather than true relationships seems unworthy, vulgar. If one can rid oneself of the sense of guilt and anxiety that makes any s-m move furtive, it should not be so difficult to broach the matter via fairly innocuous terms like "spanking."

Changes of terminology can work wonders. Everyone wants to be *gay* in America, it is the errand of our social hopes and their advertising. Homosexual groups were astute in purloining this term for their own activities. In the heart of the hedonist civilization it could hardly be denied. The s-m relationship has been less lucky here. Its relationship being a very intimate kind of cooperative happening, it demands one who can be counted on to participate in scripts and scenarios best established after some personal acquaintance.

In a recently published interview a young male masochist stated: "The earliest erotic experience I can remember as a very young child is a great love of being carried around in a laundry bag. I remember when I was a kid I always wanted to play cowboys. The idea of being captured appealed to me. I remember saying, 'Let's play cowboys and Indians.' And if I couldn't get the guy interested in it I'd say, 'O.K., just tie me up.'" Surely this is a

repetition, in contemporary American terms, of the same sort of
probing and groping so charmingly, and amusingly, illustrated at
the start of Swinburne's *Love's Cross-Currents*:

> Then, with straightened shoulders and raised chin, Reginald Hare-
> wood took up his parable. Some of his filial expressions must be
> forgiven to youthful excitement and for the sake of accuracy; boys,
> when voluble on a tender point, are awfully accurate in their choice
> of words. Reginald was very voluble by nature and easy to excite
> on this painfully personal matter.
>
> "Ah, yes, I should think so. My good fellow, you ought to have
> seen me yesterday. I was swished twice in the morning. Can't you
> see in a man's eyes? My father is—the—most—awful—Turk. He
> likes to swish me—he does really. What you'll do when you get to
> school" (here a pause), "God knows." (This in a pensive and devout
> manner, touched with pity.) "You'll sing out—by Jove!—won't you
> sing out the first time you catch it! I used to—I do sometimes now.
> For it hurts most awfully. But I can stand a good lot of it. My father
> can always draw blood at the third or fourth cut. It's just like a
> swarm of mad bees stinging you at once. At school, if you kick, or
> if you wince even, or if you make the least bit of row, you get three
> cuts over . . . I dare say you've no end of pluck, but you're nervous,
> don't you see? I don't mean you funk exactly; things disagree with
> you—that's it."
>
> Here Reginald strangled a discourteous and compromising
> chuckle and gave himself a cut with his whip that made his junior
> wink.
>
> "Ah, now, you see, that makes you wince. Now, look here, you
> just take hold of that whip and give me a cut as hard as you
> possibly can. You just do that. I should like it. Do, there's a good
> fellow. I want to see if you could hurt me. Hit hard, mind. Now
> then," and he presented a bending broadside to the shot.
>
> The trodden worm turned and stung. Driven mad by patronage,
> and all the more savage because of his deep admiration, Frank
> could not let the chance slip. He took sharp aim, set his teeth, and,
> swinging all his body round with the force of the blow as he dealt it,
> brought down the whip on the tightest part he could pick out, with
> a vicious vigor and stinging skill.
>
> He had a moment's sip of pure honey; Reginald jumped a foot
> high and yelled.
>
> But in another minute, before Frank had got his breath again,

the boy turned round, rubbing hard with one hand, patted him, and delivered a "Well done!" more stinging than a dozen cuts.

It can, in short, be as simple a start as that. The decisive factor is the presence of love.

If love is not present, sex will suffer a separation. A relationship immediately takes s-m out of the dungeon of taboo in which it has lingered for so long. This need—simply to talk to someone non-moralistic about the subject—was evidenced in the various group (or "consciousness-raising") sessions the authors of this book attended in the field.

It was suddenly surprising how many of those present confessed to being under analysis, and then it was not so. For the analyst was clearly in this case someone to talk to *who would not pass judgment*, the first step to, or substitute for, an understanding partner. Talking with someone who will hear you without criticism is a certain form of therapy. But while the two are in a sense reciprocal, understanding is not the same as love. The analyst may be able to furnish the former, but the lonely s-m person really needs the latter, to which s-m is a dependency or adjunct.

It is *not* a replacement. The nature of the correspondence ads would see it as such and this happens to be their most serious limitation. If, finally, the hunger becomes a craving (as it did for "Florrie"), and the isolate is impelled to reach out for others willy-nilly, we would counsel caution. There exists an obvious spectrum in such matters. The underground press is probably at the lower end of reliability, notably where box numbers and such evasions are proffered by the correspondent. Here sex is sought first, and sometimes simply for itself. At the upper levels one might think of announced lectures, talks and the like, given on subjects close to s-m (e.g. Dionysiac history, de Sade, taboo, censorship, magic, libertine literature, films—the gamut is clearly wide).

Utterance is, in short, essential. In the November 1972 number of the magazine *Forum* a long analysis of algolagnia by an eminent psychoanalyst concluded as follows: "We practice sadomasochism as the highest expression of love and therefore consider it to be an

intimate activity arising from the deepest fellowship of two lovers
. . . Sadomasochism can only be handled properly by those who
exist in perfect mutual confidence and love." At the risk of being
repetitive, here are Henry James' golden words again: "The
essence of moral energy is to survey the whole field."

S-M
IN
MARRIAGE

When it comes to the interjection or recreation of s-m drives in marriage, or in already established and cohabited relationships, we have to remember certain abiding elements in the human pair-bond. Simone de Beauvoir tells us with her customary brisk confidence that "the married man is less inhibited than another."

This may have been the case in her childhood, and ours, in the sense that as a male making regular love, a married man was less anxious and sexually broken-up than a bachelor. We doubt that this is necessarily the case today, least of all in contemporary permissive America. Indeed, something of the reverse would seem to obtain. Here length of intimacy may be oddly commensurate with difficulty of communication of intimacies. This is a House of Lords way of saying that one doesn't want to make a fool of oneself in front of one's favorite person.

When one has lived with another for any stretch of time certain absolutes cohere. Certain self-images are handed out, from partner to partner. These harden with age. A man could have a rich and fecund sexual life with his wife on the basis of being a certain personality, while keeping another aspect of it concealed. Such a Jekyll-Hyde would become increasingly frightened of revealing the hidden part of himself, primarily for fear of spoiling what had come to be, for him, a mutually agreeable relationship.

With a stranger such image-destruction wouldn't matter in the least.

At this point we remember Ellis' "Florrie" who, though she had no sexual relations with her husband at all, evidently adored him to such an extent that she felt she could never reveal to him her hidden masochistic yearnings. He too, after the first timid approaches to initiating a wholly ignorant and vulnerable girl into sex, seems to have been reconciled into a tender constancy, unblemished by any revelation.

For this reason it is not paradoxical that some people seem almost to enjoy confiding in those most parenthetical to their lives. We do not mean only analysts here. Occasional friends, dependents of a transitory nature, hairdressers, masseurs, casual acquaintances, are notoriously the recipients of sexual secrets often withheld from spouses. And why not? There is no penalty to pay for such.

Why is it *more* difficult to share one's deepest desires and anxieties with one's life's soul? Why is it so easy to confide in strangers? Some people spend long hours in bars for this very purpose, unlocking themselves mentally and ruining themselves physically in the process. It is simply that with a long-time partner we have constructed a façade (in T. S. Eliot's terms "a face to meet the faces that you meet") which becomes increasingly difficult to crack. Late revelations of our inner selves to a longtime partner may well come to seem inherent treacheries since the other has accepted the given persona as a working basis for the whole relationship.

We all exchange self-images with a loved one, and see such reflected back to us. There may indeed be, as de Beauvoir suggests, a sort of narcissistic valuation in this. But, on the conscious level, what we know and have to deal with is simply that there may be other feelings we have not expressed or exchanged with a mate which the habit of suppression makes increasingly difficult to share. For such participation would seem to threaten to shatter the self-image. The hidden feelings then become more deeply hidden, or what Jung would have called "undifferentiated" (unrecognized) so that containing them at any cost comes to seem preferable to admitting them and having them rebuffed by a beloved.

"Florrie" 's husband went to his death in total psychic ignorance of someone close to him for years to whom he had been devoted. This is very sad.

For it is also a disservice to oneself. And the longer such suppression lasts the more blocks to utterance will arise. Finally, in later years, sexual indifference will be speeded by such lack of earlier psychic outlet. (It's all over now.) Continence is then called normal because—according to the textbooks—in old age the sexual organs fail of office. We shall hope to suggest that this is relative rubbish. Tolstoy, Picasso, and Chaplin are three in our civilization who proved the reverse. But to avoid this syndrome, immortalized in Burns' famous poem "John Anderson My Jo," some manner of communication, we would reiterate, should be opened up. The confessional releases the obsessional. We take our text from Anthony Storr: "Men and women are only fully themselves when related to each other."

Lack of cooperation breeds resentment. If you do not share your whole personality with another (however shameful you may consider such to be at points) you are extremely unlikely to develop and continue any relationship of value. Shame is social. And sex is so fundamental to a truly human relationship that any damming-up of special sexual interests or desires will of course spill over into the entire sex act—to produce physical impotence, crises like premature ejaculation in the male, frigidity in the female, guilt at masturbation when married, and all the psychic rages resulting in turn from these frustrations.

Release of blocked instinctual drives means a flood of creativity in the psyche; this can be correlated by contrasting the fecundity (not quality) of artistic production in a Picasso with a Baudelaire. In the former it is tempting to see a libidinal extrovert and fully eventuated creative personality loving to express images of his world; the latter shows us carnal desire, constantly wounded by sexual frustration and/or possible impotence, coming through as a flame of torment. This is not to denigrate Baudelaire's superb accomplishments; it is simply to suggest that a dimension of life is absent from them or, if you wish, that they would have been even greater and more frequent, had he not felt so hurt by his society.

Any delayed revelation of one's inmost being to a partner makes it automatically more difficult for him/her, as the latter then has to deal emotionally with the humiliation of not having been considered worthy of the secret earlier. With semi-strangers (hairdressers, manicurists, maids, bar friends, masseurs) there is no prepared image at stake, so that the confiding individual feels far less inhibited. It has been a characteristic of secret service systems (like those of Germany and Japan in this century) to infiltrate just those categories of confidant we have cited. Older people, on the other hand, notoriously talk less. There are many versions of the story of the two old-timers on a long bus trip, one of whom finally sighed after about two hours, to elicit a grunt of agreement from the other and a softly breathed "You're telling me!"

Furthermore, in confiding to an almost total stranger, one with whose company you can dispense at any time, you know there is no peril. The recipient of the information is under your own control. After all, you can drop even an analyst and never see him again, let alone a hairdresser. A barfly can be fairly certain he will never see again, if he does not want to, the bosom buddy of his last Saturday night outpouring. Obviously this is not the case with an intimate of many years, where a true breach becomes a psychic menace.

The revelation of a secret from one's psychic life is perhaps particularly difficult in a modern technology, despite all the gush about our much-vaunted permissiveness, and frankness of language. Even our permissiveness is "differentiated" these days, hence *Screw*. The searchlight of science seems to have illumined every nook and cranny of the psyche, with its cold, clinical light before which the sensitive ferns and anemones of the unconscious understandably cringe and shrink. A Times Square weekly newspaper can thus calmly consider the possibility of eating shit alongside a large ad for technical devices allegedly increasing sexual sensation. A typical *Screw* interview question goes, "Did you find that 69 was performed three to one, say, over face-to-face? I mean, did you keep any figures?"

Monique von Cleef recounts the story of a client who pretended to be a rabbit. "He liked to scurry around upstairs. When I find him I say 'look at the nice little rabbit,' and he cries and says, 'I lost my mother.' " We submit that such cathections sound especially absurd in the era of space shots. The man who wanted to be a rabbit was in a different context a century ago, when most people had seen rabbits in the countryside. S-m can come to seem fairly absurd in our hyperhygienic society, with its lack of privacy (not to mention abolition of corporal punishment). Yet if one despises the curio hunter, one also condemns curiosity. Kinsey was principally a collector rather than a curio hunter in the French sense of *amateur* (which still retains the connotation of *lover of*); Wardell Pomeroy's recent book on him notes that before he even thought of sex Kinsey had collected over a million specimens of gall wasps. Would he have been embedded forever in Krafft-Ebing, one wonders, if he had been, instead, a collector of handkerchiefs?

The reason why we dilated on the case of "Florrie" above was simply that hers seems to have been the textbook tragic anagram of s-m in marriage. Wife or husband hides an interest. Anxiety about it grows. With eventual revelation, if such arrives, there is bewilderment at rediscovering someone one has known all one's life as another, unknown individual. If, as in "Florrie"'s case, a third person, a stranger, has gotten involved, the whole matter becomes top-heavy with sexual jealousy, and any understanding will require a real effort. It is significant that "Florrie" broke with "N." after the few times they met because he threatened her social life. Love partners should know that confiding a secret is a true gift to the other to whom it is imparted. Children know this, and adore secrets as a consequence. Revelation may not be easy, but it will repay large emotional dividends.

The retention of a secret is scarcely a crime, however. It is simply another social determinant. In infancy sex seeks out itself. When we are older we replay what we understand to be acceptable norms. As a hobby a medical researcher once trained houseflies to lie on their backs and balance a toothpick on their feet. The same "pure" professor might have been most alarmed at the idea of a reputable businessman paying a Dutch dominatrix to let him run around her house like a rabbit. But, as de Beauvoir has well put it, "desire is most often satisfied through deviations in which the fantasies of middle age are accentuated."

America is the first country to have put what is roughly euphemized as "swinging" into some sort of mass-production. Judging from the ads for them, so-called spanking clubs and other group s-m meetings between consenting adults are beginning to proliferate. "SPANKING & B/D CLUB—give &/or receive, single girls & couples," runs one such invitation. Presumably these furnish contacts of a sort between serious s-m people; and since the married, or those in sexual liaison, are psychologically the safest bets, these loosely structured organizations often accept only couples as members.

Frankly, we do not know what good these groups do, if any, since we have not checked many out. Not everyone likes sex public. Reports are varied. They are part and parcel of a prevalent sexual climate and should primarily be judged within such. There is some evidence coming in to suspect that they may actually be the source of more anxiety than relief, especially for women (and especially for women taken, a trifle reluctantly, to these gatherings by horny husbands). It is conceivable that to release s-m inclinations and desires *first* among others rather than with a loved person would aggravate problems, by parenthetical influence. For the true s-m person the marginal spanking club is probably contra-indicated.

There can be no doubt, however, that if such inclinations are felt they should be eventuated in some form between consenting couples themselves. In her book *The Coming of Age* Simone de Beauvoir writes, "the happier and richer sexual life has been, the longer it goes on." But the longer it goes on, the more the male realizes that he is at an increasing disadvantage in the transaction. For a woman's sexual drive is much less weakened by age than a man's. Kinsey and Masters and Johnson all showed that, *given proper stimulation,* a woman could go on enjoying sex indefinitely. Indeed, State mental hospitals are evidently replete with senile female patients suffering from precisely that erotic dementia which de Sade was finally imprisoned for.

All the more reason, then, to allow s-m as a polymorphous play activity preliminary to sex, instead of stigmatizing it as perversion. We are not encouraging a lot of old ladies to go out and buy birches for their biologically weakening husbands. We are simply suggesting, once more, taking a look at this vexed matter through the other end of the sexual telescope.

It has long been a cliché of Western thought that the elderly rake, senile and twitching, sought out perversion in order to stimulate a jaded sexual appetite. But yesterday's perversion can be today's norm (these words were written in the month when *Cosmopolitan* magazine breezily recommended sending an absent boyfriend, among other mementoes, "a lock of your pubic hair" while, beside it on the stands, a dildo-shaped "personal massager" was advertised in *Better Homes and Gardens*). The beautiful, febrile Comte Robert de Montesquiou-Fezensac, model for Huysmans' Des Esseintes and Proust's Charlus, has often been held up as the prototype of the exhausted *roué*, almost as often as has also George Augustus Selwyn (1719–1791); in the latter Mario Praz sees fixed forever "the type of English algolagnic," the Neville Heath of the eighteenth century, a man supposedly so sexually worked out and debilitated that he even paid to watch public executions in France, once doing so (according to Sir Nathaniel Wraxall) "disguised in a female dress." The Goncourt brothers, who set Selwyn into fiction, met such a cliché Englishman in real life and described his body as twitching and jerking stiffly "like the torso of an automaton."

To some extent, it must be admitted that de Beauvoir herself accepts this cliché, or part of it. Assuming that in the older man "the two stages of ejaculation are reduced to one" and that "he no longer has that piercing sensation of imminence which marks the passage from the first to the second" (how does she know?), we find her senior male citizen turning into the typically dirty old man. He looks into pornography, "he indulges in fetishism, sado-masochism, various forms of *perversion*" (our italics). Finally, after eighty, the poor fellow degenerates eventually into a voyeur. As if he had not been such all his life. A sizeable slice of the American economy would cease to function without male voyeurism.

Now there is evidence that masturbation recurs and increases in old age. In one survey of married men *Sexology* magazine found onanism virtually recommencing after sixty. Stimulations such as are provided by fetishisms or s-m need *not* be seen as so many pathetic potency symbols for the aged, like those useless condoms with feathered heads and the like once sold in a famous sex store in Kobe, Japan. What if such tendencies have always existed, yet never really surfaced until a time in life when stimulation is at a premium? After all, sex in old age is no longer biological. It thus asks to spread out from the genital.

Simone de Beauvoir's contribution to the understanding of sex in old age ("maturity" . . . "senior citizenry") has been considerable. For it is our society, with its adoration of youth, which keeps telling us that old people become impotent or frigid and, in a characteristic self-fulfilling prophecy, thereby produces a lot of impotent and/or frigid old people.

The classic cases of sexual longevity have been found (a) in certain specialized peasant communities, such as the Black Sea area, and (b) creative individuals all over, not only Picasso, Casals, and Chaplin, but those like the French man of letters Paul Léautaud who kept a journal of growing old and whose sexual life seems to have begun *after*, rather than *before*, the age of sixty. We also note, parenthetically, that our society has not coined the phrase *dirty old woman*. When menopause arrives, our women are supposed to be sexually sidelined, set in a gradual, decorative decline, whereas a man who thinks of copulation is still an accessory, if an enfeebled one, to the going civilization; maybe he can still foster a few more productive digits for the economy.

This is admittedly a loaded statement. It is of purpose so. Contemporary technology has so distorted sex while exploiting it that all context gets lost. The writers of this book would be the first to admit that it undeniably does become more difficult to jump a tennis net as the years pass by. Aging of a purely physical sort has to be taken into account when assessing any form of sexuality in either sex, as does habit—if you do it a lot you'll do it a lot; the British defector Guy Burgess had, according to the latest biography of him, a sexual appetite as gargantuan as that of the Boston Strangler (and he drank much more). The glory of the human animal is that the psyche lets us to a degree transcend the decline of the flesh.

America is probably one of the most difficult countries in which to eventuate true s-m. The present mode of the nation is a libertarian, yet totally undisciplined, hedonism. *Screw* exemplifies as much, and has accordingly reaped rich rewards. Yet, as Milton reminded us, liberty itself needs certain disciplines—let's call them here respect for human rights. Even contemporary feminism, however well-intentioned, is demanding new disciplines in place of the old. Hire women, or else. No males need apply. When de Sade tried to "solve" prostitution in the Tamoé section of *Aline et Valcour* we note that it was only by an added discipline that he could do so: all males, called for stud service by a woman, *had to* respond, as well as they could. Any true human relationship demands a discipline, a curbing or retraction of one's own drives in the interest of the other. The sweetness of love is that it makes even this a joy.

This is the larger context within which American s-m must be viewed. Between two consenting adults it represents a real effort at inner discipline. For genuine morality comes from within. This is no mere pious formula, another drone from the pulpit, but a true prescription for sexual happiness. We are not, in these pages, advocating wild sexual license—on some basis of try it and see! The fashionable attitude of the *Screw* sort operates on the axiom excoriated in Nabokov's Epilogue to *Lolita*. The more the merrier! By the canons of the world of *Screw, Kiss, Pleasure* and the rest, immorality is a sacred right, a fifth freedom; anyone may comfortably cheat on a husband/wife, regardless of the human hurt entailed. Such media would scarcely enjoy being mugged in that Times Square area where they ply their main business, but by implication would not seem to object very much to breaking a carefully constructed human relationship. In their pages the sexual explosion comes first, the relationships second, if at all.

There is no receipt for sexual enjoyment in the wham-bang-thank-you-Ma'am attitude, since there is little or no depth relationship. All is on a surface level. Such fucking can be good, bad or indifferent (or, as they used to say of the brassieres meted out to British servicewomen in the last war, "Small, Medium, Large, Great Scott, and Good God"). Directly there is depth relationship with another, there is a responsibility. Aldous Huxley once had a fictional character remark, "The higher and more advanced the civilization, the more perverted the sex." For his "perverted" one might today substitute "imaginative."

Surface fucking can't truly "improve." S-m can. We are far from advocating wild, anti-human, not to say costly, orgies, but total trust carries with it total responsibility. It is for this reason that the true sadist can be both very serious, in his precious mystery or trade, and very tender. One remembers the old code of rights accompanying duties, and vice versa.

Moreover, it is perfectly possible that s-m could assist in relieving impotence, or at least indifference, in marriage. The classic impotence cases of the past were typically married men who began to abandon sex as variety and excitement connected with it passed. According to three well-known New York psychiatrists, reporting on contemporary impotence in the March, 1972, issue of *The Archives of General Psychiatry,* such males "felt confident that novel objects or practices could revive their interest." Why not s-m?

Furthermore, the same report noted that the major manhood anxieties occurring in young Americans today were traceable to the new and increased sexual demands made upon them by the new woman. "When we explored these sexual failures occurring in a relationship," the three psychiatrists (two of them from Bellevue) wrote, "we found a common male complaint: these newly freed women demanded sexual performance. There is a reversal of roles. The role of the put-upon Victorian woman is that of the put-upon man of the 1970's." If such men could be offered a strongly dominant role in s-m practice and play, they would surely be helped. And they are going to need to be; as woman advances and requires less protection in society she is going to be more and more demanding, culturally and sexually.

This is no myth. A 1970 poll taken by *Psychology Today* showed over one-third of its male readers having difficulty achieving erection, with four out of five sexologists in an October, 1971, symposium reporting impotence on the increase. In its October, 1972, issue *Esquire* featured an article by Philip Noble, "What is the New Impotence, and Who's Got It?" A University Hospital (New York) psychiatrist was quoted as saying, "Unconscious transmissions of feminine revenge by an aggressive manner and over-assertiveness may enhance a man's castration anxiety with consequent fear of the vagina."

If s-m could be freed from the terrifying-perversion label that has been stuck on it, the mode might well become a helpful adjunct to marriage. Or, at least, to some marriages. In these cases it could be an ideal tool for preserving the vitality of the bond. For what does the latter consist of in contemporary America? Out of 162,303 California marriages in 1969 there were 81,670 divorces (dissolutions), a rate of over 50%.

And why not? Marriage is scarcely "marriage" any more, under such conditions. Today when two people of opposite sexes meet, they face the facts. They are erotically excited by discovering each other, with the result that each is The Other to the other. This is simply a way of saying that two strangers feel each other out, and find natural excitement in discovering another human being. After a long period together, they come close. They even become alike. Married couples will sometimes quite unconsciously mimic each other's body positions and gestures.

Yet coming as close as this has its penalities. In joining two selves together in harmony you risk the annihilation by absorption of one or the other. In such circumstances sex becomes a shade predictable. The pair have ceased to be surprising, one to the other.

Intelligent s-m could help to repair this state of affairs. It involves creative role-playing in a psychodrama wherein each becomes The Other to the other (or, alternatively, varieties of The Other). This is not just so much psychological hair-splitting, or name-dropping; old age makes possible a wider spectrum in this respect in marriage, than at the start of a youthful relationship. Instead of being cast as Nervous Bride, a woman finds all sorts of outlets possible, including Courtesan, Schoolgirl, Slave, or

Persecuted Maiden in general. Sheik literature can come to life. At the same time she is preserving, indeed cementing, proximity with her beloved.

Among others, de Beauvoir claims that a woman does not necessarily have to attain orgasm in order to get sexual pleasure, with the principle ensuing that "The 'preliminary pleasures' count even more perhaps for her than they do for a man." For her, that is, there is no fear of genital failure and she can consequently become increasingly generous to her husband ("less worried by his growing old").

This is perhaps a little pat. Frankly, a woman likes to have an orgasm. While she may not need this climax in quite the same way as a man does, she still feels frustrated today if she hasn't come during a sexual interlude. Her own ecstasy may not *depend* on the male genital explosion, but she does like some climax. Unresolved arousal is likely to be just as dissatisfying to her as to her husband, or lover.

When sex, then, has been freed of the biological and freed of the punitive social behest for a genital explosion, it becomes more and more immured in fantasy, "attached to functions dependent upon other drives," as de Beauvoir puts it. While we may not share her views of s-m as an aberrance, we endorse her wholeheartedly when she writes, "Normally, seeing and caressing one's partner plays an important part in sexual intercourse. It is accompanied by fantasy; sadomasochistic elements appear; and often fetishism, clothes and ornaments evoking the presence of the body. When genital pleasure is weak or nonexistent, all these elements rise to the first place."

In a way, therefore, old age can add a subtle coda to sex which helps us see its full splendor. It is possibly a characteristic of creative and imaginative people to have long sexual lives since they sense the wonderful generosity being afforded us in sexual giving. It is far more positive to regard sexuality in our later years as another *kind* of love, rather than that decline of a once bright sun which Burns provided in his famous poem (after all, his protagonists were simple peasants). The s-m husband or dominant has a true life's task in this relationship and revelation. By nature, as Storr has told us, he is almost "over-considerate." Yet his wife requires him to lead her by the hand down into the hidden mysteries of their souls, where the buried treasure glimmers.

THE STRUCTURE
OF THE
S-M EXPERIENCE

The prevalent form of s-m is what is generally known as flagellation; viz. physical punishment of, usually, the buttocks.

However, we have tried to show how clinical case histories and/or pornographic writings may convey scant idea of the width of reference in this sort of love play. A bondage enthusiast whose chief thrill is to be tied up, and is quite turned off by any actual blows, might well think of himself as into s-m. The range of erotic activities is wide, as its symbolism is obscure, including in its behavior such disparate drives as fascination with feces and adoration of tiny toes. "Fetish" is, in fact, an adopted acronym for Friends and Enthusiasts of Tiny Insignificant Shoes and Hair.

Some cultures pattern hair as a virility symbol—in some of Baudelaire's poems it is almost a vegetation myth—while others adulate baldness in males; the work of the nineteenth-century Portuguese novelist Eça de Queiroz could be brought to the bar here, as might, indeed, the movie image of Yul Brynner. In fact, virtually anything can be fetishized and spiritualized. In a now famous film Eric Rohmer fastened on a girl's knee as a man's fetish object.

This width of reference is extremely important to establish from the start, and particularly is it important to women. We have suggested that what might, at present writing, roughly be designated

the *Screw-Playboy-Cosmopolitan* axis (allowing for obvious variations in degree) advocates sexual attitudes which are duplicates, in
human relations, of industrial techniques. Both are on an inexorable feedbelt of endeavor. The hedonist leer behind these attitudes
encourages a repeat performance with as many chicks as possible—
and that some of these may be boy-chicks far from invalidates our
argument. *Cosmo* would seem to presuppose a feminine readership
not only looking for "lovers" rather than husbands, but actively
turning over lovers like so many new lipsticks. The attitude is
emotionally thinning.

Frankly, an initial requirement of s-m is to have a *depth* relationship. If this does not happen, the intimacy of the psyche will
scarcely be sensed although, fairly obviously, someone craving for
s-m will clearly get some sort of surface satisfaction from the
Monique von Cleefs of this world. What we are saying is simply
that you should not have to go to such strangers for relief.

But s-m turns its back from the start on that quantitative,
rather than qualitative, yardstick by which our society so universally judges. In the sense that it is a depth relationship it is intensely
moral, and on the side of women. It is not simply a matter of more
and better fucking, bigger and more blasting orgasms. Animals
can achieve such, and frequently do.

It was thus significant that, in a long and basically sympathetic
interview with Monique von Cleef, *Screw* magazine's Al Goldstein
treated her as a social worker, someone performing therapy. He did
not seem to realize that implicit in this attitude was the contention
that s-m was aberrant, and that no wholly mature s-m relationship
was possible. The woman was a whore, and a very high-priced one.
You go to a whore when there are no outlets for your desires in
society. For those of the *Screw* persuasion no emotional relationship in depth can be conceived to inhere within an s-m union. Unlike homosexuality or drug addiction, it is by definition abnormal,
transient, and accordingly furtive and fleeting. For *Screw* sex seems
to be dialectically promiscuous . . . what one might call so much
serial fucking. S-m, however, is not promiscuous and defends the
woman within its scope. Let us elaborate an instant on this basic
orientation.

The conception of someone like Monique von Cleef as a "leather social worker" presupposes the s-m person as one simply requiring so much psychosexual release. She was a kind of safety valve, and had no emotional involvement with her clients. Surely this is a desperate last remedy. If those people who visited her in such droves, and evidently still do in Holland, had been able to find a similar sexual release through a love relationship, they would have had no need to depend on furtive prostitution.

But *does* one want to support the separation of the sex urge from the emotional restraints of love? For love does curb the sort of random sexual activity which animals indulge in, and it does so in a very precious manner. The minions of *Screw* would surely have us live like dogs, with the maximum of climaxes with sundry individuals over a given period being slide-ruled to a sort of "happiness" meter.

Still, let us assume, and admit, that this philosophy at least recognizes—as did de Sade—the incorrigibly plural nature of the sex drive. This was long thought to be a prerogative of the male, but we now suppose the female to be equally lavish of her sexual interests. Let us assume that both sexes require some variety to avoid the boredom of routine. Surely in the s-m relationship of deep involvement with one person you can still explore the widest possibilities of the sexual imagination. You can be schoolgirl or slave, sheik or squire. Paradoxically, this is far more moral and responsible to the human condition than all the promiscuous screwing, sucking, and eating advocated as the nirvana of the liberated life in so much of our slightly panting press.

We have claimed that s-m is on the side of women, and it is. If a woman has a really imaginative s-m scene going with her partner, there are so many varieties and surprises possible, so much invention under way, that she will always be interesting to him. There is a wealth of roles open in s-m and a man (either s or m) is much less likely to get bored and stray from such a partner than with the in-out airline hostess. In s-m, each plays a world of roles to the other and it is highly unlikely that a complex scenario could be satisfactorily worked out in a matter of minutes with a person new to one—let alone someone perhaps never to be seen again. If

all the male wants, as per *Playboy* or *Screw,* is an attractive exterior
and convenient apertures, well then there are thousands who will
supply them.

We must allow the s-m person into our society in the truest
sense. The psychic intimacy which makes for a successful homosexual union, of either sex, relies on just that depth which s-m
people at present find implicitly denied to them. Theirs is supposed to be the world of the prostitute and call-girl; they are the
frightened freaks. Yet they, too, are creative beings. This is essential to realize, and integrate into our society, for a variety of reasons.
Unlike the gay, the s-m person is still almost universally considered
depraved, a lame, dwarfed, and hunchback being. To dismiss all
such people as deviants on the road to crime, as did Krafft-Ebing,
is what is really crippling.

Surely there is something immensely touching in the effort
to idealize the less beautiful attributes of a beloved person. May
not what we call unnatural perversions really be so many symbols
of great erotic love? Are they not thus, paradoxically enough, more
resoundingly wholesome and "pure"? And so in a way, more
potent? For they demand high intellectual energy and an entirely
different attitude to the human body. De Sade pointed this direction out. Even urine suddenly becomes no more than an extension
of The Other and so can be precious and valuable. The long
litanies of religious hysterics often advanced at this point (all
eating dung, licking syphilitic wounds, and the like) are the true
fodder for Stekel, Moll, Krafft-Ebing, rather than the terrified
baker's assistants and soap manufacturers of this world. In the pages
that follow we shall hope to sketch a little sanguine picture of the
width of the s-m relationship, having briefly tried to characterize
the need for its depth.

THE
SCENARIO

True s-m seems to us a sexual dyad. This may be a bias, so it is as well to admit it at once.

The mutual confidence and trust essential to the s-m scene are likely to be dissipated in any group. If suffering pain in front of others gives pleasure to some, it perhaps owes more to the entry of disparate elements, and happens because s-m proper has been diluted or even drowned out in exhibitionism (which might well be called s-m improper). For a true masochist the best that could be said about the extension of such love play beyond the pair-bond might be that it could form some sort of extra mental mistreatment and abasement.

While we do not wish in any way to force our personal predilections on practitioners, or those who would be, we should be less than honest if we did not lay our own prejudices out on the table first. Among these is the suspicion that an orgy can more often attenuate sex than enrich it. To be sexually reverberative the sadist/masochist must be the superior/inferior part of a symbiotic bond based on love. A group of people paying to watch someone unknown to them flagellated is of another order altogether, and quite outside the scope of our analysis here.

At the start of this study we were keen to make clear what Kinsey's associate, Paul Gebhard, came to see, namely that ceremony and ritual are of the essence of all s-m play. The lover, we have noted, is here in a very real sense an artist . . . the esthete of sex.

After all, postponement and delay—resulting in that apprehensive anticipation the masochist finds so delicious—are modes of control. As Gebhard puts it, "It is important to realize that pain *per se* is not attractive to the masochist, and generally not to the sadist, unless it occurs in an arranged situation." Writing in *The Village Voice*, the self-confessed practitioner Terry Kolb confirms this emphasis:

> The two consenting partners must work very hard to achieve a compatible relationship because so much depends on relating the fantasies of each partner to the other. The successful s/m act can be compared to a successful production of a drama composed by two or more authors. A great deal of intuition, ability to improvise, and cooperation is needed. In some cases, the relationship is highly ritualized, almost resembling a religious ceremony.

Exactly. Here we are in a realm beyond hurried hedonism where the lover has to sound out every part of his beloved's psyche. The s-m scene is truly what has been called a *happening*, yet one in which you have to hold back rather than over-indulge. On a basic structure a couple improvises as they go along. The notion of a performance, a mime, is quite pervasive, extending to clothing and gesture. In this private little *Commedia dell'Arte* emotions such as sternness, and submission, will be exaggerated for their over-spill effect. In serious s-m movies it is notable that the participants' movements are slower rather than faster than normal, often highly stylized. Since apprehension and suspense are so intensely turning-on for the submissive, the dominant must prolong preparation, play on these qualities of arousal with, yes, a quasi-religious devotion, or the care of an expert violinist for his Stradivarius.

Obviously, needs as undifferentiated as these depend on good communication. Hence, a deep relationship is ideal. Presumably, in the case of a professional like Monique von Cleef, she would inquire the kind of fantasy desired by the paying client—whether he wanted to run around her house like a rabbit or crow like a cock on his knees, in the manner of the protagonist in Heinrich Mann's famous original for *The Blue Angel*, namely *Professor Unrat* (1905).

Not everyone has the time or ability to devise a sexual playlet, of course, and in general the s-m scenario is of two sorts—structured or unstructured. In the former the couple can agree to go into a scene with fairly rigid outlines, even down to dialogue. The submissive can thus work out (and in a sense control) the various stages of the impending punishment, even perhaps deciding at what point to interject intercourse; the couple can agree how much begging-off, stalling, imploring, is or is not turning-on, how much pain is to be given, and shown (or mimed). Amusing versions—parodies—of structured s-m scenarios exist in the *Oh! Calcutta!* sequence, to wit "Who: Whom" and "St. Dominic's, 1917" (see Appendix).

In the unstructured or impromptu fantasy the dominant obviously carries the greater onus. He/she must take the initiative, while the submissive follows a lead, sensing perhaps more thrill in the unknown (on the principle of "It's always going to be slightly worse than expected"), responding in kind to the ordering around, the particular amount of touching and humiliation and punishment allotted and designed. For two people who know each other well, and so share an awareness of one especial s-m scene, this really amounts to about the same thing, when you come to think of it. Which brings us to specifics: What is the nature of the s-m scenario?

We decline to prescribe, beyond certain rather tentative and, indeed, manifest guidelines. Each human being is an individual, with private tastes. The spectrum of such exchanges in s-m is extremely wide and richly varied. Yet the superstitions that prevail about the s-m scene, even in the relatively educated mind, remain quite incredible. Thus we find William S. Ruben, co-author with Dr. Curtis Wood of *Sex Without Babies*, calmly writing in *Sexology* magazine for April, 1972, the following: "A normal person's reactions to sadomasochism range from shocked disbelief to curiosity about how s-m acts are performed. The methods of beatings are as varied as the participants can devise. Often, some mutilation of the masochist's sex organs is involved." The last sentence bears re-reading. Often! And "mutilation" of the organs of joy. In the face of such misunderstanding by self-elected experts, one almost gives up. It is but a step from this "sexological" interpretation to the Jack-the-Ripper cliché of the popular mind.

On the whole, the s-m scene generally depends on fairly strong character contrasts (and this does *not* mean intensity of pain or defilement). After all, you are involved in an exaggerative mime in which a lot is being lived through in a short time; and such contrasts are frequently supported by adjacent sensory fetishism (the tactuality of rubber, fur, leather), just as they are by the innumerable ads from burly steelworkers, truckers or construction men allegedly longing to be toilet slaves for a weekend (e.g., "Docile white male, 38, in frilly maid's uniform, will do household cleaning work for 10 cents an hour for dominant Dallas-area woman or couple who believe in spanking, slapping, and humiliating their slave"). *Justice Weekly* used to teem with these.

Drawing on the experiments made into environmental causation by Judson Brown (in *Punishment and Aversion Behavior,* edited by B. A. Campbell and R. M. Church), Dr. Eugene E. Levitt of Indiana University summarizes certain principles generally applicable to learned masochism in lower mammals that seem wholly applicable to the s-m scenario (most of them matters of common sense, in any case):

1. The situation in which the current behavior occurs should resemble as closely as possible the original conditioning situation. (Childhood beating on the buttocks with a rod by a woman maximizes the sexual impact of a similar situation in adulthood.)
2. The punishing stimulation should not arouse responses that compete with the sexual, like disgust or anger. (Essentially the point made by Havelock Ellis.)
3. The punishing stimulation should be of moderate intensity. Too weak punishment will have no effect. Too strong punishment is likely to evoke the competing tendencies. (Essentially the point made by Ellis' patient.)•
4. The individual must be sexually aroused or inclined at the

• This was "Florrie."

moment of punishment. [We ourselves would footnote this with the recommendation that strong s–m play can come *after* a certain amount of screwing, and result in an even more ecstatic final exchange.]

As we have endeavored to explain above, it is fairly obvious that "the original conditioning situation" will pattern a person's s-m scenario. In England, Scandinavia, Germany, and Switzerland the latter is, we would confidently surmise, strongly colored by the school situation. This can be extremely elastic, and is probably less rigid in structure than the slave bit.

For in the school scenario a dominant can be a schoolmaster or mistress with a recalcitrant, lazy, or inattentive girl pupil. If the pair-bond is male homosexual, however, a tutor can of course act out the correction of an erring or idle boy. Alternatively, if the submissive is a male masochist and the dominant a female sadist, the role-playing can be that of a governess, disciplining her boy charge (as in Miles Underwood's *The Governess*, re-edited as *Harriet Marwood, Governess*, by Anon.). *The Tutor* by "P. N. Dedeaux," meanwhile, apart from being a clever parody of *Lesbia Brandon* which even includes passages of stolen Swinburne, furnishes a considerable variety of scenarios within the spectrum of its title, the dominant male tutor here dealing with a pubescent girl charge who is dressed up obligatorily as a boy. *Gynecocracy* (alleged by some to be by Ellis) would reverse this, and has a young boy dressed as a girl and tormented by women.

Story of O by "Pauline Réage" may or may not be less successful than these works on the literary level, but gets usefully and deeply into another prevalent s-m scenario—that of the slave, though fortunately (for us) without ethnic overtones. The slave scenario is one in which complete possession, ownership, has to be felt by the submissive for it to work. The slave is a nothing thing. This seems to have considerable and widespread male masochist/ female dominant repercussions in modern America, as mentioned, and *Story of O* was understandably a best-seller here. Since this scenario is fairly strong, it is usually characterized by extremes of humiliation and, as verbal stand-in, streams of abuse and obscenity heaped on the luckless inexistent. The latter need not be male, of

course. One girl we know, graduate of a leading college, has her
s-m scene, with her blue-chip husband, so highly charged with the
slave coloring that she has increasingly to patrol the second-hand
clothing or discount stores since one of her most important moments in the scenario is to have her clothing ripped off her by her
"master."

All we can say is—live and let love. For us personally, the
"punishing stimulation" of the slave scene arouses too many social
echoes, "responses that compete with the sexual, like disgust or
anger." Something like The Black Pearl Agency which offers in
chipper fashion throughout the current underground press "Dominant, Beautiful & Bizarre" black women to whip you would
probably score a fairly low arousal valence in most countries in
Europe. S-m is non- or aracial. When Xaviera Hollander (another
Dutch Jewess) tells us that most of the masochists—"freaks or
weirdos"—who came to her for punishment were small Jewish
businessmen, the social memories intrude uncomfortably, even for
s-m people of a persecuted race; and when, concerning coprophilia,
she adds the theory that "the guys who want to be shit on are the
guys with a lot of power," the analogy seems altogether too pat,
something read in literature rather than found in life.

We also find this social staining particularly the case with the
semi-Nazi bike boys, or itinerant Hell's Angels, accoutered with
chains and para-military insignia. It may be, for all we know, that
such people are simply dressing up rather late in life, and go
through a controlled ritual with as tender a sexual conscience as
any pseudo-tutor. We must in all honesty confess that the last such
youth we talked to one night, who could have doubled for Goering
at his most melodramatic, proved disarmingly gentle and discrimi-
nate. He may well have been a most solicitous sadist. Any excess—
the shedding of blood, in particular—competes with s-m arousal to
its exclusion. Yet the popular mind still thinks of the s-m scene in
terms of blood and scars.

Equally obviously, too, "the original conditioning situation"
applies to the instruments used in any such session. Until fairly
recently the English had scarcely heard of something called a
"paddle," which they would primarily associate with canoeing.

Yet it was and is a routine item in some American fraternities, one still visibly carried around, in symbolic form, by lowly pledges. Equally surely we feel that few Americans know what a birch— so resoundingly reverberative in all senses in England—really is.

The birches Keate and Busby used, sometimes "put up" by the sinners themselves, were more like whips than brooms. This applies also to the birches used on juvenile offenders in British prisons until World War II, and penally on the Isle of Man to this day. For the true sadomasochist this kind of birch rod was perhaps the closest to poetry of all flogging instruments, and is accordingly accorded pride of place in the literature of the genre. It was made of, at most, five or six long, lean withes, toughly budded and further hardened by steeping in brine, vinegar, pickle, or other solution, birch being a water-retentive wood. Swinburne's whipping poems are full of little else.

Sometimes these supple and lively limbs would be carefully wound in wire, to make them stricter still. The dreaded soko birch was said to have been compounded of thin strips of whalebone, of the kind used for stiffening ladies' corsets of the time. If it is a fiction that girls in Victorian academies "went" as many as six dozen with these—and much of the correspondence in the *English-woman's Domestic Magazine* of the 1860's on the subject has now been shown to be spurious, dreamt up by the "Florries" rather than the Keates of such schools—it was undoubtedly the case that English girls were treated then with quite extraordinary severity. The widely attended exhibition on English girls' education, staged in London a few years ago, showed a variety of appurtenances of discipline and restraint more worthy of an Inquisition dungeon than any school classroom.

Now that the birch is almost unused anywhere in schools (or prisons) its imagery has been increasingly drained of resonance. The cane has replaced it (originally for clemency). The same might be said to be true of another erotogeneous article, or topic, once a European favorite, namely the tightly breeched and booted Amazon astride her stallion into whose plump and shining crupper she energetically whaled her whip. Literature has attested to this (principally yet not exclusively) male fantasy. Joyce gives us a bevy at the beginning of Bloom's Circe fantasy: the Honorable Mrs. Mervyn Talboys appears "*In amazon costume, hard hat, jackboots cockspurred, vermilion waistcoat, fawn musketeer gauntlets with braided drums, long train held up and hunting crop with which she strikes her welt constantly.*" She threatens Bloom "to chastise him as he richly deserves, to bestride and ride him, to give him a most vicious horsewhipping." Bloom "*quails expectantly,*" and we read the following exchange:

> THE HONORABLE MRS. MERVYN TALBOYS: I'll make it hot for you. I'll make you dance Jack Latten for that.
>
> MRS. BELLINGHAM: Tan his breech well, the upstart! Write the stars and stripes on it!
>
> MRS. YELVERTON BARRY: Disgraceful! There's no excuse for him! A married man!
>
> BLOOM: All these people. I meant only the spanking idea. A warm tingling glow without effusion. Refined birching to stimulate the circulation.
>
> THE HONORABLE MRS. MERVYN TALBOYS: (*Laughs derisively.*) O, did you, my fine fellow? Well, by the living God, you'll get the surprise of your life now, believe me, the most unmerciful hiding a man ever bargained for. You have lashed the dormant tiger in my nature into fury.

However, now that few people in our huge cities even see horses, let alone ride them for pleasure, these affects have dimmed and, as a result, even fewer humans are being ridden, as was Zola's Comte Muffat by Nana, around bedrooms any more.

Still and all, both birch and cane retain a certain purity, perhaps a pre-eminence, of affect in the s-m scene since neither was ever used for anything else other than personal chastisement. Both were purely pedagogic, that is. Whips get used on animals. Riding switches share both offices. Belts and straps have dismayingly utilitarian associations. In France the martinet, or leathern flail, is still on open display in provincial hardware stores, as an instrument for the correction of children (a far too brutal one to our taste, too) and so it still works in s-m there, if not here. French flagellantine fiction features the martinet with obvious relish. But as a general rule rarefied instruments divorced from "the original conditioning situation" are less likely to prove turning-on. Yet again, to each his own.

But when it comes to the area of the body on which to inflict punishment, even in symbolic form, we feel more confident in asserting that the buttocks, or what Ellis had to latinize as the "*nates*" (plural of *natis*), are indicated—to the point of exclusion of other areas. Now there have been whole books on buttock fetishism or what the Germans so nicely term *Gesässerotik*. This is not the place to add to the literature. But nearly all sadists are inveterate ass-men (or women). As a matter of fact, this may be why so many male homosexuals can conveniently locate themselves within s-m. It is as if, by one of nature's more congenial symmetries, the sadist carried along a built-in protective device. The fatty gluteal area, so beloved of poets and painters alike, can be chastised with least harm and, since it is also a modesty center, with most psychic reverberation, especially when well bared. And the baring is all-important in the scenario.

Where someone is terribly involved in feet, he or she might find it exciting to beat them. China is the country of the tiny bound foot and also the bastinado on the soles of the feet. This scarcely seems to have entered into our social s-m at all, even among the foot fetishists, while whipping on the breasts, strongly contra-indicated here, is something that genuinely offends many sadists, who get nothing out of it at all.

To start off with, men don't have breasts. Secondly, the fleshy frontal protuberances of women, unique among primates in our species, are said by zoologist Desmond Morris to be sexual signals only in that they are surrogate buttocks: "The protuberant, hemi-spherical breasts of the female must surely be copies of the fleshy buttocks" (*The Naked Ape*). Although this theory has come under some attack, generally from polemicists irritated to see the female cast once more in the role of subservient (?) lure, nonetheless few would now deny that fucking from behind has always been the typical or "normal" animal position ("The typical mating posture of all other primates involves the rear approach of the male to the female") and that the masochist is definitely involved in rump presentation. It is another characteristic of the sadist to like sex from the rear. You therefore punish what you *love* not what you hate.

This is an insight into s-m behavior borrowed from "Bloch" Dühren. All cultures have considered the buttocks beautiful. Suffice it to say here—and we will touch on the subject below— that for most forms of s-m the buttocks are almost exclusively the ideal, the proper area for punishment play. Knickers, drawers, various materials stretched drum-taut over what Shakespeare forever referred to as "the afternoon of the body" can be accordingly turn-ons for the sadist. Maltreatment of the breasts could be physically damaging and is certainly not recommended.

The buttocks are served by the same nerve system as the external genitalia, unlike the breasts. And unlike those secondary sexual characteristics, too, their baring is implicitly suggestive of preparation for intercourse. To turn this into a humiliating procedure, to revert an adult to a child in this way, can be one of the most exciting aspects of careful s-m, one scarcely shared by turning someone into a slave (usually adult in the reality). The rump is really the only part of the body to accept trauma with stimulation. The buttocks have become the acknowledged desiderata of the sadist since they are charged with the esthetic.

As the scenario, then, requires a divestiture of external personas, and a degree of theatricals, a second stripping, as it were, s-m people may feel tempted to use some form of anti-inhibitant— at least at first. Again, this is a personal matter, to be considered in the context of the participants' daily life. But consciousness is of the essence of s-m (else it could not draw so deep of the unconscious) and it must be borne in mind that extreme control therein is an article of faith. An estimate of external reality has to proceed contiguously beside the love play, including of course a realization of how much pain is actually being inflicted. Someone like Heath obviously lost this. Thus, high sensitivity should always be present, indeed is part and parcel of the scene, and drugs and alcohol can be distinctly desensitizing for some people. One obvious way of breaking down conscious inhibitions, and helping on the surreality, is common, however: that is some form of fetishist clothing.

Nearly all couples into s-m dig some aspect of this, however mild or peripheral. In truth, it is probably why such a high quotient of transvestism, or Ellis' "eonism," exists in masochists. For a while, via clever use of make-up, clothes and wigs, even a mere male may seem to live like a woman, vicariously. After all, we are required in s-m play to meet in a very new way a daily partner; the face across the breakfast table, ironing board, or garden hose likes to be transformed by such passionate art. Let us not forget that when Pentheus, in Euripides' *The Bacchae,* wished to see the Maenad revels on the mountain, Dionysos insisted that he should dress as a woman ("If they knew you were a man, they would kill you instantly").

Masks serve this purpose, and are frequently worn when they can be found or made. Frankly, this sort of gear is exorbitantly expensive. The cheapest such leather mask we could recently locate on the underground s-m market, a rather clumsily stitched version of a medieval scold's bridle, cost $37. It could probably have been put together by any fairly able housewife for about a fifth of that price.

Some extraordinarily affective, and effective, s-m leather masks were recently put on display (and all bought) in a Manhattan gallery by Nancy Grossman, who was quoted in *Time* magazine as saying, "Everyone is a sadomasochist. The difference between me and other artists is that I admit it." As a second skin with its own particular form of imposed nudity, and color, leather is invariably reverberative for those into s-m.

Leather-love has been variously explained in this connection but the explanations remain such, so many cases of pathology. Krafft-Ebing's "Mr. Z.," for instance, an American "manufacturer," adored kid gloves, collected hundreds of pairs, and made love to his wife with them on either side of her head; he even wrapped them round his penis for the purpose of masturbation (Case 122). Krafft-Ebing found this fetishism "based upon a psychico-physical and morbid predisposition," of course, but it seems to have resulted far more from guilt over infringing a social taboo, namely masturbation. The man had been happily married for eight years— indeed "blessed with offspring," as the learned doctor loadedly put it—and, from the evidence given, his wife didn't

mind either wearing black kid leather a lot nor being screwed with
leather around her. What worried poor "Mr. Z." and "brought
him well nigh to the verge of despair and even insanity" was that
he masturbated with gloves on the side, something which today
would probably be more likely to earn him a revered place as a
folk hero of the Masters and Johnson laboratories. As regards
women, *Cosmopolitan* would seem to encourage masturbation:
"Sex studies indicate that 47% of the females in this country
masturbate (I bet the rate is even higher—but not everybody's
talking . . . Anyway, I'm sure the other 53 percent would enjoy it
if they tried!), and girls who do masturbate fare better in bed with
a man, too!" (Laura Cunningham, July, 1971).

The same issue of the magazine equally endorses the fabric
fetishisms today:

> Certain textures have an affinity with your deepest emotions.
> Velvet, fur, satin, kid leather—all have some relation to sexual
> excitation ("Her skin was like warm velvet" . . . blah, blah). Some
> people, of course, get *fixated* on a certain texture: that is, it reaches
> their inner core of sensuality a little *too* powerfully! These people
> can often become *fetishists* and make a hobby of collecting little
> pieces of silk underwear, or whatever else they're hung up on. You
> probably have a few touch fetishes yourself: your man's tweed
> jacket, the coolness of fresh sheets.

Certainly tight black glacé kid—in boots and gloves—is a *sine
qua non* of much s-m. The creak of leather, with its inexorable
sense of compression of flesh, can produce a delectable *frisson* in
many.

There finally remains what might be called the $500 problem
of the s m scenario. By nature the sadist requires to inflict pain,
as the masochist desires to receive it. In the case of strong homosexual males the problem is less acute. But no girl wants to put
herself into the hands of a man, however dear to her, who will
possibly inflict intolerable agony. Too much pain will, in short,
prove a turn-off for her: too little a turn-off for him. On his side,
that is, her partner eagerly desires some sight of pain, in writhings,
clutchings, gasps, and moans—if not outright cries. How can the
twain come together?

It does so more often than not. To begin with, as Ellis pointed out in his "Love and Pain" monograph, in the course of memory actual pain gets buffered, shunted aside, by the subconscious. Thus, in fantasy, in pornographic writings, it grows accordingly intense in order to compensate for the sheer physical loss involved. In fantasy pain has to be extreme to be brought forward again at all. *Story of O* is a case in point. What girl cherishes the idea of wearing vulval rings? A lot of what happened to O would have hospitalized a real woman for life and on this basis alone we were somewhat horrified to see it slyly recommended as an initiation into sadomasochism, a lovers' *livre de chevet,* by a recent writer in *Cosmopolitan.* It is not the s-m story to read first, interesting as it is. There is nearly always a basis of the genuine in s-m play and we personally suspect that most intelligent men, turned on by strong pain visions in fantasy, are more than happy to settle for a fairly mild simulacrum in reality. Any good male sadist will soon feel out and assess the pain threshold of his partner, and take that as his level. What is more, with practice in the play the partner will often find this threshold pleasurably rising.

Add to this the element that the masochist can mime out more pain than is actually felt, almost mirroring the pain as it were (and a mirror is an admirable adjunct to s-m play). The pair are genuinely acting out roles. If this does not suffice, s-m can get into analogous areas where the actual pain experienced is minimal— b & d, enemas—yet which can often provide fully satisfying "punishment" systems for the sadist. We will approach such briefly in the following section.

In the old organized Paris brothels of the more costly variety there was nearly always a whipping room. A girl could be purchased to thrash. It was extremely expensive and she suffered almost nothing (despite her squirmings) since what was used was a flail or martinet which could be swung with a full arm yet was scarcely felt at all. Sometimes these instruments may be found in modern America. They can in Toronto. There is usually a short malacca handle supplied with many longish leather thongs which, when they fall together, have a dull rather than stingy impact. If it is essential to the dominant that he should seem to himself to be hitting hard, with gusto, such an implement or something like it is a must; it is probably ideal for slave play.*

Yet it is for this very reason that the most apt s-m scenario still seems to us the classic schoolroom scene, complete if possible with simulated clothing (gym tunics, knickers, and fluffy socks), where control is of the essence—you are punishing a child, mind—where there are no competing elements, such as ethnic or political, and where "the original conditioning situation" can be fully handled, with true psychic health. In such inspired play we do not "regress" to childhood, in the sense that it drowns us; rather we dip into its refreshing waters consciously, and for a moment perhaps recapture something of our lost innocence.

* With one warning hint, from personal experience: a trained dog, hearing the swish of whip or flail, can cause problems for an s-m couple, and seriously impede indulgence in the art, certainly under small apartment conditions. It is almost impossible for such an animal to know that one partner is loving another by using the whip—and this proves its own point.

"WATER SPORTS"—
UNDINISM
AND ENEMAS

The useful and charming term "undinism" can be used to cover a whole gamut of delightful diversions, from taking prolonged walks in light clothing in summer rain to urinating on a beloved in the bath. From the latest fashionable "wet look" to high colonics, in fact. "Not only," Ellis reminds us, "may rain be the symbol of urine but urine the symbol of rain." The use of undinism to describe fascination with peeing was first made, so far as we know, by Ellis himself in his long essay of that title.

Before proceeding any further into this subject, it is important to point out Ellis' wise emphasis on the symbolic. In truth, the obtuseness of Krafft-Ebing in these and other respects really attains at times a kind of genius. Thus when the thirty-five-year-old civil servant he called "Z." (in common with many others, and not to be confused with the American "Mr. Z." mentioned) came to him, Krafft-Ebing seems to have been rather exasperated not to find anything "abnormal" at all: "The patient presented nothing abnormal except symptoms of slight neurasthenia. Genitals and sexual functions normal. Patient stated that he had only masturbated four or five times when he was very young" (Case 109).

What, then, was wrong? The answer given is: "His greatest delight was to look at women with wet garments in the rain . . . He stated that he had never had any desire to steal wet female dresses or to throw water on women. He could give no explanation of the origin of his peculiarity." Neither could his erudite analyst, simply because it was no peculiarity: wet material adheres to the body, that is all. A wet bathing costume on a woman probably attracts more male glances than a dry one. To add insult to misunderstanding, Krafft-Ebing calls the man a case of "*petticoat fetishism.*" It is quite unclear why—any more than why the designation of "sickie" applies to the client cited by Xaviera Hollander, in her *The Happy Hooker,* who "simply wants me to sit in a chair, while he sits naked facing me in another chair, and puff on a cigarette and blow the smoke in his face while he plays with himself."

"Z." 's case is cited as a literal use of water. Ellis studied the psychic influence of water in general, yet also its special reference and appeal to sexual excitement, or what we today call water games: pissing on a love partner in some way or simply watching (or making) another pee. By Krafft-Ebing's canon such a person would be ready for the gallows. Ellis himself took the term from the name used for water nymphs by Paracelsus, in the sixteenth century. It is convenient enough for our purpose here.

In passing, one might add that there can be no doubt but that Ellis showed unusual fascination with this subject, and may even have been a devout urolagnic himself. There is an almost suspiciously close resemblance between the reminiscences of the forty-four-year-old man at the end of the "Undinism" essay and those of "Florrie" earlier. The former wrote to Ellis:

> I have been interested to observe how in France the country-women commonly make water standing. One sees a woman stop as she is walking, a cataract gushes down to the ground inside her skirts and she walks on unconcernedly. Or a woman will stand talking to a friend and a stream flows from between her feet. Working in the fields, too, they piss standing, not squatting like an Englishwoman.

"Florrie," who had seen her young brothers pee with childish delight over each other's hands, had the same French associations. She told Ellis of discovering, as a girl, a novel *urinette* in Portsmouth (of all places!) where "one had to stride across a boat-shaped earthenware grating." After which, she repeatedly urinated in public, as follows:

> I had to make my exit from the garden directly into the road. By this time further delay had made matters worse. I felt that I could not wait any longer. There were no shops near, only houses, and I could not find any sheltered spot. I at once realized how utterly impossible it would be to squat down, so I determined to make the attempt standing, though I felt very nervous and doubtful as to my probable success. There was no rain to help matters, and the pavement was white and dry . . . No one was in sight, and I determined to be as quick as possible, but to my mortification it wouldn't come. I suppose I had put off too long. At last, after waiting what seemed to me a tremendous time (although probably only a few seconds!) I felt it beginning to come. For fear of detection I had refrained from standing with my legs a little apart, and the result was that a great deal went into my drawers and soaked them straight off. Afterwards, the stream penetrated, and came with terrific force on the pavement, and terrible were my feelings when I saw it meandering from under my skirt . . . In towns I generally take refuge on a doorstep or in a doorway where no one is likely to enter. I did this once on an early closing day when the shops were shut, and thought how lucky I was since no one would enter or come out. Although the shop I chose was closed the blinds were up and the goods displayed. So I looked in, but my attention was in reality absorbed in an entirely different manner. It was some time before I could persuade myself to begin, and then I started cautiously, but even so I was alarmed when I saw the stream flowing rapidly down the passage, over the step and on to the pavement. Rain was coming down. . . .

Whether or not the analyst's interest in all these "terrific streams" was such as to distort some of the verisimilitude of his patients' accounts, we have to concede Ellis, from the start, as some sort of an expert on undinism (he clearly identified the attraction of the "uncontrollable" in a urinating woman). The man who could, according to his learned "The Bladder as a Dynamometer" in *The American Journal of Dermatology* for May, 1902, measure the vesical energy of jets of piss with the care more usually associated with lexicography or numismatics deserves our undying respect. Ellis evidently laid one female patient on her back to learn, with obvious satisfaction, that "The average distance of the jet was 48 inches (which agrees with that of some women in the erect position) and the maximum, with very full bladder and some general excitement, as much as 75 inches, which indicates an energy probably not often exceeded by the female bladder."

But his prize undinist was a lovely Cornish girl, with "the Spanish type of *ensellure* or saddle-back" to her limpid buttock basin, called "A.P." This graceful mermaid could positively jet like a man, erect, with raised skirts, pulling back the labia and fairly hissing her pee at a wall. Again, the measurements seem intensely exact. "In the garden her achievements were much more remarkable. Thus, on one occasion, she was able to spurt the stream to a distance of 75 inches" (one notes the identical figure, making for a kind of urinary tie). One senses a real pride on Ellis' part in his description of this watery beauty, "A.P."

But we do not mean to make fun of the subject. Our animal ancestry, our life in the womb, both continually send their water reverberations through our sexual enchantments. No lover need feel ashamed of these half-conscious urges and delights. We all know the joy children take in urinating over those dear to them, like parents or nurses, while the same liquid kisses were apparently a real part of primitive ritual. In Hottentot marriage ceremonies the priest had to pee on bride and bridegroom alike, in blessing— truly his own form of holy water. To savage societies vesical power and sexual potency seemed to go hand in hand, not such a far-out medical notion, after all, when you know that a first symptom of prostate trouble in the male is sometimes a weakening (or doubling) of jet. One can but add, meanwhile, that in supposedly more civilized cultures less polymorphously inclined children sometimes grew up to think of fucking as urinating into the vagina.

The clinics of Vienna again dirtied these pretty obsessions, of which no one should feel in the least guilty. Water imagery pours through Greek myth. The old British *London Life* was replete with letters from hydrophiliacs—people who love getting wet. Some fulfill this desire by standing fully clothed under a shower. The old grade "B" movies of the past frequently featured a woman being dunked or soaked (a large number of John Wayne vehicles adding a spanking). Women wrestling in mud—that *Schlamm-kampf* for long the outstanding feature of Hamburg's Reeperbahn area—are notoriously aphrodisiacal, and if such be thought to be simply a typical trait of the perverse Teuton, it should be observed that not many years ago some American sororities used to have mud races for initiates, after which they were hosed clean by senior girls.

Rubber or vinyl raincoat fetishism clearly comes under this head, and probably the indulgence in rubberwear generally. No doubt, all sorts of other interests do also. That is the point of polymorphous play. Children rush to touch anything that pleases them, just as grownups enjoy stroking cats; when materials tend to vanish from the imagistic repertoire, nylon replacing silk today, new elements will seem odd when first fetishized. To isolate some-one who loves to wear raincoats (an illiteral translation of the rubberized mackintosh) under the category of a fetishist deviant is a social directive, not ours. Fascination with urine and feces are clearly allied, as is the licking-off of any exusion, from tears to sweat. As soon as it has been born, the human child needs to know that it is a discrete, finite entity. All oozings menace this concep-tion. Thus all are taboo, from tears to semen (even nails have had taboo attached to them).

We do not propose to enter here into what might be called the eschatology of this scatology. Since Freud first dealt with anal eroticism—*Anal-erotik*—in a 1909 paper there has indeed been a diarrhea of different theories. How does it actually help practicing s-m people to know that licking excrement has been paralleled by saints and medicine men (Krafft-Ebing)? That coprophagia is com-mon among the insane? That fresh urine has been taken as medi-cine, as well as hair restorer and general stimulant, widely through-out the globe? Once again, for our purpose it is more helpful to know the *functional* element, what character the undinist or urolagnic attaches to certain affects.

It seems that sound is one of the most stimulating of these, that helpless soft hushed rushing as the cascade descends. "Florrie," we have noted, liked to hear her piss strongly crackling down on to dry leaves, in some deserted wood—"Real control seems gone; one feels it *must* come even though the whole world were present. One would stop it if one could—a sudden footstep, a shadow falls, 'Oh, *do* stop!' one says to oneself, 'there's someone coming!' But no, it is not to be. The inexorable force wills otherwise, the stream continues to flow unabashed, and the gentle compulsion is pleasing." According to Margarethe Petersen, one Danish urolagnic, an energetic lady of nearly eighty, preferred to let fly "on orange or apple rinds, enjoying the fragrant odor." De Sade would have approved. The synesthesia (or crossing of senses) involved here shows the "spread" technique and the true poetry of the affects. Indeed, there was once an English euphemism for urinating—"I'm going to give a Chinaman a music lesson."

Binswanger records yet another female patient who liked to carry a small milk can around with her, pissing into it at intervals and then tossing the results out the window. One merely hopes she had good aim. The majority of undinists of this sort who have come before analysts would seem to have been women, probably because of the greater taboos involved and the gratifying excitement in infringing them. Urethral eroticism is said to be particularly high in English girls—"Florrie" was one, of course—and it was for long genuinely difficult for a woman to find anywhere to relieve herself in some towns in England. A hotel was about the only hope. Stekel surmises that urolagnia exists in about 20% of all adults, with the proviso that "unsatisfied people, especially women, most often urinate. Micturition is often performed by adults as a sort of substitute for coitus." He mentions a frigid woman who went into orgasm *only* when her husband pissed on her.

Almost any retention is exciting. Obligatory retention of an enema is a common s-m scenario, or by-play of it, and the holding of urine similarly draws attention to and colors with pleasure the eventual discharge (it would be a hypocritical adult, let alone a child, who denied a degree of pleasure felt in doing "a good shit"). All such on the basis of Ellis' excellent maxim, "what we fight against we fortify." What woman, caught short in some horror of a Midlands suburb in England, would not echo this? The whole cycle has a sexual pattern too obvious to need reiteration here.

It is clear that urination can be used in love play in a variety of modes of sexual symbolism. Generally, prostitutes report urolagnic masochism, that is, male customers who ask to be pissed on. In a press interview Xaviera Hollander, if she is to be credited, cites a "famous TV producer who came to my house and he requested nine girls . . . He wanted nine girls to pee on him . . . he would have loved anything as long as there was a golden shower" (the same anecdote is recounted in *The Happy Hooker* where the count is put up to "a dozen pretty girls").

We are moving into a completely new society and frankly cannot see any harm in such imaginative play which involves a liquid primitively used as a mark of honor and in its constituents, as one medical authority has observed, differing little from beef bouillon, but for a higher content of uric acid. It is doubtless much less harmful a punishment for an erring submissive to be peed on, than to be physically chastised by a tyro of the rod. For the submissive to have to lie, say, in a bath and be urinated on by a beloved can provoke a feeling of total humiliation and, accordingly, delicious shame.

Nor should we forget, here, the important role of urine retention. To be made to hold either urine or feces against the threat of punishment (for failure to do so) can become a palpitating agony of delight for a submissive. Then to have to soil the self fully clothed, as in effect did "Florrie, to have to revert in this way to a child when a grown person, can be thrilling indeed.

As anyone who has experienced involuntary incontinence when recovering from hospital anesthesia must admit, the feeling of sheer helplessness is very vivid. The submissive worships this, and it forms the key to the understanding of intelligent enema play. "I remember standing in a country lane," wrote "Florrie" to Ellis, "ostensibly searching for blackberries, and being caught by a passer-by. There was no escape; I was in full swing. I shall never forget my sensations. The stream seemed to be drawn from me without my consent, and *yet with even more pleasure than if I were doing it freely.*" The italics were "Florrie"'s and Ellis observed them. She continued to dilate on the subtle charm of being deprived of control, the ineluctable and inexorable magnetism a submissive feels when, lost to shame, she or he must give up to the tides of vital natural conquest. The true dominant will know how to feel out and exploit with tenderness this feeling of breathless helplessness which is at the core of the masochist experience, and can convert into pure ecstasy at will.

Let us not deny, however, the pleasures of urolagnia to those less interested in s-m, who simply want to enhance sexual play in this manner, like Ellis' 44-year-old male correspondent:

> Before marriage, indeed, though I had had a certain amount of sexual experience I had none of urination in company with a woman. In fact, it was not until I had been married some little time that I discovered the delights of it. Not that there had been any shyness between us. On the first night we were married my wife sat down for this purpose quite simply and naturally, and I followed. And if we were in the country together we would water the roadside side by side. Then, one day in the country, when we had been married about four months, I invited her to sit on my knees to urinate, as I sat on the ground with my knees hunched up. When the smoking golden stream gushed forth she was irresistible, and it had hardly ceased when, to my wife's astonishment, I pulled her eagerly back into my lap and bestowed a different libation on her.

The words "simply and naturally" ring clear here. Can we say they do the same in those exhibitions of feces frequently staged these days for shock effect? In the spring of 1972 a photographer saw fit to exhibit in Greenwich Village pictures of his wife squatting and urinating on a barn floor, while a few blocks off, at the Westbeth Galleries, another showed dozens of shiny shit bowls filled with his own turds.

When it comes to coprophagic acts, taboo deepens and thickens, and even de Sade, as we sense throughout *The 120 Days,* was not really able to pierce its tendentious mists, any more than he was those surrounding the matter of bestiality (sex with animals seems truly perverse since it is non-human and, above all, their permission was not properly obtained beforehand). It is said that Ezekiel fasted on dung and Caligula ate his wife's. Neither man seems to have been a prototype of sanity, exactly.

And such is surely the point. When certain animals eat the

excrement of their young, it is usually in the interest of hygiene and survival, thus extremely sane. But in twentieth-century "scientific" human beings such asceticism of the saints could only occur in a state of extraordinary sexual rapture, or intoxicated exaltation. We frankly find it hard to credit Monique von Cleef when she is quoted as follows in a recent interview:

> I remember one of my slaves, a nice executive who lived on East 53rd Street. He wasn't feeling well, so he asked me to go to his house with some fresh hot shit. I put it in my attache case and took it the few blocks to his house. It seemed strange to be walking down Third Avenue with all those people rushing past me, no one knowing I had shit in my case. When I got to his house, I spoon-fed it to him, and he felt much better, or so he said.

This is not to deny that defecation may become dynamically exciting to members of both sexes, and all ages. Ellis hypothesized that the muscular release in expelling accumulated excreta is a sort of simulacrum of the sexual process (Moll, Taxil, and others in evident agreement). In the old Sphinx brothel in Paris, as doubtless in others elsewhere, there was a *tabouret de verre* or form of glass flooring, from beneath which clients could closely watch women defecating. De Sade gave us the same, and it is not too difficult to make modest copies (even with a Pyrex dish) in any small New York apartment today. It but remains to add that Farouk, ex-King of Egypt, bought at auction the major part of the instrumentalia of the Paris Sphinx.

No more detailed a corroboration of Krafft-Ebing has probably existed than the Sphinx, and what has been supplied since, in Paris at least, has been but a pale echo of that great bordel. In the 1960's a famous Corsican *souteneur* or pimp called Nachat Martini (among other aliases) emerged as a vice king catering to supposed perversions—homosexuality at his Pigalle nightclub Madame Arthur's, authentic flagellation at the Drap d'Or, and urolagnia almost everywhere. When he was wiped out in an internecine gang feud, his widow Hélène de Cressac tried to continue a certain polymorphous perversion, but ran up against Madame de Gaulle.

It is by now a platitude to observe that America is a technology

and that a technology cannot handle its contradistinctions like
death and defecation. There is nothing over-complicated about
this. One simply notices the degree of avoidance of such in our
society becoming slightly paranoiac. As our relatives and friends
die, they are hustled out of their apartments into elevators, strapped
on "funeral-parlor" barrows under black leather like so many
pets, and we come to see that death is deeply taboo in America
since it directly defeats the announced civilization. We can fly to
the moon, but we still have to die, and defecate. The latest re-
frigeration notion—being put into cold storage for 400 years—
reads, then, like a sort of manic resurrection myth *de nos jours*.
While death is hushed up in our cities, it is virtually indulged in
throughout rural cultures, such as those of Mexico, Sicily, Corsica,
and of course Ireland. In Japan the mourner prolongs the re-
minder that death is essentially a change into another state, a view
inherently disallowed by a democratic technocracy since what
could be better than our Great Society? Hence, too, the celebrated
Forest Lawn semantic and those hyperexaggerated mortuary cus-
toms which spawn their death-euphemisms, like *passed on, no
longer with us, loved one,* and the like. Echoes of this fear exist in
the excremental.

Both Swift and de Sade saw the futility of this. We think we
have solved our nature by doffing taboos as so many passing prejudices, and imagining that we can eliminate (or blinker ourselves to)
eruptions of violence. "Just as though," Georges Bataille reminds
us, "our whole humanity did not spring from the reaction of
horror followed by fascination linked with sensitiveness and intelligence . . . In order to reach the limits of the ecstasy in which
we lose ourselves in bliss we must always set an immediate boundary
to it: horror."* We can unlearn prejudice since it was learned in
the first place. But taboo involves the whole of our being, and the
most sacred aspects of our psyche.

If only this dynamic were understood, we should not have
supported by our taxes small armies of official snoopers all trying
to detect something called obscenity, world statesmen (to say noth-

* The quotation is from the Preface to the third edition of *Madame Edwarda* (Paris:
Pauvert, 1956) by "Pierre Angelique," viz. Georges Bataille.

ing of Lord Longford) would not have made idiots of themselves in public by attributing communism to pornography, and prosecuting authors for blasphemy as a sort of substitute for obscenity. "Pornography," thundered Enrique Green, brother-in-law in 1966 of the Brazilian President, "is the real basis of communist infiltration," thus agreeing with Congresswoman Kathryn O'Hay Granahan, Chairwoman of the Subcommittee on Postal Operations, and instrumental in the conviction of Ralph Ginzburg, that obscenity is "part of an international communist plot." In the same year as this resounding statement was made author Gerard-Kornelis Van het Reve was prosecuted under Article 147 of the Dutch Penal Code for blasphemy when it was considered likely that he would escape an obscenity charge.

Echoes of our fecal fear are everywhere and since enematic sex is the most difficult side of s-m play to articulate successfully, it demands a degree of rapture. It is painful to regard something repellent as part of our nature, and in *The 120 Days* de Sade tried to shock us into the transgression of this recognition.

There are normally two types of people who like to play with enemas prior to sex and the first need not concern us unduly here, since they are outside s-m. In both cases all water sports addicts know that after a second or third infusion enemas need not be repellent at all, since they come out relatively clean.

In the first category is the woman who likes the sensation of repletion, of being filled up inside by another medium than—and often as well as—sheer male gristle. Retention of an enema administered with a fat nozzle during intercourse seems to give such women especial joy at orgasm. A rubber sheet is advisable. Similarly, there is the non-s-m male who simply finds enemas a pleasant occasional ancillary to anal sex. Obviously water sports emphasize the posterior, and enema-men are ass-men A slippery sphincter and well-lubed rectal tube are ideal for both partners in buggery.

But anal sex is really outside algolagnia *pur sang*. It is still deeply tactile. In common with animals we really share two skins, for the inner integument, reaching from mouth to anus, is lined with analogous cells to the outer and it is a feature of our species that the skin is more sensitive where the inner layer surfaces.

Margaret Mead claims that women are tactually sensitive all over. However, the facile flippancy with which buggery is treated by our new permissiveness is medically irresponsible. *The Sensuous Woman* gloatingly assures its subway strap-hanging readership that "nice people are copulating anally every day of the week and nothing horrible or even unpleasant happens to them." They are lucky. The rectum is swarming with bacilli and it would be a foolish male, indeed, who buggered regularly sans condom. And what is *not* told us, in all these cheerful and authoritative-sounding yips from our new pseudo-sexologists, is that for the addicted sodomite the internal churnings and vise-like grippings of his organ by a spasming rectal sheath can be, if properly timed and controlled, a rare sensation. It should be added that sodomy is against the law in several States.

In s-m play the enema is, as a rule, lightly punitive. Here "the original conditioning situation" seems to be American also. Any one who has undergone an extended stay in any modern American hospital will admit that the use of the enema therein is prodigal. A treatise on family medicine by a professor of gynecology born in the late nineteenth century and published in Philadelphia in the early twentieth, contains the following recommendations for the toilet training of children:

> Just as the child's volition to eliminate must be scrupulously supervised, so also must his refusal to eliminate on command be remorselessly rectified. The problem will inevitably arise, at one time or another, that the subject, being commanded to function, will protest his "inability" to do so. To meet this contingency, the parent can either inspect the toilet after each "visit," or—better yet—stand over the child throughout it, with a switch. When the subject pretends an inability to pass solid waste, then the author commends the use of an *enema*. Two quarts of soapy water, administered on the spot as painfully as possible (for the properties of the *anus* as a sexually responsive area cannot be too vigorously prohibited), should suffice to correct the most recalcitrant bowel, and a diet of bran and prunes at each meal for a week afterward will effectively prevent a recurrence of this phenomenon. Toilet paper, needless to say, should be as abrasive as possible, and in abundant supply.

This is so s-m as to seem phony. But a safely copious injection can make a submissive look curiously pregnant and, if the water is warm, even make the recipient sweat. Aldous Huxley's *The Devils of Loudun* commented on the sexually suggestive use of enemas by Holy Church in winkling out witches, and Ken Russell's film made from this book provided a weak echo of such. Enemas have nearly always figured punitively in erotic literature. The French novel *L'Anglais décrit dans le château fermé* was a classic of this genre, as was also a long intense Orties Blanches title which devoted almost every page to a succession of enemas given as punishment—they were taken in every way imaginable, being given at one point to two girls at a time, off twin tubes. Here is a contemporary American description of a punishment enema, taken from a catalog of photo sets sold through box number in the underground press:

> Anita has been much too sassy lately. To her embarrassment, this very voluptuous Cuban girl has to bend way forward and to spread her naked buttocks wide to show her little black hole. After which, she is bound with ropes. A long greased nozzle is then inserted in her tender derrière and moved back and forth until it is way up her rectum. Her master shows her the swollen water bag which he has just hung way above her and filled up to the brim with a mixture of hot water, glycerine, and soap suds. Even though she has taken a number of enemas before, they have never been *that* voluminous. The clamp is now open, and the water gushes in her belly. After each quart, the clamp is closed for a while and to humiliate her even more Anita is vigorously spanked. Despite the cramps and the stinging slaps, she has to take the whole bag to the last drop and keep the solution in her churning bowels for fifteen minutes, with the threat of another large dose, given with a much bigger nozzle, if anything leaks out.

Such would be about the typical s-m scenario for anyone into water sports, the final rush to the john providing pleasant humiliation. On the side are endless variations in administration and materials, of course, some finding the metal canister far more reverberative (less modern) than the rubber douche bag. We ourselves saw an affecting eighteenth-century brass clyster in France years ago, with a powerful ring piston and a slight crook, for some reason, in its lengthy beak. It was still in service on the occasional costive daughter.

The old French *irrigateur* is extremely hard to find these days, being an old-fashioned do-it-yourself clyster. You simply filled the reservoir, set a spring mechanism, inserted the nozzle, and waited for it. It must have been highly uncomfortable since the jet was produced under some pressure and there were no control clamps as supplied on the modern tube. The latter are highly recommended, for the submissive may simply be unable to take the whole libation at a single gulp, as it were, and become increasingly turned off by having to do so; failure can be incorporated into cause for later correction, of course.

Whether one uses the conventional bulb syringe or the colonic tube attached to a nozzle, and inserted slowly and gently via short jets of the solution, it is as well to consult some small medical dictionary before experimenting for the first time. The literature on the subject is characteristically fanciful, and the idea of taking quarts and quarts of some of the recipes we have heard of (including, in one case, club soda!) is both ridiculous and dangerous. An enema should never be given in s-m play on a full stomach, and glycerine or olive oil or turpentine enemas are strongly contraindicated. Excessive griping is, of course, exhausting, and a guaranteed turn-off. Mixing glycerine with soap suds, as in the above quote, is noxious and unnecessary, while turpentine, strongly aperient, should *never* be added to soap and water . . . it simply floats on the top and causes painful spasms. Lukewarm water is really all the s-m addict needs. Two pints for a start. Capacity increases with practice.

Fortunately, there is no difficulty or opprobrium in obtaining enematic materials as there often is with other s-m gear. Surgical shops abound in any city of consequence and frankly all they care is that you're a paying customer. The bulb syringe is preferred by many, since you can easily control the injections which the dominant can squirt directly, with a free fist. Furthermore, there is here too that strong flushing feeling which draws so many women to the high colonic parlors. In the latter, of course, literally gallons course through colon or gut. Finally, we have even seen a small treatise, American, on how to "build" the enema nozzle of your choice. One of these made some sort of final pun on skin communication. It was a cigar holder—designed for the mouth, to be inserted into the other end of the human being's inner tube.

B & D

The term b & d as an abbreviation for bondage and discipline is gaining currency, certainly in the underground press, for s-m. E.g.: "*Demanding Detroit gal, 5' 6", 110, 34-22-34, waist length blonde hair. Interested in TVism, rubber/leather wear, boots and corsets. If you desire a restrained good time with a little B&D given for good measure, write now!*" (*The Capricians* magazine). The term is, rather, a homonym. We propose to discuss it but briefly here inasmuch as it leads towards, rather than away from, our central subject.

By bondage some of the early encyclopedists like Krafft-Ebing meant no more than psychological enslavement to another. A book like Stephen Barlay's *Bondage,* already cited, has really almost nothing to do with b & d at all. The latter comprises a very wide spectrum based on that pleasure in restraint noted as algolagnic by Ellis, embracing a whole range of fetish stimuli from corsets, boots, rubber garments, masks and gags, to those outright pony girls of "John Willie" mentioned. The last are frankly so close to impossible of eventuation that they remain purely fantastic, and Eugene Levitt remarks the same of "leather bar" or extreme enclosure in leather, calling it "qualitatively as well as quantatively different from the normal type [of sadomasochism]."

This is a pleasant change from the voice of the outraged schoolmaster we so often hear in *Screw*. Reviewing *The Leatherman's Handbook* by Larry Townsend, a sort of guide to "leather bar" s-m, the latter publication's Michael Perkins rants and raves like any T. C. Mits, in fact just like that indefatigable opponent of any porn whatsoever, David Holbrook himself:

> Ordinarily I'd keep shut of opinion about another's sexual preferences, but Townsend asks for a rap. Leathersex, it seems to me, is suited best to emotionally retarded people so fucked up their sexual preferences leave the realm of what should be tolerated by anyone of intelligence . . . it's obvious that there are parts of our inner selves that should be suppressed; that was, after all, one of the assumptions upon which the beginnings of society ("You can't throw crap where I sleep")—and the idea of society—were based. It would be easy to say each to his own, and I have no difficulty doing that with the usual run of S&M material; but when it comes dressed in leather boots and leather jackets, popping wide garrison belts, then I flash back to other leather scenes in this century which didn't remain harmless expressions of the inner self society had repressed. Would that some society had repressed Hitler before he assembled the leather freaks into the Gestapo.

Etcetera, etcetera. The seething syllogisms behind this passage are almost incredible. Where is Krafft-Ebing when we want him? Really, *Screw*'s attitude toward sex might be summarized as: You can do as much as you like, provided it's our way. Leather is for "freaks." Case Something-or-other.

But let us concede that some form of fettering does have strong symbolic content for s-m. Moreover, the requirement of "the original conditioning situation" is here present, for presumably there are still children today who are stood in a corner, or told to keep their hands still, legs together, and the like. We wager there are few dominants who have not at least toyed with the idea of securing their submissive's hands behind the back.

After all, the acceptance of cultural standards is a form of "restraint" itself and we note that corset fetishism has always been far bigger in England than here. The old *London Life* was full of remarkable photos of women with wasp waists (allegedly even down to the sixteen or seventeen inches desirable a century ago, when Veblen commented on them), seated upright in shiny black glacé kid corsets stiffened with bone or steel. Morse Peckham imagines such a fetishist saying to himself, "I have transcended the limitations of my culture; I have been imaginative and creative; my powerful genital response to drawings of black leather corsets is proof that I have a freedom which ordinary men do not have." And the commentator adds, "Thus he puts his acceptability of the stimulus into harmony with acceptability of response." On a single point along the stimulus continuum, as it were, the b & d fetishist has elected to unite the sensual and esthetic.

This is quite apparent in confessions from various forms of stuff or bondage addicts, and such people understandably feel themselves artists. A boy asks to be tied up in a game of cowboys and Indians; but it is an adult who has exerted and put out erotic activity in this direction later in life. Again, we are observing not encouraging. One extremely articulate fetishist writes as follows to Krafft-Ebing:

> Though in me, and, in fact, in all "fetishists," the sensual and aesthetic effect must be strictly differentiated, nevertheless, that does not prevent me from demanding in my fetish a whole series of aesthetic qualities in form, style, color, etc. I could give a lengthy description of these qualities demanded by my tastes; but I omit it as not being essential to the real subject at hand. I would only call attention to the fact that erotic fetishism is complicated with purely aesthetic tastes. (Case 117)

"John Willie" used to like to imagine and depict girls tied up around doors in such a way as to simulate doorstops. He featured many photographs of such, as he did another of his stimuli—the u.d. skirt (viz. a girl's skirt, pre-mini, raised upside-down to her neck and secured by a belt there, thus immobilizing her enclosed arms, a form stolen by Ian Fleming at the start of one of his more bondage Bond stories). "Willie"-Coutts would rightly have yawned at psychological explanations of why he in particular enjoyed these bondage positions more than others—"as not being essential to the real subject at hand." His unconscious had chosen them as a strategy.

As more of the correspondence of this gifted and strange individual "Willie"-Coutts (whom we once had the pleasure of meeting) comes to light, we find evidence of a passion for bondage similar to "Florrie" 's whipping "craze." We have seen, for instance, a detailed ten-page letter from him, in his beautiful, microscopic hand (entirely worthy of de Sade), giving minute instructions for making a submissive—in his case a girl—helpless by cording. As he here writes, "we preferred cords to straps and straps to chains. Chains allow too much movement unless special contrivances such as you seem to have are used." A student of Houdini who knew what fetterings even that supreme escape-artist disliked, "Willie"-Coutts obviously favored extreme constriction—which for beginners might be somewhat dangerous: e.g. "If a clove hitch is tied around each wrist the more the captive struggles the tighter it will become that's all." He illustrated these letters exquisitely, going into detail worthy of a Krafft-Ebing "Case," e.g.:

> There is one hell of a tie which is very effective. The victim's hands are tied behind her back and then she sits cross-legged like Buddha and her ankles are tied in this position—Then her feet are tied to the calves of her legs—squat down and you'll see what I mean. Then (rather a difficult operation) she is turned over on her face. Because her feet are tied to her calves she must keep her knees separated—in fact her legs really form a triangle her two thighs being the sides and her bound feet, calves and ankles being the bottom. Once on her face her wrists are tied back as tightly as possible to her ankles, arching her back. Then she is turned over on her back again—and all those items of interest are beautifully displayed.

Since, then, the forms of bondage are so diverse, the range so wide, it would be presumptuous to prescribe what are truly matters of taste here. Some like ropes, other chains. Still others prefer leather straps. Certain recommendations might be in order perhaps.

Tying someone up like a parcel can take forever, unless you were in the U.S. Navy, which we weren't. And when it comes to undoing all those knots. . . . If chains are reverberative, rather than straps, as in some slave scenario perhaps, we strongly advise securing these symbolically, rather than actually. The kind of clip you can find on a dog leash suffices. Anything that involves a padlock and a key can be awfully inconvenient if the lock jams. We can testify as much ourselves.

One night we were introducing into our play a pair of handcuffs bought in a toy shop. They had come with two keys which up to that point had always worked perfectly. This time, however, first one key and then the other broke inside the locks. The result was one well-handcuffed wife. It was indeed lucky she was wearing a long evening gown since visits to two local fire stations proved necessary, though abortive, and each time a fireman tried to open one of the cuffs, a ratchet would tighten a notch. Finally, we had recourse to the nearest police precinct. Beyond reminding us that the possession of handcuffs was locally illegal, the boys in blue couldn't have been more courteous; they had, however, to send out for a special car containing an expert in what was known, it seemed, as a "ring-job." Having first identified their make (Japanese), the officer opened up the cuffs easily enough. It was all accomplished in a spirit of pleasant banter; by an extraordinary coincidence it was Halloween.

The intrusion of fear, uncertainty, is a turn-off for a submissive and there are understandably few who will let themselves be tied in initial s-m exchanges. Complete trust is a must. Consequently, bondage is better in such cases when it is symbolic—that is, the submissive could get out of the bonds, but they still feel constricting. In this respect we recommend those admirable elastic or rubber luggage thongs sold in nearly every auto shop.

Simplicity, too, is of the essence of the b & d structure. A very elaborate harness will nearly always go wrong; something that impedes normal activities, like eating and drinking, toilet functions, is often all that is needed. "John Willie" used to specialize in simple bondage positions that were at the same time extremely esthetic: one such consisted of straps round wrists and ankles, after which the submissive sat down and leant forward with wrists in front of the shins. A long stick, or old broom handle, was then slid under the backs of the bent knees. Immobilizing, effective, and yet oddly touching. But as anyone into b & d at all will agree, the simple securing of the wrists behind the back is often more than sufficient; it greatly reduces mobility, such as raising from a kneeling position and the like.

As to how to acquire b & d materials, we have examined a number of catalogs in the field and frankly found that many of the expensive items listed could be home-made by anyone with average intelligence. Moreover, they tended to supplant rather than enrich imagination, and to dictate the nature of the s-m play (e.g. penis harnesses, only suitable for a male submissive). A San Francisco mail order firm called Fobos-A Taste of Leather seemed purely geared to "leather-bar" motorcycle fetishism, advertising boot chains, handcuff belts, and other dangerous-sounding gadgets. Oddly enough, very few flagellatory items were offered at all.

The most serious and solid-looking catalog inspected was that of a company called Karaval, in Houston, Texas. They were found to be reliable and prompt, if inordinately expensive, a spanking block costing as much as $65. However, the range was wide and interesting, including thumbcuffs which are highly portable and were used in Victorian girls' schools in England (but carry the key risk again). The celebrated "saddle strap," frequently featured in *London Life* and *Bizarre,* and dear to b & d enthusiasts, could be seen in a variety of simple spanking harnesses sold by Karaval.

Only really applicable to female submissives this is a strap that comes up tightly between the legs and separates the buttock cheeks for more effective application. Slave sandals, locking bibs, anti-sitting harnesses, posture collars, humility collars, one simple harness that kept a submissive kneeling, were all easily seen via clear photographs in this imaginative catalog, as well as a number of ancillary s-m items such as leather slave aprons, bibs, and serving skirts, discipline instruments, and electric prods (battery-operated —an effective and long-standing device for training dogs). Obviously caution must be used in selecting and sending for any of these materials; we can hardly imagine any b & d addict calling in the nearest Better Business Bureau if a chastity belt or pair of dungeon chains proved unsatisfactory. When it comes to the purchase of flagellatory instruments pure and simple, this risk can usually be obviated, however.

S-M
MATERIALS

Buying s-m gear can be simpler and much less dismaying than it sounds. Certainly in America, where the customer is more likely to be right than elsewhere. After all, it isn't such a big deal to go into a riding wear shop and pick out a whalebone switch with tasseled trainer.

Conceding that certain s-m people have particular hang-ups in this area—the British for canes and birches, the French for martinets, the Americans for whips and paddles—it is still remarkable how many of these instruments may be hand-made with a little ingenuity. Styrene rubbers straps are the easiest thing in the world to make, have an excellent sting and make a solid smack.

Years ago, when we wanted to create a tawse, that tailed strap of Scottish lore and legend whose tips used to be hardened near a fire for better effect, it proved surprisingly easy to get the necessary lump of leather from a shop selling sandals in a northern State. A birch, or its close simulacrum, can be made by almost anyone in the countryside, while leather shoelaces can be put to an obvious variety of uses in flails and martinets. The cane poses a problem.

Before World War II there used to be a shop at the top of New Bond Street, in London, which specialized in superb glossy canes, set out in rows behind glass. It was haunted by admirers, doubtless all more or less "wet with sweat" in company with

Krafft-Ebing's wretched baker's assistant. We can make few very serious recommendations here except that s-m people should be and generally are constantly inventive. Some s-m friends, stuck for instrumentation in a Midwest motel, found that the curtain cords filled the bill more than admirably.

While in Rome, do as the Romans do. Frat paddles are easy to obtain in America. Years ago we purchased, on the other hand, a bi-thonged quirt through a California mail order house. The ad had stated: "It can be easily used in close quarters and it can be carried tucked through a belt or in a back pocket." A feeble instrument we found it to be, for all of $14. Later, in Mexico, we saw a similar bisected thong being applied to the crupper of a mule with effect, outside a house we had rented. The nonagenarian astride the quadruped was delighted to be relieved of this simple and reverberative instrument (made the more so by wear) for the peso equivalent of a dollar. He had owned it most of his life and use, as usual, had conferred affect. It was very real, and is so still.

At present writing it is quite easy to obtain almost anything the s-m person would like to use in New York City. First, there are the "theatrical" shops, and we would recommend this approach to anyone in a jam. S-m is a sort of theater, when all is said and done. Even long bull-whips may be hired, against deposit. In most major cities you can find some "novelty" store which is likely to sell, or even rent out, such ominous artifacts.

In the larger urban centers it is surprising the number of stores stocking umbrellas and sticks which also have a small selection of canes, whips, and cravaches. In New York the justly famous and splendidly named Uncle Sam's Stick Shop boasts two emporia where, among the racks and rows of umbrellas and sticks, a wide variety of sound s-m instrumentalia can be inspected before purchase by the *aficionado*. Paul Krassner's *The Realist* once ran a piece on Uncle Sam's Stick Shop, when it was a tiny store on West 46th Street. The Pleasure Chest opposite Lutèce on East 50th Street currently has much s-m gear.

The main thing is to be a buyer. A few years ago a self-styled hippie motoring the Southwest published an article on his experiences in *The New York Times* travel section. Bearded, in tie-dyes and wearing love-beads, he had been worried about reactions to his appearance. It was apparent that directly he entered a store to *buy* he effectively reclassified himself from hippie to purchaser. He was met with complete courtesy throughout a fairly square section of the country.

We ourselves have bought from Uncle Sam's Stick Shop on 57th Street and for the faint in heart it is quite easy to pose there as an out-of-town tourist picking up some kinky New York souvenirs. The salesman is there to sell. And it seems to us perfectly proper—indeed, symbolically the burden of this book—that you should be able to go into a place called Uncle Sam's Stick Shop, buy a cane on an American Express credit card, and use it in a Holiday Inn.*

* As these words go to bed, as it were, it is of perhaps analogous interest that the latest "sex shop" we have unearthed in New York is being run on Columbus Avenue by a black Sears, Roebuck assistant buyer for six years. It is stiff with s-m gear.

A "TIDY" PAIN

In the course of this book we have tried to confront areas of the human subconscious hitherto regarded as taboo—disgusting, inaccessible, and dangerous. The span of our own lives, comprising an astonishing increase in sexual tolerance in the public domain, lent us confidence in this task. Two children whose hands were diligently placed outside the bedclothes by attentive English nannies grew up to see every form of what Krafft-Ebing would have codified as aberrant not simply permitted in modern America, but actively encouraged, in best-selling books. In the vast panoply of pleasures suddenly opened to men and, especially, women, can we be certain our culture is taking the right course?

Clearly we cannot yet tell. You do not reverse a civilization in a day. Response learning takes time. Woman's orgasmic potential has only just begun to be truly "liberated." The Victorians may have suppressed it, but at least they did not regard the bed as a competitive arena. We on our side must now ask: Are the new freedoms on the side of the psyche? Or are they simply on the side of the dominant technology? Was Jung right when he wrote, "the spirit of our time believes itself superior to its own psychology?"

No pat answers are possible here. T. C. Mits seems to believe vaguely in our new sexual freedoms but he also still considers s-m people "freaks." His attitude is that of Xaviera Hollander who, in *The Happy Hooker*, prides herself on her liberated outlook, yet calmly writes: "Sadists and masochists, referred to by the *cognoscenti* as 'S and M,' or 'slave and masters,' are the most prevalent of the freak syndrome, and 90% of those that I know are slaves, preferring to have punishment inflicted rather than mete it out." And T. C. Mits, who is not a hooker, finds it all more and more complicated since the new sexual freedoms simply ask him to do more. They become new aggressions. Havelock Ellis was concerned that they should not be so. We ourselves have tried in the course of these pages to clarify what one of his female respondents termed a "tidy" pain. And at the risk of repetition we would again cite as central to our argument Joan Malleson's comment: "potency in a man is limited *because a sadistic element linked with it requires also to be repressed.*"

Let it not be so. Such is all we ask. Let us allow our sexual prodigality to extend wider as well as higher, as it were, and to embrace that form of love play atavistically within us all. Let us allow the lover to be a new sort of artist. Our society may be a little healed in the process.

Up to this point s-m has wisely refrained from turning into one more "movement." May it long do so. There have been the usual consciousness-raising groups in the field, but those we have attended turned out to be routine *kaffee klatsches* on the matter, healthy and harmless, so many miniature Scarsdales on s-m. Fortunately s-m does not, like other liberationist movements, seek power. It seeks only freedom. It thus does well to eschew the vulgarity of the barricades.

For directly sex enters politics, certain things happen. A human being risks turning into a function, a necessary unit in the acquisition of political liberty. Indeed, the barricades must be backed by the vulgus or they will soon be overthrown. Blacks, women, gays can rightly retort that without them, without concerted political action, they would have got nowhere.

The penalty paid is, alas, a certain Durkheimian anomy—one

starts to yawn at all the jargon. "The end of a philosophical epoch," writes Susanne Langer, "comes with the exhaustion of its motive concepts." Our advertising so rapidly demeaned the meaning of words like *liberation* and *freedom*—e.g. "The Liberator" (Cupid's Quiver gyna-cosmetic), "The Freedom Spray" (Massengill feminine hygiene deodorant spray, with, of course, hexachlorophene)— that some underground newspapers understandably vetoed the appearance of such terms as sales lures in their pages. As these words are being written, FREE ANGELA buttons are on sale alongside FREE CLIFFORD [Irving] buttons in one Manhattan store. Button-selling was what was important. By implication both Angela Davis and Clifford Irving are anesthetized as so much fodder for the Johnnie Carson Show.

Which is where our sex, a serious activity, is at: a couple discussing in the most intimate detail their love lives with David Susskind in front of 40 million viewers or more. "Must we all continue to drag out our secret desires and turn them into boring rituals and public issues?" asks Laura Cunningham. "Can't anything be private, intimate, just simply our own anymore? Apparently not." As she observes, our psyche risks standing as naked as our flesh today. Men and women are encouraged to love or leave each other not on a human basis but in a role relationship—you don't quit a unique individual, you leave a Liberated Lesbian, a Male Chauvinist. Even *Cosmopolitan*'s repeatedly recommended older "lover" for the girl office worker is really a role rather than a person. This too is sad.

But sex is separated from love by politics in other ways. Politicizing sex is to structure and intellectualize it, to "differentiate" it as we try to with violence. If we can give people comfortable lives, violence will go away. We have cited Anthony Storr's acute expose of these pretensions, in his *Human Aggression*, wherein he reveals the uselessness of our permanent illusion that our aggressive instincts can somehow or other be socially managed away. "Aggressive expression," he writes, "may be as necessary a part of being a human being as sexual expression." And he goes on to remind us that:

One of the unfortunate features of the human condition is that the natural exploratory behavior of human infants has to be curtailed, especially in conditions of civilization, where the hazards of traffic, electricity, gas, stairs, and many other complex dangers have been added to those which are found in primitive, rural circumstances.

In another, equally brilliant way, the novelist Anthony Burgess had told us the same in his remarkable *A Clockwork Orange,* almost unnoticed until Stanley Kubrick made his suggestive movie from it. Government by satisfaction is fraught with all sorts of dangerous open ends of which our politicians seem all too blithely ignorant. Burgess' Alex, introduced to us as a fifteen-year-old member of a street gang committed to finding pleasure in socially contradistinctive activities, epitomizes today's disaffiliated Western youth when he says:

> badness is of the self, the one, the you or me on our oddy knockies [lonesomes], and that self is made by old Bog or God and is his great pride and radosty [joy]. But the not-self cannot have the bad, meaning they of the government and the judges and the schools cannot allow the bad because they cannot allow the self.

Far be it from us to propose that intromission of s-m into sex will cure every social ill. All we are saying is that it is a sexual mode which recognizes pain. It offers no card to carry. It is simply a way of love based on the most intimate knowledge of the human soul. A private religion, without priests or altars, only a few spat-upon acolytes, its secret confessional does not pretend to be some panacea to be propagated, and anyone who thinks that we have here tried to solve the world's problems by s-m can be said to have understood this book but dimly.

What we have tried to do is to lift a last veil between human individuals, to calm violence by love. This is a desperately esthetic task and it is small wonder that so many of the failures, outlawed by their society, ended up in Krafft-Ebing's chamber of horrors. In a convoluted but impassioned passage Georges Bataille suggests that sooner or later we have to come to true terms with our being— we have to love one another or die:

Hell is the feeble idea God involuntarily gives us of himself. But on the scale of unlimited loss we come again upon the triumph of *being*—whose only failure has ever been to be in tune with the movement that would have it perishable. Being joins the terrible syncopated dance of its own accord, the dance we must accept for what it is, conscious of the horror it is in key with. If our heart fail us, there is no torture like it. And the moment of torment will always come: how would we overcome it if it were to fail? But all of being ready and open—for death, joy or torment—unreservedly open and dying, painful and happy, is there already with its shadowed light, and this light is divine: and the cry that being—vainly? —tries to utter from a twisted mouth is an immense *alleluia*, lost in endless silence.

This is a difficult and poetic saying, yet profoundly true. Bataille acknowledges that we have a human nature—how could we overcome horror and torment and violence "*if it were to fail*"? S-m play enacts symbolically this terrible, ideal freedom. In his understanding of the erotic symbolist we have felt that Ellis stands almost alone. He saw that the s-m person was an outlaw, an aberrant, particularly in the sense that he was exercising an extreme of individuality. Behind him lay the atavistic yearnings—"his species, his sex, his nation."

For the erotic symbolist Ellis most generously wrote this epithalamium and epitaph:

His most sacred ideals are for all those around him a childish absurdity, or a disgusting obscenity, possibly a matter calling for the intervention of the policeman. We have forgotten that all these impulses which to us seem so unnatural—this adoration of the foot and other despised parts of the body, this reverence for the excretory acts and products, the acceptance of congress with animals, the solemnity of self-exhibition—were all beliefs and practices which, to our remote forefathers, were bound up with the highest conceptions of life and the deepest ardors of religion . . .

Yet, regarded as a whole, and notwithstanding the frequency with which they witness to congenital morbidity, the phenomena of erotic symbolism can scarcely fail to be profoundly impressive to the patient and impartial student of the human soul. They often seem absurd, sometimes disgusting, occasionally criminal; they are always, when carried to an extreme degree, abnormal. But of all the manifestations of sexual psychology, normal and abnormal, they are the most specifically human. More than any others they involve the potently plastic force of the imagination. They bring before us the individual man, not only apart from his fellows, but in opposition, himself creating his own paradise. They constitute the supreme triumph of human idealism.

APPENDIX

From the Fields of Infamy

The following extracts are examples
of what has been categorized as s-m in this book,
treated with joy and some degree of art;
far from being sad "case histories" they mostly employ fantasy
and are unashamed in their delight in the mode.
Needless to say, many were censored on their publication.

FROM
CHARLES BAUDELAIRE

Les Fleurs du Mal
1857

The Damned Women

Lounging like pensive cattle on the sand,
They turn their eyes to the horizon of seas,
And their feet seek each other and their close hands
Now languish with softness, now quiver with gall.

Some, their hearts captivated by slow secrets
In the depths of bushes chattering with streams,
Go gathering the first loves of timid childhoods
Exploring the green wood of tender trees;

Others, like nuns, slow and grave, move
Over rocks swarming with visions,
Where St. Anthony saw rise up the lava
Of the purple naked breasts of his temptations;

There are some who, to the resin's shaking glimmer,
Call, from the silent hollows of old pagan caverns,
To you, O Bacchus, who soothe remorse,
For help out of their shouting fevers.

And others, whose bosoms crave the scapular,
Who hide a whip under their long clothes
And mingle, in the dismal wood and lonely night,
The foam of pleasure with the twists of pain.

To you, virgins, demons, monsters, martyrs,
To your great spirits spurning reality,
Searchers of the infinite, devotees and satyrs,
Now full of cries, now full of tears,

To you whom to your hell my soul has followed
My poor sisters, I give you my love and pity,
For your dark sorrows, your unslakeable thirsts,
And the caskets of your love of which your hearts are full!

To Her Who Is Too Gay

Your head, your gesture, your air
Are beautiful as a beautiful landscape;
The smile plays in your face
Like a fresh wind in a clear sky.

The fleeting care that you brush against
Is dazzled by the health
Which leaps like clarity
From your arms and your shoulders.

The re-echoing colors
Which you scatter in your toilet

Cast in the hearts of poets
The image of a ballet of flowers.

These silly clothes are the emblem
Of your many-colored spirit;
Silly woman of my infatuation,
I hate as much as love you!

Sometimes in a pretty garden
Where I dragged my weakness,
I have felt the sun like irony
Tear my chest;

And the spring and the green of things
Have so humbled my heart,
That I have punished a flower
For the insolence of Nature.

Thus I would wish, one night,
When the voluptuary's hour sounds,
To crawl like a coward, noiselessly,
Towards the treasures of your body,

In order to correct your gay flesh
And beat your unbegrudging breast,
To make upon your starting thigh
A long and biting weal,

And, sweet giddiness,
Along those newly-gaping lips
More vivid and more beautiful,
Inject my venom, O my sister!

FROM
GEORGE COLMAN

Squire Hardman
1871

Hail, Goddess of the stern and bended brow,
Revered and worshipped, yet unnam'd till now
Ev'n in this land where Thou hast most acclaim,
And where the rites conducive to Thy fame
Have grown to be a kind of national game,
Hail, dear Domestic Discipline, the nurse
Of Albion's fame (for better or for worse)
And cast a fav'ring spell upon my verse!

And Ye, the votaries of her Deity,
Her lovely priestesses, where'er ye be,
Whether in castle, cottage, boarding school,
Nursery or workhouse, Ye that bear the rule
O'er British youth and British backsides: hail,
You strait-laced Tyrants of the head and tail!
To you I dedicate these tingling rhimes
Made for the delectation of the times,
So that they may, as other Farces do,
Amuse the public for a month or two,
Though if perchance posterity allows
Such merit in them that they still arouse
In future minds (congenial to the theme)

An int'rest in the Flagellant *régime*,
Pray let me pay their debt of gratitude
To One pre-eminent in the multitude
Of members of your whipping Sisterhood.
Aye, *Mary Anne!* ev'n Thee let me invoke
With whom I've shared the matrimonial yoke
For nigh ten years, nor ever ceas'd to find
Fresh cause for jubilation since we join'd
Our hands and fortunes, and our tastes combin'd:
To Thee, then, if these lines should live indeed
To warm the future's blood, and fill a need
For all subscribers to the Flogging Creed,
I consecrate the song; and may it find
A lasting place among those works design'd
T' erect the carnal spirits of mankind.

Now Gentle Reader, lend me first of all
Your fancy's vision—what the "Lakers" call
"The inward eye," "the bliss of solitude,"
Or what else dignifies a moonstruck mood—
At any rate, pray lend me it, and gaze
On the two pictures which my poem lays
Before you (as 'twere in the Playhouse): so,
Turn down the lights, the curtain raise, and now—
See *The Good Governess* at close of day,
The supper eaten, the toys put away,
The ev'ning lesson heard, the prayers said,
And her young charges all sent up to bed,
And she now reading from the little book
Wherein their daily crimes are summ'd: who took
That liberty, and who that extra jam;
Who lost his temper and let fall a d——n;
Who pull'd his little sister's hair, and *lied*
When tax'd with it—and so much more beside,
You see how well her patience has been tried.
Yet mark the pensive smile that steals apace

Over the features of that modest face,
That face so stern and somber that you'd vow
'Twas downright plain, unless you saw it now!
Ah see, indeed, how the becoming blood
Tinges her neck and rises in a flood
To nurture in each cheek a lovely Rose,
See how her breath more swiftly comes and goes,
How her mouth softens and her glowing eyes
Have gain'd in brilliance and increas'd in size;
And when she rises, how her form has grown
In majesty, and in that motion shown
A very Juno rising from her throne!
She walks, 'tis Music, and she stands, 'tis Art;
But what is *this* which strikes you to the heart
In yond fine pose, so graceful and so grand?
Is it the cane that quivers in her hand?
At any rate, see how the dear girl's beauty
Wakes at the prospect of her *painful duty*:
Smiling she turns, and softly trips upstairs;
And let that Reader follow her who dares.

I, for my part, am loath to play the spy
On the good woman, and I'll tell you why.
There are some scenes, as ev'ry Author knows,
Whose power is multiplied, whose pathos grows
Through presentation by some means oblique:
E.g., Iphigenia's dying shriek
Heard off the stage—th' effect is full of power;
Or take the little Princes in the Tower,
Smother'd by hearsay: how that moves the heart!
And Sophocles' Medea shews the art
Of moving sympathy's profoundest springs
By knocking off her children—in the wings.

Imagine to yourself a Guest, therefore,
In the same house, and one dividing door

Betwixt his chamber and the children's room,
A Bachelor of fortune, one to whom
Such sounds as from th' adjoining chamber come
Are music sweeter than the heavenly spheres'.
He stops, enraptured by the cries he hears,
His heart in's mouth, his whole soul in his ears:
Each whistling stroke, each howl and plea and sob
Make his blood boil, his very being throb;
For he, by taste and moral judgment both,
Favors the drastic governance of youth:
The study of the whip was, to his mind,
The "properest study" of all womankind,
And woman's *proper sphere*—a boy's *behind*.
Greedier than courtier for the Royal smile
Was he for flogging in the good old style;
Welcomer than to bride her wedding bells
To him the sounds of discipline, the yells
And shrieks of a well flagellated boy.
This was his Hobby, this his greatest joy.
So, little wonder that you see him stand
Mute-motionless, his chin within his hand,
His ears upon the stretch, and in his eyes
A vision of domestic paradise;
And when you understand this tranced guest
Was still unshav'd, and only partly dress'd,
'Tis still less wonder that the jolly sinner
Should be, that ev'ning, rather late for dinner.

And there, dear Reader, are the pictures twain
I promis'd you. Ah not (I hope) in vain
My efforts to arouse and entertain;
And if you ask me how I came to draw 'em,
This Governess and Guest, as if I saw 'em,
And think the portraits too high color'd—well,
That Guest was I, and that cane-bearing *belle*
Was she who—but perhaps I'd best relate
The tale in proper form, at any rate.

So down to dinner did I take my way
To join the company, and tho' *distrait*
With all my mind still fixed on fustigation,
Manag'd to take part in the conversation;
And when it flagg'd, as talk is bound to do
In country houses all the country through,
I cunningly contriv'd to interject
That topic to which Mothers ne'er object:
"Your La'ship, and the children? Are they well?"
"Aye, Mr. Hardman, thank ye; but to tell
The truth, I'm far from being satisfied
With their Miss Lashley." Here she paus'd and sighed.
"The pretty Governess, you mean?" I ask.
(My real int'rest I think best to mask)
"Well, plain or pretty, she must leave us soon—"
"How's that, my love?" his Lordship asks, the spoon
Arrested half way from the serving platter:
"Miss Lashley leaving us? Why, what's the matter?"
"The matter? Why, if you must know, my dear,
'Tis that I find her—well, much too *severe*."
"Severe—a fiddlestick!" my Lord exclaims:
"Whate'er her methods, I approve her aims.
Hardman, d'ye know my Billy has the names
Of all the Kings from Norman William down,
And Bob can tell an adverb from a noun!"
"And at what cost, my Lord?" his wife puts in:
"The boys are black and blue from discipline!"
"No matter. Faith, Miss Lashley's in the right.
I never knew the boys half so polite:
Even little Oliver, who's only three—"
"—She takes him every night across her knee!"
"But John, the French and Latin that she's taught him—"
"—Granted, my dear, but have you seen his b——m?"

Amidst a gen'ral laugh the subject dies;
But it was plain who carried off the prize:
In this, as in all manner of retort,

My Lord was silenc'd; and I saw, in short
This governess so apt at flagellation
Was soon to be without a situation;
And as the meal and conversation sped,
A wondrous plan was hatching in my head.

Up rose the sun next day, and so did I,
And hasten'd downstairs hoping to espy
The fair adept whose image all that night
Had filled my dreams with motions of delight;
And, whether by some leading from Above
(Or elsewhere, if the pious disapprove),
I' th' garden, all alone, I found my love.
—I greet her with my most majestic bow;
She answers with a curtsey, fine and low:
I break the ice by mentioning the weather,
And in no time we're walking on together.

O blessed hour when first I knew my Dear!
The image of that morning, cool and clear,
Is at this moment present to my sight;
I see once more, with all the old delight,
The dewy garden in the light of dawn,
The pale sky and the little clouds thereon,
The slanting sunlight pouring in a flood,
Gilding the grass and silvering the wood;
And clearer still than all, I see once more
The dark blue capuchin my darling wore,
Within whose hood her face peep'd like a flower.
Again I feel the dear disturbing charm
Of that first walk together, arm in arm;
And once again, transpos'd in time, I hear
The low, sweet voice which then enthrall'd my ear,
As we paced slowly o'er the dewy sod,
Discoursing on the Virtues of the Rod.

Tho' I already knew my "cruel fair"
Was no fond, visionary Doctrinaire

In matters of correction, soon I found
Her theory was, like her practice, sound,
Full of good reasons back'd by ancient saws
And moral apothegms and natural laws.
She preach'd most eloquently on the text
Of "proper measures"; and on this pretext
Seem'd to find full occasion to reveal
The fleshly taste behind the moral zeal;
But then, just when her accents made me feel
She look'd on whipping as an amorous bout,
She alter'd, and to plunge me into doubt,
Like Dante to his sinners parcelling out
The various, nice intensities of fire,
She speaks of boys.—"Look ye, Sir, they require
At different ages different instruments:
I give good measure in my punishments,
But would not task an infant with the weight
Of cutting whipcord: 'tis beyond his state.
No, no, indeed: although I do not shun
The strictest methods, when all's said and done
The naked palm is best for baby's skin;
Not till the boy is four should we begin
To use the leathern strap; and for the cane,
He must be eight ere he can stand the pain."
Tho' charm'd, I cast down a dissembling eye,
"Aye, aye, you're in the right," I make reply,
"But, Ma'am, you spoke of whipcord: tell me, pray,
What is the age when *that* should come in play?"

She smil'd at that. O what a heavenly smile,
How well combin'd its gaiety and guile!
And in her eyes what sparkles of delight
Strove with the glow of wanton appetite!
Yet when she spoke, most circumspect and quiet
Her tone, as if the theme were dress or diet
Or other humdrum matter of debate:
"Why, Sir, the circumstances will dictate

The wisest course of action. Much depends
On the degree to which the boy offends;
His growth, his health and habits, too, control
The choice of instruments; but on the whole,
'Tis my opinion, and has always been,
A boy should have the horsewhip at thirteen."
And thus we talk'd. Ah, how my Heart did swell!
Her discourse charm'd me more than I can tell.

And still I took occasion oft to view
Her animated face, approv'd the hue
Of her complexion, brown but clear and warm,
Nor fail'd to note the beauties of her Form:
The length of limb, the slenderness of waist,
The amplitude of thigh—naught went untrac'd
By each inquiring and enraptur'd glance
I turn'd upon this queen of flagellants.
And, Reader, 'twas not long before I knew
My destiny, and what I had to do;
And tho' at first I found me rather queasy,
Once I had spoken, all the rest was easy.

My fortune and estate I did present,
So much in Consols and so much in rent;
My way of living, quiet and retir'd,
And how a wife was all that I desir'd,
"No fond conceited girl whose feather head
Runs upon fashions and such ginger-bread,
No pert, well-dowered, London-loving Miss,
With dreams of naught save the metropolis,
Of Op'ra boxes, balls and carriages;
But some mature and sober votaress
Of home-grown pleasures in a homely dress—"
And here, observing how the brown and red
Blent in her cheek, "Some woman grown," I said,
"Some woman clear of head and firm of hand,
Whose natural disposition to command

Should find its scope and exercise within
Domestic rule and *family discipline.*"

At these last words (insidiously stress'd)
I mark'd the sudden swelling of her breast,
The half-surpris'd unveiling of a glance
That met my own, like lance encountering lance;
And so I leapt into my peroration:
"In short, Miss Lashley, all my admiration
Is, as I find, directed to those spheres
Wherein the *educative* bent appears;
There have I sought my Bride, my happiness,
Have ask'd, 'Who better than a Governess?' "

FROM
AUBREY BEARDSLEY

Under the Hill°
1904

Of The Operetta

The Théâtre des Deux Mains was a bijou little playhouse which
breathed an elegance altogether Regency. Not more than ninety
feet by sixty, its proportions were exquisite. The walls were spaced
out by panels picturing the gilded shapes of amorous cupidons
and caryatides, between which hung portières of dusty-yellow
Utrecht velvet embellished with loops, tassels, fleurons and for-
malized heraldic figures; the ceiling, softly domed and figured
with wreaths and curlicues of creamy plaster, was a little low.
Everything was arranged in the most intimate way, for the pit
had been suppressed altogether, and behind the single row of
stalls began the boxes and loges, each able to hold four or five
persons.

Although the floor sloped down to a minuscule orchestra pit,
maintaining the classical separation of audience and actors, the

---

° The manuscript was, in fact, incomplete at Beardsley's death in March of 1898; install-
ments had appeared in *The Savoy* early in 1896, but clearly the literary climate was such
in England at the time that integral publication of the whole was impossible. In 1904
John Lane published some posthumous Beardsleyana with the comment that *Under the
Hill* was "deemed unprintable by the editors." It was, however, quickly translated into
French. A complete version is to be found in the New York Public Library, thanks to
Dr. A. S. W. Rosenbach, but the whole has only recently truly surfaced in a fine Grove
Press edition (now out of print).

stage was so close as to give you the impression of being a part of
what was going on; and in fact, when Venus and her party slipped
in during the entr'acte, the audience was still deeply moved. The
lights were only half up, and everywhere was a buzz of comment
and criticism, expressions of appreciation, ejaculations from behind masks, smiling retorts and suggestive grimaces. The occu-
pants of some of the boxes had even drawn the curtains, from behind which came the sound of slaps and smothered laughter!

Tannhauser was delighted with everything, especially with the
box-openers; for here, instead of the grumpy old women to whom
the playgoer has become used—though not, I dare say, reconciled
—were a dozen or so beautiful young creatures in plum-colored
jackets and yellow tapering trousers that strapped under the instep
and fitted smoothly across their behinds; their build, their delicate
features, and the short ringlets that played around their shoulders
left their sex a matter of doubt; but this ambiguity, de la Pine
explained in a whisper, was matched by their readiness to sus-
tain the role of either.

Then the lights went down, the music began, and the curtains
rose on the second of the two acts, discovering the interior of an
orphanage where a dozen or more ravishing children, dressed in
an old-fashioned and modest manner, were performing a graceful
gavotte. Circling, dividing, forming and re-forming in intricate
patterns and arabesques, they engrossed the stage with a charming
collective movement, making quaint erotic gestures and accompanying their dance with the sweet treble of a cheerful little song.
Soon the fun became more lively and more risqué, the couples
detaching themselves for a few minutes in the center of the stage
to excute some really naughty pantomime, while the others
clapped their hands in time, beat their little slippers on the floor, and
laughed in a simple, wordless cascade of melody which was tossed
to and fro, from the boys to the girls and back again, with infinite
varieties of expression and cadence.

But all at once there was a roll of drums, the lights on the stage
changed to a deep rose, and a drop-curtain swept aside, revealing
two statuesque female figures in long white gowns, who had been
watching. A wild arpeggio from the harp, like the susurrus of an

autumn wind, succeeded, and the chorus of children, wailing, shrank back in a calculated disarray towards the wings; then the Matrons advanced slowly, to a solemn, throbbing pizzicato of bass viols.

Their appearance was truly wonderful. With faces painted dead white, mounting false chins and noses which almost met over tiny mouths, their foreheads graced with rows of curls like inverted question marks, and wearing enormous mob-caps which quivered and swayed on their heads, they moved slowly upstage, nodding portentously and making gestures of outrage. A round of applause greeted them, for these were Mrs. Bowyer and Mrs. Barker.

And now the former took a striking attitude, the harp sounded a few notes, and she delivered a glorious recitative, her majestic contralto filling the theater as she expressed her indignation and horror, her well-nigh disbelief in the testimony of her eyes, while she clasped her hands, raised them in the air and dropped them to her sides, rolling her eyes and shaking her head; an occasional interpolation from Mrs. Barker's golden soprano cut across her words, and then the two voices joined in a somber and stirring duet in which execrations were mingled with promises of punishment and invocations of the spirit of birch.

The duet ended with three long notes in alt, uttered by the Matrons in unison. This was the call to the servants, and as the applause of the audience reached its climax four strapping girls carrying rods rushed on the stage. Now, the orchestra struck up a jolly bourrée, to whose accented rhythm was executed a short and lively bacchanale, the orphans retreating and fleeing, the servant girls pursuing, grasping, and losing; cries of alarm, triumph, and vexation mingled with the invigorating music, the dance became a wild rout of flying forms, a whirling kaleidoscope of smock and sash, of bare limb and lacy pantalette, from which at last two of the serving wenches emerged, each with an orphan securely horsed on her back, and the music ceased with a plangent crash of cymbals.

To the sounds of an exquisite solo by the premier violin, the two captives, a boy and a girl, were now lovingly and ceremoniously untrussed. Ah, what a delightful operation this was! What ravishing contours were exposed, what quiverings, what tremblings and trepidations, what rosy reluctancies, as the plump fesses emerged and the two dear children were prepared for the neat birch rods in the hands of Bowyer and Barker!

Then all was quiet; the tableau arranged itself, each captive flanked by Matron and domestic, the remaining children creeping close as at the bidding of fear and fascination, and Mrs. Barker, her rod upraised, began to deliver a thrilling lecture full of the old-fashioned phrases of nursery eloquence. By degrees her emotion mounted, as if like a Homeric hero she were exciting herself by her own threats and vauntings; her voice rose, throbbing and fulminating in somber *crescendi*, her arm gesturing with motions ever more purposeful, until at last, as a superb and stately period rolled to its close, the twigs descended with a rich and urgent hiss, and the flagellation commenced to a softly resumed music.

Tannhauser, already blushing with pleasure, followed everything eagerly, loving the strokes that fell so roundly, admiring the art with which the voices of *fesseuse* and *fessé* blended, this one rising, that falling, in a chromatic progression that decorated in obbligato the gentle but insistent beat of the bolero whispered by drums and muted strings. Now, the birch seemed to dominate all the sounds and movements, as if it, and not the conductor's baton, were leading the music, evoking the cries of distress and satisfaction, and directing the reedlike swaying of the chorus from side to side and the leaps and bounds of the disciplined urchin. The Chevalier found himself beating time with the toe of his slipper.

Then the music and cries increased in volume as flutes and oboes joined in, echoing and mingling and competing with the singers, and all at once two other voices added themselves, as Mrs. Bowyer began to thrash the other culprit; and now the rhythms multiplied themselves in ingenious counterbeats and syncopations, notes short and long were exchanged like the repartees of a fugue, and at last, as agonized trills, roulades and fiorituri poured from the two children, the stirring quartet came to an end, its final strains engulfed by roars and bravos from the audience of deboshed *cognoscenti*.

Fresh melodies and fresh victims succeeded rapidly. The plot became confused, the story lost itself, the incidents grew more outrageous, as birch rods were supplanted by long, supple canes, these by limber straps, and these in turn by many-tongued martinets. At length, when matters had apparently reached some kind of crisis, there were only the Matrons, the four servants, and a beautiful youth, quite nude, occupying the stage. Forming a circle around him, they drove him to and fro between them with blows of their martinets, laughing silverly, until after a minute or two the boy sank down in an exquisite pose, quite motionless. The lights began to dim, Mrs. Bowyer made a sign with her hand, and in the hush the domestics let down a scale from the proscenium, fastened the youth's wrists to it, and drew him up on tiptoe. The stage was utterly dark for a moment; then a clear rosy light illuminated the three principals, and one saw the two Matrons were armed with long, supple whips.

The audience was tense and silent; Tannhauser himself felt his breath quickening as the blows began to fall. For now make-believe had turned to reality! He reached for the hand of Venus, which squeezed his in moist sympathy, as they both stared at the stage, hearing now the veritable sounds of punishment and the true accents of pain. The youth's body shook, twisted and trembled, his feet danced and kicked, the two whips sang in alternation, and piercing cries filled the little theater, pleas for mercy, prayers for forgiveness, promises of amendment, all alike met by the Matrons' measured replies, calm and judicial, full of ironical sympathy and encouragement, a suave, antiphonal rhetoric made deliciously paradoxical by the steady accompaniment running beneath it, the repeated whistle and report of whipcord on flesh.

"Oddsfish," said Cosmé in a whisper, " 'tis artistry with a vengeance, that throws art to the winds." De la Pine nodded, smiling and rubbing his hands.

There was wild applause as the representation came to an end and the fainting youth hung limply in his bonds. Then, as the lights went up and the two Flagellantes advanced to the footlights, hand in hand, bowing, they were greeted by cries of "Unmask, unmask!" —and the next moment, when they twitched off their comic vizards, Tannhauser saw the two old frights replaced by a pair of handsome, smiling women who at once began to ogle the unattached gentlemen in the side-boxes. Bouquets were thrown from several directions; they were received with bows and courtesies by the divas, who held them to their breasts and then, smiling archly, held up the little notes concealed in them, blowing kisses and flourishing their whips playfully at the admirers they had made.

"If you keep on looking at those creatures that way," Venus smiled at the Chevalier, "I'll be jealous."

Tannhauser's only response was to draw the curtains of the box violently, to seize the Queen in his arms and press burning kisses upon her neck and shoulders.

"Oh!" she cried after a few moments. "Not here, not here!"

"No," said Mrs. Marsuple, putting her head through the curtains at that instant. "I've engaged the Ducal Suite upstairs. I saw you, my dears, and I knew *just* how you'd be feeling. Come on!"

FROM
EDITH CADIVEC

Confessions and Experiences[°]
(ca. 1920–24, first published in 1930)

As a baby, up to the age of eighteen months, I was fat as a dumpling. Then I began to walk and lost weight. I was my mother's likeness and her pampered darling. Thus our family was divided into two camps: on the one side father and Gabrielle, on the other, mother and I. My sister was "a chip off the old block"; she had inherited his character traits as well as his physical features. The law of similarity fully applied to them: father and his daughter Gabrielle were wholly in accord with each other. They never found fault with each other and no conflicts and differences ever troubled their relationship. They understood and loved each other in their own way. I do not recall my sister ever having been punished or even scolded by father. Father was extremely fond of Ella, he saw himself in his child and loved her all the more.

However, I was too different from my sister for my father to be able to love me. Also, I did not love either my father or my sister and stuck to my mother like a bur. I had the burning feminine need to love and be loved. For me, mother was the quintessence of tenderness, warmth, of all love and security. In earliest childhood I had the vague idea of disappearing forever in the body of my beloved mother so that I could be sheltered against all that was threatening and hostile, especially against father and sister, who were not allowed to follow me to that sanctuary.

As a small child, to the extent that I can remember, I liked to

° New York: Grove Press, 1971.

hide under my mother's clothes. For me it was a passion of which
no blows could break me. So far as I know mother was obliging,
indeed it even happened that she pressed my head and face with
a special ardor against her warm body, and I felt that the contact
with the soft child body also gave her a feeling of pleasure. The
only time she did not allow this was when father was present, and
then she acted as if she were pushing me away and were angry
with me. Actually, she would hold my head firmly between her
legs, bend over my back and smack my naked bottom so soundly
that it burned.

Father was pleased to see that mother punished me in this way.
He would always encourage her by saying, "Give her a good tan-
ning, you're spoiling her too much. The child should not grow up
so pampered!"

And after the smackings he would place me, howling, in a
corner. After a while mother would fetch me from my corner and
become so extravagantly affectionate with me that her kisses and
stormy caresses took my breath away. She rubbed and stroked
my smarting bottom and kissed it for so long and so hard that
perforce I broke out into a fit of ecstatic laughter. Even when I
lay next to her in bed, body nestled against body, I became drunk
with bliss when I could feel her breast and touch the soft, hairy
bulges of her sex with my little feet.

All these sweet things appeared so natural that it never occurred to me to say a word about them. Just as sugar is sweet, and
one repeatedly craves for this sweetness, so was mother for me
the sweetness, the bliss for which I constantly hungered. I climbed
onto her lap as often as I could and buried my face in her soft,
warm breast. Mother locked me in her arms most tenderly, at the
same time she kissed me and pressed me against herself so tightly
that it almost hurt. She did all this secretly, only when she was
alone with me and father and sister could not see it. For father
tolerated no coddling and for the most part I hated him when in
an apparently angry voice he would forbid mother to do this.

No caresses were ever exchanged between father and sister.
Theirs was an affection of another kind which had absolutely
nothing of a sensual character about it. The love between mother

and me was unconsciously erotic: the eruptive maternal love on the one hand and my passionate childish demand for it on the other, exclusively an affection for mother—an aversion for father and sister who threatened to tear me away from her.

Once, when I was three or four years old, I again slipped under my mother's clothes and hid myself there. I clasped her legs tightly and wanted neither to let them go nor to come out from under. Finally my mother pulled me out and became so angry that she boxed my ears and gave me a sound thrashing. Ashamed, thrashed soundly, shaken, I stood before her as if hypnotized by her unusual cruelty and sternness.

The chaos of my own feelings utterly confused me. The sultry warmth and the body-scent of my pregnant mother, the contact with her stern hand, whose blows seared my skin, left such strong impressions on my childish mind that the remembrance of them is vivid to this day. Then the yearning for the maternal body, the eternal yearning again to become one with the beloved mother becomes so strong and compelling that I fall into rapture. But at the same time, I sensed, trembling, mother's rejecting sternness, her power and cruelty, which aroused fear and shame in my innermost being and churned all my feelings.

Mother's pregnancy and the birth of a little brother, who lived only one day, was another erotic childhood experience for me. One morning my sister and I were awakened from slumber and led to mother's bed in order to greet the screaming tiny new member of the family. He did not please me one whit. I merely inquired, anxiously, whether he had been cut out of mother's body because I had noticed blood on the sheets.

I could not restrain myself from asking father, "How does one know that it's a boy?" He answered me evasively, that after all one could easily tell by looking at the face. But I did not believe his lie.

The next day little brother lay wrapped in swaddling clothes, as a corpse in a coffin. We were allowed to look at him again and were then sent out of the room. In an unguarded moment, however, afflicted with childish curiosity, I sneaked back into the room, scrambled up a chair and with a searching hand I felt the body of the tiny corpse under the swaddling clothes. I saw nothing, but distinctly felt the forms of the male sex. Everything transpired in fear and great excitement. I slipped out of the room as stealthily as I had entered it and I was satisfied with my knowledge. Nobody had noticed anything.

No other child came after the little brother.

When Gabrielle was five and a half years old my father began to give us both elementary instruction. He taught us reading, writing, and arithmetic and I had to learn at the same pace as my older sister. I preferred to play with the dog and the cat and still rejected learning. But father forced me to apply myself. Ella learned easily; she was quick to grasp things, matter-of-fact, and able to concentrate. I was led astray by my fantasy, pursuing my chimeras, and father was put out by my lack of attention. The result was praise and preference for my sister, while father lavished censure, loveless invectives, and blows on me.

Wicked impulses arose in me. At times I was gripped by a real mania to annoy father and Ella. I lied, I took away from my sister everything that she received as reward from father, destroyed and tore everything that gave her joy. I was defiant, disobedient, hostile, and malicious. I scratched and pinched my sister, pulled her hair, and out of sheer wickedness I did things to her that grieved and offended her. She would then always complain about me to father. He would grab me like a predatory bird and, without uttering a word, clamp me tightly with his left arm against his hip so that I kicked and struggled in the air. Lifting my dress, he would belabor my buttocks soundly with his powerful hand. I screamed and defended myself with all my might until he set me down. This enraged me extremely since I did not want to be beaten by father. I did not let him touch me and after the forced punishment I hated him all the more. Only the respect which had been implanted in me kept me from spitting on father and regaling him with kicks. I did this to good measure in my thoughts and thus assuaged my wild fury.

Gabrielle was seven years old when she was accepted in the second grade of public school. Father had me enrolled in the first class at the same time so that we two sisters could attend school together. At that time my father lived on the outskirts of Vienna in a locality where we remained for five years.

In her report cards Ella always brought home the best marks. She was a model of good behavior and good upbringing and was praised from all sides. For my part, the marks in my report cards were lower, I was the embodiment of wildness and willfulness and I was always being scolded, punished, and slighted. I had the painful feeling that nobody loved me except my mother who was always affectionate to me in the same way, and always stern with me in the same way when her anger was aroused.

Often she too would push me away when I was especially naughty and place me in a corner or lock me in my room after duly thrashing me. But when my sobs died down, she would fetch me from the corner, take me in her arms and inundate me with her accumulated wild tenderness. I almost lost consciousness under her passionate kisses, but I felt the bliss of the maternal embrace. How confusing her cold sternness appeared to me in the trembling expectation of the stormy opposite that unfailingly followed! Her boundless motherly love shook me to the innermost depths.

As the result of her neurasthenia mother ailed more and more in mind and body. The attacks of mental illness following the birth of the last child increased the effects of her terrible affliction which grew more and more drastic, and the bigger I grew and the more I understood, the more frightening mother's invalidism appeared to me. I clung to her skirts and forcibly obtained from her the affection for which I hungered. And when in moments of clarity she again pressed me tightly against her breast, kissed me and clasped me to herself so passionately that it cut off my breath, I felt as if my whole body were shaking in a spasm of bliss.

Because of the indifference resulting from her affliction, mother in no way concerned herself with everyday matters; neither the household nor the rearing and instruction of her little girls mattered to her. Everything was left to father, who even had to attend to our clothes and underthings, and battle with the servants.

In school I was inattentive, I daydreamed, and took litle joy in planned learning. However, because Gabrielle's industriousness and irreproachable conduct in school exceeded all expectations, father looked proudly into the future of his true daughter. He began to teach her Latin and French, while I was allowed only to listen to the lessons and not to participate.

At that time I showed little interest in subjects which could not prove their usefulness through practical application. I liked much better to concern myself with the active life around me. I took a lively interest in my schoolmates, the members of their families, and their way of life. I never neglected to ask my school comrades about their parents and brothers and sisters, about the sternness or tenderness in the family, in order to ferret out whether they were punished for certain types of misbehavior and in which way this punishment was administered, whether they loved their father or mother more, or whether they themselves were favored or punished by the father or mother. These were the favorite questions which I asked of every child. And my thirst for such knowledge was always satisfied.

Gabrielle found less sympathy among her classmates; she was not interesting enough and her exemplary goodness bored most of them. Moreover, Ella spent little time with children, preferring adults. I was overtly "bad" but guileless, and sympathetic to the fate of others. Hearts flew toward me although I was not especially charming. I was never evil and never malicious. The leitmotif of my behavior lay in the injunction: love thy neighbor as thyself. That was practical reason.

At home there was a lively traffic of families with whom my parents were friends and they often came to visit us with their children. But especially the reciprocal invitations among school friends often gave me an opportunity to practice my inclinations. Gabrielle felt best when she was near father. I, however, ran around with children of my own age, or younger, and even with small tots whom I directed at my pleasure and ruled over.

I always chose my favorite game in such a way that a dominating role fell to me. The mother-and-child game was very popular as long as I could be the mother and play this role even from the birth of a child onward. I padded my breasts and belly, got sick as the situation called for, and finally let the child be cut from my body. It was always a doll swathed in the cloth forming the padding on my belly and which was removed at birth. I let the newborn infant suckle at my breast. Suddenly the child was big, the doll was replaced by a playmate who thereafter was made to feel all my maternal sternness. This game ended with a quarrel and disagreement between "mother" and "child," and it met with scant approval from the rest of our playmates.

Even playing school was a source of pleasure for me as long as I could play the strict, pitiless woman teacher draconically swinging the cane over her pupils. But this game too never lasted long because the ill-treated "pupils" soon ran away from it in tears, declaring that they no longer wanted to join in the game because the "teacher" really and soundly whacked them.

After such failures I would immediately propose another game of which I was equally fond: doctor and patient! I always wanted to be the doctor, another girl played the mother who brought her sick child to me. My chief pleasure in my role as doctor lay in thoroughly examining the body of the "patient," where I always concerned myself—at length and thoroughly—with the most private parts of the body. In this way I acquired an extraordinary knowledge of the anatomy of female and male genitalia and satisfied my secret longing to see, to touch and, at times, also to pinch the stark-naked bottoms of boys and girls. Everything transpired in full secrecy and no child was allowed to betray anything of the examination. But this game likewise ended with the refusal of the "patients" to accommodate the "doctor" because "he" hurt them by subjecting them to small tortures.

From the age of eight to ten I was often invited to the homes of my girl friends. To be sure, we harmonized well but quarrels were nevertheless unavoidable. We disagreed, quarreled, and after scuffling in such a way that it was no longer possible to determine who originally had been at fault, we complained to the mother of the house. She would rush over to us and first of all ask about the cause and the originator of the quarrel. As the guest I felt secure against any insult and boldly complained about the quarrelsomeness of the other children. I accused them of so many bad things the mother, angered and excited by my charges, without further ado would belabor the rudely bared bottom of her offspring with a birch rod, a cane, or the flat of her hand before all those present.

The ear-piercing screams and the struggling of the girl or boy being punished, the stark-naked bottom, glowing red and flashing under the stern mother's hissing birch, the fascinating power of the punisher, all this taken together had a wholly irresistible effect on the children. They were, of course, afraid of beatings but the spectacle of someone else receiving a thrashing was a prickling stimulant and constant attraction to them.

I myself stood rigid, as though hypnotized by the suggestive event; I was fascinated and incapable of moving, shaken and overcome by the tremendous impact which the maternal punishment had exerted on me. I preserved the image in my fantasy, my mind was in a tumult. I could hardly understand myself. Full of admiration, I gazed at the stern mother; passionately I wished that I were in the place of the child being punished! At the same time there arose in my consciousness the remembrance of my own mother whose body scent and warmth formerly had so intoxicated me.

And at night in bed I imagined again the event that had so shaken me during the day. In my fantasy I was the mother of the naughty girl who had been birched because of her bad behavior. I relived the whole procedure of the shameful punishment. I saw myself as a stern mother, I guided my hands under the child's clothes, unbuttoned her drawers, pulled them down, stretched the bitterly weeping girl across my lap, bared her whole bottom, grabbed the birch and belabored the bottom with slanting blows until the skin burned. The more the girl showed her fear and resisted, the more she wailed and screamed, the more her naked bottom glowed and smarted, all the more sharply and searingly did the stinging blows of my birch fall, all the more did her shrill and piercing screams sound like lovely music in my ears. I became hotter and hotter with such fantasies, a wondrous thrill of voluptuary pleasure shot through my body. I understood that an inner relationship existed between the birching of a naked bottom and the prickling feeling of happiness that suffused my soul.

Toward a smaller child I liked to feel like a mother to whom

it is handed over against its will. I also wanted to have such unlimited control over a child. Sometimes it happened that a child
was naughty; I immediately led it to its mother and complained
about its naughtiness. Back then every angered mother would
soundly thwack her tot's bottom without standing on ceremony. I
wanted to bring about these thwackings, it gratified me when
they happened and the punished child broke into a wild scream—
not so much, of course, because of the thwackings but out of
shame that it had to submit its bare bottom for such punishment.

I would feel myself drawn to this mother admiringly. I would
nestle against her, sensing what she experienced when she made
her offspring feel the weight of her absolute maternal authority.
How beautiful the mother-child relationship in which one, in
childlike trust, felt secure and sheltered and looked up in rever-
ential love to the person held in respect, embodied by the stern
mother!

My mother died when I was nine years old. She had been mentally deranged many months before her life was fully extinguished
by a heart attack after years of invalidism. Her death was beyond
my comprehension. I cried night and day without knowing why.
The whole house seemed to me to be shrouded in sadness, useless
and desolate. I did not want to remain in it any longer without
mother.

Father and Gabrielle coolly and rationally made all the necessary arrangements after mother's death. They did not weep but
showed their everyday faces and it seemed to me as if they viewed
the death of this poor invalid as a wished-for deliverance. Nevertheless, it was a hard blow to all of us.

My father's sister, Aunt Regina, the widow of a district judge
who had died early, came over to the house after my mother died,
as she had so often done before, in order to see that everything was
all right. The household was greatly neglected, the wardrobe of the
children was in a bad way, and our upbringing left much to be
desired. This time Aunt Regina remained several months with us,
more for her brother's sake than for that of her motherless nieces.
She found us not at all properly brought up and worthy of love
as her own son Peter, who was already grown up. Auntie, however,

could not cope with the task of running her brother's household permanently and she soon returned to the loneliness and peace of her widow's residence. This certainly was the reason why father decided to marry for the second time only one year after mother's death.

The step-mother was a lady of thirty-five. When father took her home she had just become the widow of a seventy-eight-year-old doctor, to whom she had been married four years. Formerly she had been the governess of many children of socially prominent families.

Outwardly she was pleasant without actually being pretty. Practical, materialistic, and clever as she was, she had married father only for reasons of security. She was a model of a good housewife, a good cook, a foe of dust and of stockings with holes and tyrannized the whole house with her inveterate love of order. She shook me out of my daydreaming and urged me to take up needlework. Gabrielle had to help with the housework and knit stockings. We were no longer allowed to be idle and to play.

We sisters quickly discovered that the step-mother was a lady of great energy and sternness who always knew how to make her will prevail. She demanded prompt obedience, good behavior, and an iron industriousness from us. When she was angry and bored through us with her looks, her cold, steel-green eyes could look at us with a sternness that made hot and cold shivers run down our spines. Our freedom was limited and now we had to come home punctually, on the minute.

Despite her zeal in child-rearing the step-mother did not show the slightest affection for us children. But she was ostentatiously affectionate with father. He was happy at her side, wholly henpecked; he even handed over to her the education of his daughter, which up to now he alone had directed.

When our mentally ill mother was still alive the atmosphere at home had been oppressive and unhealthy, full of mysteries and horror. Fantastic shapes crept toward me from all corners, the disorder in the rooms was appealing and uncanny at once: I avoided touching the objects in them, bewitched as in a fairy tale. A needlework begun would lie for weeks in one place, untouched and covered with dust, the cat would lie down on it and fall asleep. Our toys were strewn all over the floor and our school things lay dreaming in a corner. The step-mother brought order and purposefulness into the idyllic peace of these slumbering things. She discarded, and radically, all which stood in the way of her practical sense.

A few months after the entrance of the step-mother into our house it happened that Ella, now thirteen, did not come home punctually at one o'clock for the midday meal. It was served and eaten as usual and when Gabrielle finally came home, around one-thirty, she was served afterward and had to eat alone. The step-mother darted angry glances but did not utter a word as long as father was present. Gabrielle excused herself to father, explaining that she was late because she had accompanied a school friend home and believed that this explanation had settled the matter. As she finished her lunch with good appetite, father and step-mother returned to their bedroom to rest as usual after meals.

After this rest, when father had left the house, the step-mother came into the room where Ella and I were busy with our homework. She went directly up to my sister and, flushing red, angrily asked her: "At what time are you supposed to be home?"

"At one o'clock," answered Gabrielle calmly.

"Good! And at what time did you come home today?"

"At one-thirty, because I walked my girl friend home."

"Yes, indeed! But you know that I have insisted again and again that you be at home at one o'clock punctually! Now, come with me!"

The step-mother grabbed the resisting Gabrielle by the arm and dragged her to the bedroom next to the living room in which we had been sitting. It was clear to both of us that now something terrible was about to happen. Gabrielle, too, sensed that something frightful was in the offing for her. I stared into space, stiff, as if paralyzed in every joint. My heart was in my mouth, and the air was laden with an oppressive mystery that took my breath away. Ella began to cry, to plead, and to promise that she would certainly never do it again. But the step-mother did not listen and silently dragged Ella along with her. After she and Gabrielle disappeared into the bedroom, she locked the door.

The surmise that a thrashing was in the offing became a certainty. An oppressive stillness prevailed all around me, so that I could hear every sound coming from the bedroom. I heard the sound of a chair being pulled out and then I heard how the step-mother was speaking to Gabrielle:

"Now, little girl, my patience is at an end! If you will not hear, you must be made to feel. Now you'll taste the birch on your naked bottom. Maybe that will make you mind my words better!"

Immediately the bedroom resounded with urgent pleas and implorations for forgiveness. Gabrielle's promises to mend her ways were heard, her weeping grew louder and louder, her screaming ever more heart-rendering. A convulsion went through my body, I trembled like an aspen leaf.

"Here!" called the step-mother in the bedroom, and Gabrielle, in a mysteriously fear-ridden tone, whimpered and wailed: "No! No! You can't . . . unbutton my drawers! . . . I'll be good . . . good and punctual . . . as you want, mother! I won't ever do it again! But not the . . . drawers . . . no! . . . no!"

A piercing shriek ensued, betraying that Gabrielle's naked bottom had received the first blow with the birch, and indeed the first birching that had been given in our house by our step-mother. Indeed it was also the first time that Gabrielle had received a taste of the rod—but not the last!

I listened in a state of frantic, tense excitement to the whistle of the birch as it came swishing down, blow after blow, on my sister's bared body. *Swack! . . . swack! . . . swack!* So many were the blows that descended on Gabrielle's bottom that it seemed to me that the birching would never end. I will never forget that day—my soul enflamed and my blood raged as in a fever . . .

A wholly new epoch was ushered in by this event. From then onward the step-mother thought of no other punishment for us children than the birch and always on the fully bared bottom. Since that day hardly a week went by without my sister or me being summoned into the bedroom by the step-mother. Gabrielle, who was older, always had to unbutton her drawers by herself whereas my step-mother pulled them down from me, the younger, as from a moppet. When I received the rod for the first time, I almost could not endure it. The blows which had the effect of molten lead on the naked bottom singed my flesh like an infernal fire.

We were never birched when father was at home, but we lived in constant fear of inviting a punishment. One day Ella complained about the step-mother to father because she, now a big girl of almost fourteen years, had been birched. She did not want to put up with this anymore. But father calmly answered, "You must have surely deserved it, my child." That day when father left, the step-mother summoned Ella to the bedroom and birched her again and so soundly that she never again complained about the step-mother to father. Thereafter she meekly submitted to her punishments.

I always waited for such events, which stirred my soul so deeply, with taut nerves. I observed the step-mother's features searchingly and tried to read in them the riddle of her inner being. Never did her eyes beam more brightly, never did the smile around the corners of her mouth play more conqueringly than when she could belabor her step-daughters' bare bottoms with smarting blows from the birch. Then she would beat with a slow deliberateness and the strange sensations she felt filled me with awe.

Later, when I recognized the nature of my own being, when my eyes and mind had been opened wide for this sweet enjoyment of the rod, the image of my step-mother often cropped up in my mind. Then I would see her glowing cheeks, her flashing eyes, and I understood the zeal with which she sought occasions for calling us, big girls of thirteen and fifteen, into the bedroom. No doubt that was the step-mother's greatest enjoyment. Later I also learned that as a teacher she had likewise used the rod to punish her unruly pupils.

Strange to say, in this moment my thoughts turn to the drawers which my sister and I wore at that time. We never wore the open flap drawers which were prescribed in the convent. Ours fit tightly around the thigh and bottom, bordered with pretty lace, tied with ribbons: the front flap folding under the back as customary, the rear flap folding under the belly. A seamstress came to the house periodically to sew our outer clothing and our underwear. This seamstress was summoned to the house shortly after the step-mother's arrival in order to make drawers and other undergarments for us. My sister had to hold her dress high and try on the drawers so that the step-mother, in the presence of the seamstress, could see how they fit.

After a close examination and testing the step-mother ordered the seamstress to cut the side-slits of the drawers lower by a hand's breadth so that—as she put it—the drawers would not split upon being pulled up or pulled down. We made wholly futile objections against having such large side-slits, but the step-mother was adamant. This episode comes to mind now along with a crystal-clear explanation of her design! Obviously the only reason for the large side-slits was that they would enable the step-mother to pull down the rear drawer flap even lower. So at that time the step-mother was already thinking with "love and solicitude" about our bottoms hidden in the drawers and about her birch rod! At that time none of us had been birched and it is probably for this reason that the underlying purpose of the deep side-slits had not occurred to me earlier.

After the introduction of these "practical drawers" one could pull down the rear flap to the middle of the thigh once the front slip-knot was loosened. And when dress and blouse were then raised up to the waist, the full bottom lay smooth and bare down to the middle of the thigh—invitingly ready for the rod.

Gabrielle received her first punishment on a bottom that had been bared accordingly. Since Ella had refused to, the step-mother herself had grabbed her and untied the front knot of the drawers, pulled down the rear flap, after which she stretched Ella across a chair, dress and blouse raised high above her waist. Thus the field of action was laid bare. In the evening, of course, I was bent upon finding out whether traces of the birching were still discernible on my sister's bottom. At bedtime I made her lift her long nightgown and with horror I saw a number of clear, fine streaks, partly red, partly reddish-blue, and also some that were all blue. Especially and strongly noticeable, however, were the yellow-blue spots on her right buttock which was precisely where the points of the birch branches had lashed in.

It was understandable that such a sight should excite me and fill me with a quaking fear. Which one of us would be the next to have her naked bottom birched so soundly? Oh, numberless times, I too was stretched over the chair like Gabrielle and received the birch on my bare buttocks! In the beginning both my sister and I found it puzzling when the step-mother mysteriously came into the room or even merely stuck her head in the door, motioned with her forefinger and called out, "Edith, come over here!" Little by little, however, we understood what it signified: the birch rod, the rear flap of the drawers pulled down in order to lay bare the bottom, always face downward, across her lap or—especially as we grew older—across a chair! And while she once more rebuked the culprit for her misbehavior, she bared the bottom with great care while deploring the necessity to birch such a big girl on her naked—yes, on her naked—bottom. She would lay such a special emphasis on "naked" that one simply felt like crawling into the earth for shame.

At that time it seemed to me that a complete transformation had taken place in my soul. Until then I had been a small schoolgirl. My thoughts were divided between homework, my playmates, my sister, and matters affecting our household. New conditions had developed since the introduction of birching by the stepmother; the strict upbringing imposed on us played the most prominent role. In the beginning, however, this circumstance was considered merely as an exciting intensification of our education, as something unavoidable to which we had to submit with resignation. My sister Ella never grasped this circumstance in any other way.

As the years went by only I was consumed by the erotic power of birching! Why? This question has often occupied my thoughts. Is it an accident or did I possess this tendency from birth? Or was it placed in my soul from the ovum onward and had it waited only for this impetus in order to break out with elemental force? I do not know.

At that time I had still another experience that shook me deeply. One day father and step-mother had retired to their room after the midday meal as usual. Someone then came to us in the room and asked to speak to father. I was eager to be of service so, unthinkingly, I entered the room, the door of which was not locked, and surprised my parents in the act of sexual intercourse. The bed in which this was happening faced the door. I caught sight of my father moving rhythmically up and down astride the body of the step-mother. Paralyzed by shock, I stood there rooted to the spot, rigid as though bewitched, unable to utter a sound. The act was well under way. I wanted to scream but had no voice. I wanted to run but my legs failed me . . .

Minutes—perhaps an eternity—went by when the step-mother seemed to notice the open door. She raised her head, caught sight of me in the door, troubled and staring at the repugnant scene, and roared angrily: "Get out! What are you doing in here!!!"

Father leaped off the bed in a flash, rushed at me, grabbed me by the arm, shoved me out the door and then turned the key in the lock twice.

Shivering from head to toe, confused and torn apart in my innermost being, reeling, I ran into the garden, threw myself on the grass and wept . . . wept . . . wept . . .

After I had calmed down somewhat, I heard the step-mother calling my name from the house: once, twice, thrice! Mechanically I obeyed and went into the house, where she was waiting for me. Without saying a word I let myself be led to the bedroom because it was quite clear to me that I could expect a sound thrashing for this "disturbance." For all that the punishment on this day became for me the fateful hour of my life! In this hour I found myself on *le seuil de la conscience*, and now I stepped beyond this threshold of consciousness.

I had never known the feeling with which I received my punishment that time. The words uttered by my step-mother appeared to me in a wholly different light than was otherwise the case. To this day I hear the words, those wicked words—quasi-wicked I suddenly felt!—uttered by the step-mother when the door was locked and I was alone with her: "Aren't you ashamed that you violated my command not to come into the bedroom? You can't deny that I forbade you time and time again to set foot in the room unless you were summoned! Or can you? You're too big a girl not to obey instantly. Now you'll get your well-deserved punishment for it. Unbutton your knickers!"

In a state of frenzied excitement I tried my best to calm the step-mother. Instinctively, however, I felt that under no circumstances did she want to release her prey. Finally the step-mother shrilled into my face, "Are you going to unbutton your drawers, yes or no!" Her tone was so brutal that I suddenly started with shock. A ringing slap in the face accompanied her words.

The step-mother heard my sobs and urgent pleadings with visible pleasure; she sensed my quaking fear and understood that I was ashamed to deliver my naked bottom to her blows. Pitilessly, in the grip of a wild sensuous excitement, she finally achieved her desired goal. In well-delivered blows she made her birch dance hissing across my bare buttocks . . . a thrill shot through me like a hot spring and I felt the excitement being experienced by the birch-wielding step-mother flow over me as well. To me it was a wholly incomprehensible experience. I floated in a state of unimagined bliss and cried heart-rendingly for sheer joy. The blows fell over and over again on my stark-naked bottom and every blow became a sweet pain for my own mounting and awakening voluptuary pleasure.

At the end of the punishment I ran reeling into my room, threw myself on the bed and did something with such a compulsive necessity that there was no way out. The ticklish feeling of happiness in my sex swelled into a driving force, the flogged bottom burned like fire—I pressed my legs closely against each other and did not understand at all what was happening to me. I had never known such a feeling before! I did not yet clearly know that it was voluptuousness increasingly urging itself on in order to release a flow of still greater enjoyment. I made frenzied efforts to bring on this feeling . . . I did not yet know the technique, and finally I wept bitterly in the throes of an unappeasable sexual excitement.

The tickling, the urging and throbbing in my sex rose to an ever greater and more powerful crescendo, my vulva was swollen, my clitoris stiffly erect. I rubbed my legs against each other, it felt good, but all it did was to heighten the tickling sensation and finally I could not stand it anymore! My hand had to reach for the tickling spot in order to ease the tension but even this action required ever greater pressure; I rubbed the vulva with the finger and the more I rubbed, the more frenziedly did my fingers go to work in the center of my voluptuousness, the more beatific became the feeling of happiness, a moan escaped my lips and the images of my fantasy filled my senses with a never suspected ecstasy. My hand was under the compulsion to rub faster, ever faster, at the focal point . . . I was still fully a novice—until at last the orgasm convulsed my whole body in an avalanche of pleasure. Thereupon my senses faded away . . .

I had never before experienced such a wondrously blissful hour, and when I awoke from the dream, I ambled about like a drunk. Only then did I become aware of the heavenly voluptuary pleasure in birchings and by degrees this passion saturated my whole sensory life. And from this hour onward I began also to understand the step-mother, and spontaneously felt myself drawn to her. I began to love her—although I still received the blows of her birch rod on my bottom! It hurt as much as before, and yet I could not prevent myself from snuggling against her, from kissing and caressing her.

The step-mother seemed to perceive the change in my feeling. When she called me into the bedroom, she always held me close to her, called me her "darling," kissed me and deplored the fact that she was forced to bare my bottom. She caressed me tenderly, and in the midst of these caresses she would furtively slip her right hand under my dress in order to pull down my drawers . . . She furtively "caressed" my drawers down, as it were.

FROM
EDITH CADIVEC

*Eros, The Meaning of My Life**
(*first published 1931, but written earlier, as above*)

Mother turned the book around this way and that and examined it from all sides. It did not take her long to grasp the dimensions of the disaster.

"Casanova! Casanova!" she shrieked wrathfully to the rest of the family members present. Her horror before this state of affairs choked her breathing, her pale face had flushed crimson. Finally she regained her self-control and turning toward me, she asked: "What kind of book is that, you depraved child, and where did you find it? Was this the so-called homework that worried you so much? Answer me. Now!"

So saying, she gingerly took the infamous book between her fingers and held it under my nose. Defiantly, I turned my back on her. The others just stood there as if rooted to the floor, gaping at the scene. If I had been alone with my mother, I would have found impudent excuses and answered her boldly and brazenly. But the shaming reprimand in the presence of my father and my smirking siblings, this public disgrace, totally disarmed me. Tears welled up in my eyes and I remained in my corner, burning with shame and in a state of utter confusion.

"Talk up! Answer! Where did you find it? I'll give you the birching you deserve in front of everybody here."

The threat of the rod on my naked backside was not the worse threat that loomed before me. Face to face with my mother alone

* New York: Grove Press, 1969.

I had humbly submitted to the most violent floggings. But now, as an older girl of twelve, I defended myself against a flogging in the presence of my father and my sisters. Mother perceived the reason for my refusal to submit and observed me with an icy stare. Then her eyes glinted with fury and, in a sudden movement, she tore out a handful of pages from the disreputable book. She turned to my father and declared in a tone of great resolve, not without a touch of hypocrisy: "This has to stop, once and for all. If you don't take energetic steps now, we'll have worse trouble later with our little hoydens. And this one here is more trouble than all the others."

"It's true. The others don't give you half the trouble that this devilish Senta does," Father agreed. "I believe she deserves a thorough arse-warming—and right here and now. But I shouldn't be the one to do it."

"Why not? After all, you are the father, aren't you?"

"Indeed, but I can't punish her because I'm not angry enough with her. You can punish her in my presence, that will shame her all the more and take some of the arrogance out of her. Whip her behind to shreds . . ."

The maid appeared on the threshold to announce that dinner was ready at the very moment my father pronounced the last word. The whole family left for the dining room on the floor below; only I remained in my corner, in defiance of them all. Mother was the last to leave; at the threshold she turned around to me once more and after taking cognizance of my stupid stubbornness, in a very severe and peremptory tone, she declared: "As punishment you will not eat with us today. You will remain in your room until I come back. Is that clear? Don't drive me to extremes or I'll let you have here and now what you certainly can expect later."

Shame welled up in me. I felt my face glowing like a red-hot coal. I could only stammer contritely: "Oh, Mother, please forgive me just this once . . ."

She came up to me, and tried to bend me under her left arm. But she quickly realized that my resistance blocked her from carrying out her obvious intention. When I broke free of her grip, she released me and slapped me resoundingly several times on both cheeks with all her might, temporarily deafening and blinding me. I reeled back under the blow, half dazed, sobbing, and inwardly seething. My mother took advantage of this moment to leave the room.

Hastily, I hurled myself at the door in an attempt to hold her back, but she was already outside and had locked me in the room, turning the key in the lock twice. Full of anger and shame, my senses in a tumult, I threw myself on the bed. Through my brain raced the wildest thoughts of revenge against Dora who had forced the book on me. I imagined myself flogging her naked backside to shreds and this image suffused my whole being with pleasurable sensations.

Little by little, however, a deep depression came over me. I rose from my bed and went out to the balcony, where I sank into a wicker chair. The fresh air cooled my brain and cheeks. I could hear the loud conversation from the dining room, which lay directly under my room. I leaned over the side of the balcony and saw that the window was open. I heard my mother's voice saying:

"It's absolutely impossible to get on peacefully with Senta. Who owns the book, who lent it to her?"

My father's voice followed hers through the open window. Instead of trying to answer her rhetorical question, he struck a warning note: "You mustn't hesitate for an instant to use the rod unsparingly, and sooner or later the children themselves will be thankful to you for it. Mere words, tossed out like bubbles in the air, have no effect on them . . . A good arse-warming helps them remember warnings better than anything else . . ."

This exchange was followed by complete silence; the noonday stillness was broken only by the clink of the cutlery and the clatter of dishes. My anger reached a pitch of absolute fury. I was hungry, sleepy, and utterly exhausted . . .

I was suddenly awakened from my drowsiness by the rattle of the key in the door. Blinking, I recognized my mother's silhouette. She was standing in front of me, holding a long birch rod. The whole family followed behind her, like a pack of sensation-seekers, my father and my five sisters. Their faces mirrored that singular prurience which I myself felt at the prospect of witnessing a flogging.

My mother came up to me without uttering a word and grabbed me firmly by the wrist. With a jerk, she tore me away from the chair and boldly swung me to the center of the room, whereupon she said in an icy command: "Unbutton your bloomers and lay face down and straight across the bed. Out with your naked bottom. I'll give it the whipping it deserves because of your shameful deed!"

Her wicked words plunged me into an abyss of shame. I also realized that any resistance would be useless, since I deserved the thrashing and therefore had to submit to my mother's commands. Trembling, I stuck my hands under my clothes, fingering them confusedly as I tried to find the buttons of my bloomers. My mother waited in front of me impatiently, the birch rod poised in readiness to strike, accompanying the mute scene with utterances that deepened and intensified my shame.

My hands, hidden under the dress, finally found the buttons of my bloomers. I undid them, and my underclothes rolled down to my ankles. Then I bent over the edge of the bed and lifted my dress high above my arched bottom, exposing it fully to the view of all those present. Mother came to my side and after raising all encumbering pieces of clothing still higher, she began to swing the rod viciously.

Swish! Huit! Swish! Huit! Huit! soughed the thin birch branches as they landed on my exposed buttocks. Each blow seared my flesh like a hot iron and the wild sensation of pain first elicited plaintive whimperings from me. Although I squirmed and twisted like a snake and kicked wildly in all directions, I could not ward off this hail of hissing blows as they fell mercilessly on my tender backside. I burst into a terrifying scream and rolled up into a ball in a desperate effort to defend myself.

My father spontaneously rushed to her help; he grabbed me around the waist and his powerful arms easily bent me into a position which inflected my body in the correct angle. Then, in a state of great excitement, he belabored my already burning buttocks with his strong hand.

Under his crackling blows I began to scream, to kick about again, and to defend myself with all my might. My screams were so loud that the cook came running upstairs and stuck her head through the chink of the door to find out what the uproar was all about. When she saw that Father was giving me a sound thrashing, she went back to her kitchen pleased with the sight.

I find it very unseemly for a father to inflict corporal punishment on his daughter's naked bottom, especially if she is on the edge of puberty. A girl can be punished by birching up to the time of her marriage—this I believe is sound and salutary practice —but always on condition that it is the mother or the governess who administers the beating.

My father released me only after his rage subsided. I slumped to the floor and rolled on the carpet. I rubbed my sore buttocks, without thinking of the indecent spectacle I was offering the onlookers in view of my wild despair and confusion. It was the most terrible birching I had ever received. Never in my life had I ever received a similar sound thrashing, in double portion to boot.

"Get up now and pull up your bloomers, Senta. I hope you will take good note of this," said my mother in a soothing tone of voice. I got up dizzily and felt my backside; it was heavy and swollen, like a red-hot ball. I pulled up my bloomers with a feeble motion and arranged my clothes properly. Father came up to me, and in a pacifying tone of voice he admonished me emphatically: "This should teach you a lesson, child. You have been very severely punished, but eventually you will see that your parents have acted correctly. And now, try to mend your ways."

Overcome by tender family feelings, I took a few steps toward my mother, threw my arms around her neck, and hid my face in her bosom. I sobbed heart-rendingly. She loosened herself from my embrace, kissed me fleetingly on the forehead, and left the room with the others.

Once I was alone I fell prey to an extraordinary sensual excitement. A tickling stimulus in my private parts threw me into a turmoil. I pulled down my bloomers, threw myself on the bed, lifted my clothes over my head, and spread my legs. I daydreamed wonderfully about Dora's stark-naked bottom being flogged as never before . . . Fancy conjured up the most voluptuous images of a birching . . . My fingers unconsciously played with my clitoris, the area around which was moist with sexual excitation for a long time, until my consciousness was buried under an avalanche of voluptuousness.

When I went to school the next day, the teacher made it quite obvious that she was fully and exactly informed about the disagreeable story of the forbidden book. She pointed at Dora and branded her as an evildoer before the whole class. Someone had taken the trouble to hand the book over to the teacher and to disclose the secret to her with all proper discretion. She took the Casanova book from her desk and fastened it up on the wall . . .

At that time thrashings were not only administered in families, but also in schools. Dora, a thirteen-year-old girl, had not only lent the book to me but had secretly removed it from her father's library. When the teacher called her to account for it, Dora flatly denied it and named as the real culprit another girl who had nothing at all to do with the matter. After reaching the end of her patience, the teacher announced that Dora was to be punished before the whole class.

During this announcement all eyes in the classroom fell on Dora, whose pretty face reddened with shame. She bowed her head with a saintliness that was hypocritical sham, because I could notice that under her lengthy whimpers she was winking over to me and striving mightily to suppress an outburst of mocking laughter. She believed that I had betrayed her. I was in a state of wild excitement and trembled all over with a lustful craving for a look at her naked bottom.

At the close of the lesson the teacher pulled from her desk a fresh birch rod, obviously prepared in advance, summoned Dora to stand before her, adjusted a chair, and then ordered her to kneel on the seat. In a trice the poor girl's clothes were flung high above her back, her bloomers were pulled down and her rotund buttocks revealed to view. Dora remained in this position for several minutes, exposed to the scrutiny of all her classmates. She had a white, well-formed bottom, voluptuous and beautiful in its lines, as I had envisioned it in my fantasies. Dora contracted the charming buttocks so close together that the dividing line almost disappeared, and she sobbed bitterly into her handkerchief.

As the teacher's rod swished on the smooth, white rotundities, Dora grew desperate and began to scream so loud that the nerves of all the onlookers quivered with excitement. Her screams ring in my ears to this very day: "Forgive me . . . *Fräulein* teacher . . . please forgive me! . . . oooh . . . ooh . . . ohohoh . . . I won't . . . do it . . . again . . . ooooo . . . forgive me . . . ooooooooooooo,"

Her act of contrition, however, had come too late because the teacher now took no notice of her shrill screams. Unflinchingly, she landed spirited blows on the repentant sinner's scarlet red buttocks . . . *Swish!* . . . *Swish!* . . . *Swish!* . . . *Swish!* . . . Her flogged bottom danced and hopped according to this beat time, now expanding and contracting, now spreading the hams apart, now protruding toward the class and pulling itself in, only to meet again with the pitiless birch.

As if in a frenzy, the teacher counted, loud and slow, the blows that she landed on Dora's bottom, so slow indeed that she always counted two blows for one. She lashed Dora's red-hot and welt-covered buttocks pitilessly and vigorously without pause and her frenzy seemed to know no bounds.

Finally the procedure was over.

The teacher looked as though she were drunk and she was breathing heavily. Dora rose to her feet with feeble movements, dried her tears, and rushed, unnoticed, out of the room. I, however, had enjoyed this punishment scene.

It had a terrific impact on me and sent me into raptures. Even long after I fed upon the remembered voluptuousness of the scene. I clearly saw the glowing, welted, dancing, twitching buttocks. I distinctly heard Dora's mad moaning in my ears, and with this vision in mind I sexually excited myself.

At this moment, of course, it is not possible for me to report on each case in which our teacher's birch rod threatened the smooth bottoms of her charges of both sexes, and just as little on the many pretexts which our parents knew how to find when it was a question of administering the favorite arse-warmings to us. But the older I grew, the more intensely I felt that I was no longer able to separate my sensual excitements from the corporal punishment administered to stark-naked bottoms.

When I was fourteen years old, a cousin of the same age visited our house during vacation time. He was tall and very handsome, and in him I had a welcome playmate. My mother was very fond of him and kissed and fondled him frequently. I soon noticed that when she kissed him she stroked and pinched his butt at the same time, and that the boy on such occasions clung very closely to her.

In the evening, when my sisters and I went to bed at nine o'clock, she always accompanied him to his room. Kurt, my cousin, later told me that his aunt remained in the room until he lay in bed wholly undressed. Then playfully she kissed his naked bottom and gently slapped it.

Yet this was not my mother's only aim. She earnestly wanted to birch her nephew. It goes without saying that she finally found a pretext, whereby I was also guilty. One day as we were playing, Kurt threw the ball through a window. I was his play partner and I had incited him to do it. Enraged, Mother called us into the room where she waited for our arrival with her cat-o'-nine-tails.

On this day I witnessed my handsome cousin being flogged on his naked behind by my mother. This was my undoing. If I say this, it is also certainly true, even though my earlier experiences had already made their contribution. It was the first time that I became distinctly conscious of the sensations that swept over me when I saw this fourteen-year-old boy with his pants pulled down and buttocks exposed, confused with shame and fear, awaiting punishment.

My mother pulled Kurt toward her and forced him to bend over her knee. Her severe words sounded almost like verbal caresses and my cousin's flattering pleas for forgiveness were exceedingly exciting, sensually. I floated on the surface of hitherto unknown oceans of bliss, and I did not understand what was happening to me . . .

When Mother began to flog the boy's bottom, the buttocks surged like waves before my eyes, turning and twisting in enigmatic movements, expanding and contracting, dancing and leaping crazily under the cracking blows of the whip . . . Kurt pressed his belly very close against Mother's knee in a backward and forward motion, and his plaintive cry sounded like a voluptuous moan . . . I felt the sensual stimulus powerfully in my private parts. I felt the pulse beat of my raging blood hammering in my vulva. I felt close to fainting and almost threatened to sink to the floor, overpowered by the excitement.

Finally the birching of my cousin came to an end and Mother called me to her side. I took a few tottering steps in her direction and noticed a big wet spot on her clothing, which stemmed from Kurt; crying with pleasure, I threw myself over her lap. I felt the abyss of my sensuality opening up and I surrendered myself as prey to my sensations.

Without pulling up his trousers, Kurt came to my mother's assistance. He grabbed me firmly by the wrists and brutally shoved his knee against the nape of my neck in order to force my face toward the floor. My clothes were pulled up, but my mother's nervous hands did not find the buttons of my bloomers right away . . . The preparations seemed endless. Mother, my cousin, and I lost consciousness of our surroundings. The frenzy of the flogging gripped the three of us and transported us to a state of rapturous bliss.

As though hypnotized, I remained breathless, without moving. All I could do was to tremble helplessly in frenzied excitement. Suddenly like a lightning flash, I felt the cool air blowing on my naked bottom. My smooth buttocks quivered with a pleasurable sensation and pressed convulsively against each other. The first blow smacked against the tightly drawn arches of my backside with an unheard-of force. Defenseless, I opened my mouth to scream, but Kurt drowned my wail under his weight. The subsequent blows fell like hailstones on my squirming and twisting backside, which helplessly surrendered to its tormentors.

About twenty blows rained on my burning buttocks without letup, in a rising tempo. My head was clamped between my cousin's knees, my body rocked back and forth on the lap of my rod-wielding mother, without the possibility of finding a balance . . . The reciprocal engagement between the biting leather thong and my glowing buttocks seemed never to end . . .

At times, under an especially strong blow, I became limp, my muscular tension relaxed. I spread my legs far apart. My knees lost their stiffness and I pressed my vulva in wild excitement against Mother's knee. Moaning, I yielded myself completely to the pricking hail of blows. I rocked and raised my backside up and down until in a final thrust against her knee I stiffened my whole body anew and strained every nerve in order to receive the last blows in the wildest orgasm of pleasure.

My bottom burned like fire, but I no longer distinguished between pleasure and pain. I felt only the mad sexual excitement which grew from second to second into the incommensurable. I heard my mother breathe heavily, and my own heart was beating as if it would burst . . . Finally, in a moment of unendurable tension my mother left off flogging me and I reached the peak of sexual ecstasy in the clamp formed by my cousin's knee.

I sank into a state suffused by a feeling of absolute eternity . . . I don't know how long it was before I came to normal consciousness. I did not breathe, I lay there bathed in perspiration, everything reeling around me. Slowly the magic spell waned. I slid down from my mother's knees and left the room with a tottering step. I staggered forth and threw myself drunkenly on my bed. I remained in the same position all night, motionless, without taking a breath. My consciousness was in a state of total dissolution and thrills of delight rolled over me like huge, heaving waves . . .

In the middle of the night, walking in my sleep, I crept into my cousin's room and wordlessly laid myself alongside him in bed. He, too, was lying sleepless and dreaming blissful dreams in a waking state. He clamped his arms around me and whispered the revelations and sensual experiences of his fourteen years into my ear. He told me undreamed-of things about love and voluptuousness as his hand played with my sex, producing the very pleasures of which he spoke. He also guided my hand to his stiffened member and taught me the caresses which gave him pleasure. His warm flow of semen spurted in fits and starts over my fingers and I remained rigid with excitement . . . I remembered the moist spot on my mother's clothing after Kurt's punishment, the explanation of the occurrence was obvious . . . Pleasure racked both our bodies in the torrential flood of the orgasm.

We were bound together by secrecy after that experience. Kurt had a hidden penchant for cruelty and he took a mystic joy in practicing physical tortures. He inflicted them on himself before my very eyes and described the pleasure that he experienced in so doing. In order to feel this painful pleasure continuously, he had dreamed up the idea of trimming his trousers with pins which would penetrate into his flesh with every movement that he made. He loved fanatically to be birched on his naked bottom by my mother or to watch corporal punishment being dealt out to others. Without indulging in ambiguous thoughts or reveries, he sought only the sensation of pain, which alone brought him to the thrill of pleasure.

When we were alone, he invented bizarre and dangerous exercises, during which he spilled his semen before my eyes. He subjected his body to the weirdest tests and at the same time he tried his best to hurt me by devising all possible tortures. He stuck pins in my bottom, or dug deeply into my flesh with his sharp fingernails, while he himself for hours endured the strange puzzling torture of feeling his penis and testicles tightly bound with string to his body. For him it was a pleasure to suffer and to make others suffer.

My heart was seized with a feeling of physical love for the boy who was of the same age as myself. I perceived that there was no contradiction between pleasure and cruelty, but that both were fused into one, like body and soul.

FROM
PAULINE RÉAGE

Story of O*
1954

Their destination was not the apartment near the Observatoire where O had first met Anne-Marie, but a low-lying two-story house at the end of a large garden, on the edge of the Fontainebleau Forest. Since that first day, O had been wearing the whalebone corset that Anne-Marie had deemed so essential: each day she had tightened it a little more, until now her waist was scarcely larger than the circle formed by her ten fingers; Anne-Marie ought to be pleased.

When they arrived it was two o'clock in the afternoon, the whole house was asleep, and the dog barked faintly when they rang the bell: a big, shaggy, sheepdog that sniffed at O's knees beneath her skirt. Anne-Marie was sitting under a copper beech tree on the edge of the lawn which, in one corner of the garden, faced the windows of her bedroom. She did not get up.

"Here's O," Sir Stephen said. "You know what has to be done with her. When will she be ready?"

Anne-Marie glanced at O. "You mean you haven't told her? All right, I'll begin immediately. You should probably allow ten days after it's over. I imagine you'll want to put the rings and monogram on yourself? Come back in two weeks. The whole business should be finished two weeks after that."

O started to ask a question.

"Just a minute, O," Anne-Marie said, "go into the front bed-

* New York: Grove Press, 1966.

room over there, get undressed but keep your sandals on, and
come back."

The room, a large white bedroom with heavy purple Jouy
print drapes, was empty. O put her bag, her gloves, and her clothes
on a small chair near a closet door. There was no mirror. She
went back outside and, dazzled by the bright sunlight, walked
slowly back over to the shade of the beech tree. Sir Stephen was
still standing in front of Anne-Marie, the dog at his feet. Anne-
Marie's black hair, streaked with gray, shone as though she had
used some kind of cream on it, her blue eyes seemed black. She
was dressed in white, with a patent-leather belt around her waist,
and she was wearing patent-leather sandals which revealed the
bright red nail polish on the toenails of her bare feet, the same
color polish she was wearing on her fingernails.

"O," she said, "kneel down in front of Sir Stephen."

O obliged, her arms crossed behind her back, the tips of her
breasts quivering. The dog tensed, as though he were about to
spring at her.

"Down, Turk," Anne-Marie ordered. Then: "Do you consent,
O, to bear the rings and the monogram with which Sir Stephen
desires you to be marked, without knowing how they will be
placed upon you?"

"I do," O said.

"All right then, I'm going to walk Sir Stephen to his car. Stay
here."

As Anne-Marie got up from her chaise longue, Sir Stephen
bent down and took O's breasts in his hands. He kissed her on
the mouth and murmured:

"Are you mine, O, are you really mine?" then turned and left
her, to follow Anne-Marie. The gate banged shut, Anne-Marie
was coming back. O, her legs folded beneath her was sitting on
her heels and had her arms on her knees, like an Egyptian statue.

There were three other girls living in the house, all of whom
had a bedroom on the second floor. O was given a small bedroom
on the ground floor, adjoining Anne-Marie's. Anne-Marie called
up to them to come down into the garden. Like O, all three of

them were naked. The only persons in this gynaeceum—which
was carefully concealed by the high walls and by closed shutters
over the windows which overlooked a narrow dirt road—the only
persons who wore clothes were Anne-Marie and the three servants:
a cook and two maids, all of whom were older than Anne-Marie,
three severe, dour women in their black alpaca skirts and stiffly
starched aprons.

"Her name is O," said Anne-Marie, who had sat down again.
"Bring her over to me so I can get a better look at her." Two of
the girls helped O to her feet: they were both brunettes, their
hair as dark as their fleece below, and the nipples of their breasts
were large and dark, almost purple. The other girl was a short,
plump redhead, and the chalky skin of her bosom was crisscrossed
by a terrifying network of green veins. The two girls pushed O
till she was right next to Anne-Marie, who pointed to the three
black stripes that showed on the front of her thighs and were repeated on her buttocks.

"Who whipped you?" she asked. "Sir Stephen?"

"Yes," O said.

"When? and with what?"

"Three days ago, with a riding crop."

"Starting tomorrow, and for a month thereafter, you will not
be whipped. But today you will, to mark your arrival, as soon as
I've had a chance to examine you. Has Sir Stephen ever whipped
you on the inside of your thighs, with your legs spread wide? No?
It's true, men don't know how to. Well, we'll soon see. Show me
your waist. Yes, it's much better!"

Anne-Marie pressed O's waist to make it even more wasplike.
Then she sent the redhead to fetch another corset and had them
put it on her. It was also made of black nylon, but was so stiffly
whaleboned and so narrow that it looked for all the world like an
extremely wide belt. It had no garter straps. One of the girls
laced it up as tight as she could, with Anne-Marie lending her
encouragement as she pulled on the laces as hard as she could.

"This is dreadful," O said. "I don't know whether I can bear
it."

"That's the whole point," Anne-Marie said. "You're much, much lovelier than you were, but the problem was you didn't lace it tight enough. You're going to wear it this way every day. But tell me now, how did Sir Stephen prefer using you? I need to know."

She had seized O's womb with her whole hand, and O could not reply. Two of the girls were seated on the lawn, the third, one of the brunettes, was seated on the foot of Anne-Marie's chaise longue.

"Turn her around for me, girls, so I can see her back," Anne-Marie said.

She was turned around and bent over, and the hands of both girls vented her.

"Of course," Anne-Marie went on, "there was no need for you to tell me. You'll have to be marked on the rear. Stand up. We're going to put on your bracelets. Colette, go get the box, we'll draw lots to see who will whip you. Bring the tokens, Colette, then we'll go to the music room."

Colette was the taller of the two dark-haired girls, the other's name was Claire; the short redhead was named Yvonne. O had not noticed till now that they were all wearing, as at Roissy, a leather collar and leather bracelets on their wrists. They were also wearing similar bracelets around their ankles.

When Yvonne had chosen some bracelets that fit O and put them on her, Anne-Marie handed O four tokens and asked her to give one to each of the girls, without looking at the numbers on them. O handed out the tokens. The three girls each looked at theirs but said nothing, waiting for Anne-Marie to speak.

"I have number two," Anne-Marie said. "Who has number one?"

Colette had number one.

"All right, take O away, she's all yours."

Colette seized O's arms and joined her hands behind her back; she fastened the bracelets together and pushed O ahead of her. On the threshold of a French door that opened into a small wing which formed an L with the front of the house, Yvonne, who was leading the way, removed her sandals. The light entering through the French door revealed a room the far end of which formed a kind of raised rotunda; the ceiling, in the shape of a shallow cupola, was supported by two narrow columns set about six feet apart. This dais was about four steps high and, in the area between the columns, projected further into the room in a gentle arc. The floor of the rotunda, like that of the rest of the room, was covered with a red felt carpet. The walls were white, the curtains on the windows red, and the sofas set in a semicircle facing the rotunda were upholstered in the same red felt material as the carpet on the floor. In the rectangular portion of the room there was a fireplace which was wider than it was deep, and opposite the fireplace a large console-type combination record player and radio, with shelves of records on both sides. This was why it was called the music room, which communicated directly with Anne-Marie's bedroom via a door near the fireplace. The identical door on the other side of the fireplace opened into a closet. Aside from the record player and the sofas, the room had no furniture.

While Colette had O sit down on the edge of the platform, which in this center portion between the columns made a vertical drop to the floor—the steps having been placed to the left and right of the columns—the two other girls, after first having closed the Venetian blinds a trifle, shut the French door. O was surprised to note that it was a double door, and Anne-Marie, who was laughing, said: "That's so no one can hear you scream. And the walls are lined with cork. Don't worry, no one can hear the slightest thing that goes on in here. Now lie down."

She took her by both shoulders and laid her back, then pulled her slightly forward. O's hands were clutching the edge of the platform—Yvonne having attached them to a ring set in the platform—and her buttocks were thus suspended in mid-air. Anne-Marie made her raise her legs toward her chest, then O suddenly felt her legs, still doubled-up above her, being pulled taut in the same direction: straps had been fastened to her ankle bracelets and thence to the columns on either side, while she lay thus between them on this raised dais exposed in such a way that the only

part of her which was visible was the double cleft of her womb
and her buttocks violently quartered. Anne-Marie caressed the
inside of her thighs.

"It's the most tender spot of the whole body," she said, "be
careful not to harm it. Not too hard now, Colette."

Colette was standing over her, astride her at the level of her
waist, and in the bridge formed by her dark legs O could see the
tassles of the whip she was holding in her hand. As the first blows
burned into her loins, O moaned. Colette alternated from left to
right, paused, then started again. O struggled with all her might,
she thought the straps would tear her limb from limb. She did
not want to grovel, she did not want to beg for mercy. And yet
that was precisely what Anne-Marie intended wringing from her
lips.

"Faster," she said to Colette, "and harder."

O braced herself, but it was no use. A minute later she could
bear it no more, she screamed and burst into tears, while Anne-
Marie caressed her face.

"Just a second longer," she said, "and it will be over. Only five
more minutes. She can scream for five minutes. It's twenty-five
past, Colette. Stop when it's half past, when I tell you to."

But O was screaming: "No, no, for God's sake don't!" screaming that she couldn't bear it, no, she couldn't bear the torture another second. And yet she endured it to the bitter end, and after
Colette had left the little stage, Anne-Marie smiled at her.

"Thank me," she said to O, and O thanked her.

She knew very well why Anne-Marie had wanted, above all
else, to have her whipped. That the female of the species was as
cruel as, and more implacable than, the male, O had never
doubted for a minute. But O suspected that Anne-Marie was less
interested in making a spectacle of her power than she was in
establishing between O and herself a sense of complicity. O had
never really understood, but she had finally come to accept as an
undeniable and important verity, this constant and contradictory
jumble of her emotions: she liked the idea of torture, but when
she was being tortured herself she would have betrayed the whole
world to escape it, and yet when it was over she was happy to

have gone through it, happier still if it had been especially cruel
and prolonged. Anne-Marie had been correct in her assumptions
both as to O's acquiescence and as to her revolt, and knew that her
pleas for mercy were indeed genuine. There was still a third reason
for what she had done, which she explained to O. She was bent on
proving to every girl who came into her house, and who was fated
to live in a totally feminine universe, that her condition as a
woman should not be minimized or denigrated by the fact that
she was in contact only with other women, but that, on the contrary, it should be heightened and intensified. That was why she
required that the girls be constantly naked; the way in which O
was flogged, as well as the position in which she was bound, had
no other purpose. Today it was O who would remain for the rest
of the afternoon—for three more hours—exposed on the dais, her
legs raised and spread. Tomorrow it would be Claire, or Colette,
or Yvonne, whom O would contemplate in turn. It was a technique
much too slow and meticulous (as was the way the whip was
wielded) to be used at Roissy. But O would see how efficient it
was. Apart from the rings and the letters she would wear when
she left, she would be returned to Sir Stephen more open, and
more profoundly enslaved, than she had ever before thought
possible . . . Marie, who was responsible for the two basic models
of dresses, knowing where Sir Stephen's preference lay in using O,
had proposed a type of slacks which would be supported in front
by the blouse and, on both sides, have long zippers, thus allowing
the back flap to be lowered without taking off the slacks. But Sir
Stephen refused. It was true that he used O, when he did not
have recourse to her mouth, almost invariably as he would have
a boy. But O had had ample opportunity to notice that when she
was near him, even when he did not particularly desire her, he
loved to take hold of her womb, mechanically as it were, take hold
of and tug at her fleece with his hand, to pry her open and
burrow at length within. The pleasure O derived from holding
Jacqueline in much the same way, moist, and burning between
her locked fingers, was ample evidence and a guarantee of Sir
Stephen's pleasure. She understood why he did not want any
extraneous obstacles set in the path of that pleasure.

Hatless, wearing practically no make-up, her hair completely free, O looked like a well-brought-up little girl, dressed as she was in her twilled stripe or polka dot, navy blue-and-white or gray-and-white pleated sun-skirts and the fitted bolero buttoned at the neck, or in her more conservative dresses of black nylon. Everywhere Sir Stephen escorted her she was taken for his daughter, or his niece, and this mistake was abetted by the fact that he, in addressing her, employed the *tu* form, whereas she employed the *vous*. Alone together in Paris, strolling through the streets to window shop, or walking along the quays, where the paving stones were dusty because the weather had been so dry, they evinced no surprise at seeing the passers-by smile at them, the way people smile at people who are happy.

Once in a while Sir Stephen would push her into the recess of a porte-cochere, or beneath the archway of a building, which was always slightly dark, and from which there rose the musty odor of ancient cellars, and he would kiss her and tell her he loved her. O would hook her heels over the sill of the porte-cochere out of which the regular pedestrian door had been cut. They caught a glimpse of a courtyard in the rear, with lines of laundry drying in the windows. Leaning on one of the balconies, a blonde girl would be staring fixedly at them. A cat would slip between their legs. Thus did they stroll through the Gobelins district, by Saint-Marcel, along the rue Mouffetard, to the area known as the Temple, and to the Bastille.

Once Sir Stephen suddenly steered O into a wretched brothel-like hotel, where the desk clerk first wanted them to fill out the forms, but then said not to bother if it was only for an hour. The wallpaper in the room was blue, with enormous golden peonies, the window looked out onto a pit whence rose the odor of garbage cans. However weak the light bulb at the head of the bed, you could still see streaks of face powder and forgotten hairpins on the mantelpiece. On the ceiling above the bed was a large mirror.

Once, but only once, Sir Stephen invited O to lunch with two of his compatriots who were passing through Paris. He came for her an hour before she was ready, and instead of having her driven to his place, he came to the quai de Bethune.

O had finished bathing, but she had not done her hair or put on her make-up, and was not dressed. To her surprise, she saw that Sir Stephen was carrying a golf bag, though she saw no clubs in it. But she soon got over her surprise: Sir Stephen told her to open the bag. Inside were several leather riding crops, two fairly thick ones of red leather, two that were long and thin of black leather, a scourge with long lashes of green leather, each of which was folded back at the end to form a loop, a dog's whip made of a thick, single lash whose handle was of braided leather and, last but not least, leather bracelets of the sort used at Roissy, plus some rope. O laid them out side by side on the unmade bed. No matter how accustomed she became to seeing them, no matter what resolutions she made about them, she could not keep from trembling. Sir Stephen took her in his arms.

"Which do you prefer, O?" he asked her.

But she could hardly speak, and already could feel the sweat running down her arms.

"Which do you prefer?" he repeated. "All right," he said, confronted by her silence, "first you're going to help me."

He asked her for some nails, and having found a way to arrange them in a decorative manner, whips and riding crops crossed, he showed O a panel of wainscoting between her mirror and the fireplace, opposite her bed, which would be ideal for them. He hammered some nails into the wood. There were rings on the ends of the handles of the whips and riding crops, by which they could be suspended from the nails, a system which allowed each whip to be easily taken down and returned to its place on the wall. Thus, together with the bracelets and the rope, O would have, opposite her bed, the complete array of her instruments of torture. It was a handsome panoply, as harmonious as the wheel and spikes in the paintings of Saint Catherine the Martyr, as the nails and hammer, the crown of thorns, the spear and scourges portrayed in the paintings of the Crucifixion. When Jacqueline came back . . . but all this involved Jacqueline, involved her deeply. She would have to reply to Sir Stephen's question: O could not, he chose the dog whip himself.

In a tiny private dining room of the La Pérouse restaurant,

along the quays of the Left Bank, a room on the third floor whose
dark walls were brightened by Watteau-like figures in pastel colors
who resembled actors of the puppet theater, O was ensconced
alone on the sofa, with one of Sir Stephen's friends in an armchair
to her right, another to her left, and Sir Stephen across from her.
She remembered already having seen one of the men at Roissy, but
she could not recall having been taken by him. The other was a
tall, red-haired boy with gray eyes, who could not have been more
than twenty-five. In two words, Sir Stephen told them why he had
invited O, and what she was. Listening to him, O was once again
astonished at the coarseness of his language. But then, how did
she expect to be referred to, if not as a whore, a girl who, in the
presence of three men (not to mention the restaurant waiters who
kept trooping in and out, since luncheon was still being served)
would open her bodice to bare her breasts, the tips of which had
been reddened with lipstick, as they could see, as they could also
see from the purple furrows across her milk-white skin that she
had been flogged?

The meal went on for a long time, and the two Englishmen
drank a great deal. Over coffee, when the liqueurs had been
served, Sir Stephen pushed the table back against the opposite
wall and, after having lifted her skirt to show his friends how O
was branded and in irons, left her to them.

The man she had met at Roissy wasted no time with her: without leaving his armchair, without even touching her with his
fingertips, he ordered her to kneel down in front of him, take him
and caress his sex until he discharged in her mouth. After which,
he made her straighten out his clothing, and then he left.

But the red-haired lad, who had been completely overwhelmed
by O's submissiveness and meek surrender, by her irons and the
welts which he had glimpsed on her body, took her by the hand
instead of throwing himself upon her as she had expected, and
descended the stairs, paying not the slightest heed to the sly
smiles of the waiters and, after hailing a taxi, took her back to his
hotel room. He did not let her go till nightfall, after having fran-
tically plowed her fore and aft, both of which he bruised and belabored unmercifully, he being of an uncommon size and rigidity

and, what is more, being totally intoxicated by the sudden freedom granted him to penetrate a woman doubly and be embraced by her in the way he had seen her ordered to a short while before (something he had never before dared ask of anyone).

The following day, when O arrived at Sir Stephen's at two o'clock in answer to his summons, she found him looking older and his face careworn.

"Eric has fallen head over heels in love with you, O," he told her. "This morning he called on me and begged me to grant you your freedom. He told me he wants to marry you. He wants to save you. You see how I treat you if you're mine, O, and if you are mine you have no right to refuse my commands; but you also know that you are always free to choose *not* to be mine. I told him so. He's coming back here at three."

O burst out laughing. "Isn't it a little late?" she said. "You're both quite mad. If Eric had not come by this morning, what would you have done with me this afternoon? We would have gone for a walk, nothing more? Then let's go for a walk. Or perhaps you would not have summoned me this afternoon? In that case I'll leave. . . ."

"No," Sir Stephen broke in, "I would have called you, but not to go for a walk. I wanted . . . "

"Go on, say it."

"Come, it will be simpler to show you."

He got up and opened a door in the wall opposite the fireplace, a door identical to the one into his office.

O had always thought that the door led into a closet which was no longer used. She saw a tiny bedroom, newly painted, and hung with dark red silk. Half of the room was occupied by a rounded stage flanked by two columns, identical to the stage in the music room at Samois.

"The walls and ceiling are lined with cork, are they not?" O said. "And the door is padded, and you've had a double window installed?"

Sir Stephen nodded.

"But since when has all this been done?" O said.

"Since you've been back."

"Then why? . . ."

"Why did I wait until today? Because I first wanted to hand you over to other men. Now I shall punish you for it. I've never punished you, O."

"But I belong to you," O said. "Punish me."

FROM
ANONYMOUS

Harriet Marwood, Governess[*]
emended ed., 1967

But Harriet, fully aware as she was of the influence she had over her ward, was nonetheless determined to place herself once and for all in a position where she would never again be challenged by a rival. The intrusion of an Alicia Barrington into the schedule of her plans was, she saw, an occurrence that must not be repeated.

For the next two days she left Richard to himself; and, as she had foreseen, he improved the occasion of his freedom by continuing to see the young woman by whom his vanity was so subtly flattered. This circumstance caused Harriet neither surprise nor disappointment; she was well aware of his weakness, egoism, and indecision—and indeed these very traits, which she had herself encouraged for years, were such as she desired and valued in the man of her choice. Accordingly, one morning she announced to him that she had made arrangements for them to go bathing.

"Everything is in readiness, my dear," she told him. "Let us go to the beach at once."

Richard was delighted. The weather had turned very warm, and for some time he had been distinctly envious of the bathers who were enjoying the water. He accepted the parcel Harriet had made of their effects, and set off eagerly at her side.

His pleasure knew no bounds when he discovered that she had engaged a bathing-machine immediately beside the Barringtons' own. Now at last, he was thinking, Harriet would meet Alicia. He looked for the young girl, but she had not yet arrived; as he

[*] New York: Grove Press, 1967.

set up the beach umbrella and disposed the blanket and cushions under Harriet's direction, he kept casting glances along the parade, and was at last rewarded by the sight of Alicia and her two friends approaching.

The young people greeted each other effusively; introductions were made, and Richard was tremulous with excitement at the idea of Harriet and Alicia having become acquaintances. Soon the party separated to change into bathing costume.

In the privacy of their bathing-machine Harriet undressed herself leisurely; Richard, his eyes modestly averted, waited until she was ready, and only then allowed himself to survey her with his habitual air of furtive adoration. And on this occasion she was indeed a striking figure. The plain black costume, clinging closely to her body, displayed her magnificent outlines to the greatest advantage, accenting the strong thighs, the well-turned hips, and the deep swell of her chest which bore her superb breasts with the rigidity of a cuirass; a kerchief of oiled silk, passed around her head, completed the elegance of her appearance. She looked at Richard with a smile.

"And here is your own bathing dress," she said, picking up a jersey and a pair of belted trunks made of soft snow-white wool. "Put it on, and we will go."

He obeyed swiftly; but when he was ready he turned to the long strip of mirror in some doubt and trepidation. What he saw did not greatly reassure him. The short-sleeved jersey, moulded smoothly to his torso, was designed with an eye to modesty and came to his very neck; but the trunks, as if to redress this excess of decorum, were another matter: extremely tight, they were quite adequate in front, but at the back, where they were cut unusually high, the nude and swelling curves were displayed with an effect of such daring that he quailed, turning to Harriet with a questioning look.

"Perfect!" she said, her glance taking him in from head to foot. "Now put this on, and let us go." And she held out a bathing-cap of thick white rubber, of the style which fastens under the chin.

He recoiled in dismay. "But . . . but, Harriet . . . " he began to protest.

Her face became stern. "Did you hear me? Put on your cap at once, sir! I am taking no chance of your getting sunstroke or earache, believe me. Come now, quickly!" With these words she picked up her cape and threw it over her shoulders.

Richard, suddenly seeing the leather whip hanging from the same peg on which her cape had been, hastened to don the rubber cap without further parley. Then he turned to the mirror, and surveyed his image with astonishment.

The figure that he saw reflected was, except in the matter of breasts, almost indistinguishable from that of a girl: there were the same slender arms, the full hips, the long, tapering legs, and crowning all this the feminine face framed by the outlines of the bathing-cap. He stepped back, turning an imploring look on his guardian.

But she was gazing at him with a peculiar expression. "My dear," she murmured, advancing suddenly and taking him in her arms. As she fastened her lips to his he felt her hand pass lightly behind him. When she withdrew her mouth she held him by the shoulders, looking at him with humid, swimming eyes; then she kissed him again with a fierce, possessive ardor, her hand, pressed now to the back of his capped head, uniting their mouths closely. When she drew away the second time, her face was still beaming with desire and admiration.

"Ah, you are adorable that way, Richard," she said. "Come, let us go now."

And so flattered and moved was he by Harriet's whole-souled approval of his appearance that, forgetting all his embarrassment of the minute before, he stepped out on the beach with an utter absence of self-consciousness: almost, indeed, with an air of pride. Without a qualm he heard the little murmur of astonishment that rose from Alicia and her two friends when they saw him; looking at them coolly, he passed without a flicker of his eyes, smiling his greeting at them, and then matching his step to Harriet's in obedience to her announcement that they would first take a short walk along the beach.

As they walked, Richard was pleasantly conscious of the looks that were turned on Harriet and himself from every side. And in fact they were a striking couple—the tall, masterful young woman whose cape, falling open occasionally, gave a glimpse of the superb body beneath it, and the tender youth who walked beside her, apparently unaware of the charms which his costume displayed with such a bold and interesting effect. And had Richard known the impression made on most of the onlookers he would have been no less complacent; he was, however, unaware that his figure and costume gave color to the belief that he was a girl himself.

When they returned to their place on the beach Harriet removed her cape and spread it under the umbrella. Richard noticed the interest with which the three slender, immature girls regarded his guardian's beautifully modelled figure as she walked to the water's edge ahead of him. They waded in together.

"Do not go any deeper than this, Richard," she told him when the water reached their waists. "I will be back soon." She immersed herself with a single graceful movement, and began swimming away with a strong, leisurely side-stroke.

Richard, regretting his inability to swim, remained in the shallows and dipped up and down. Greatly refreshed by the cool salt water, he was nevertheless fearful of letting his head go beneath the surface; he was inclined to be afraid of the water.

And now Alicia, blonde and willowy in her pale-blue bathing dress, led her friends into the sea. Soon they were splashing, laughing, and ducking each other close beside him; and soon, too, Alicia called out to him to join them in their ducking game. With a feeling of innocent pleasure he found himself pressing the yielding heads beneath the surface for an instant or two; and when it came to his own turn to be ducked, holding his nose and taking a deep breath at Alicia's friendly bidding, he found an equal pleasure in feeling the strong young hands bearing down on his capped head.

Indeed, there was a great deal of happy shouting and carefree laughter among these young people as they sported in the blue water and the brilliant sunlight! What fun it is to play like this with girls, Richard was thinking when, hearing his governess calling him, he saw she had returned. With a wave of his hand to his playmates, he left them at once and waded over to Harriet.

"Well, Richard," she said in a pleasant tone, ignoring his companions who had suddenly grown silent, "it is time for you to have a swimming lesson. You must learn to swim, you know."

"Oh yes, Miss," he said. "I should so much like to learn."

The suppressed titter that escaped one of the girls made Richard flush. But Harriet, paying no attention, merely said to him, "Wait here while I put on my cap." In a moment she had returned, a plain black cap framing her handsome face in which he now thought to detect a certain mysterious resolve.

The girls gathered around them as, obeying Harriet's instructions, he lowered himself in the water beside her, and then, with his chin supported above the surface by her hand, began moving his arms as she directed.

"Very good," she said. "And now, move your legs in the same way." And supporting his body with her other hand, she encouraged him with words of approval. Then all at once she withdrew her hand from beneath his chin. With an effort he managed to keep his head above the surface, thrashing out wildly with his arms; then his head sank, he swallowed a mouthful of water, and when Harriet at last released her hold he came to the suface gasping and choking.

Harriet smiled. "We shall try that again, Richard," she said. "Come now."

"Please . . ."

"Not a word, sir."

The three girls remained silent, exchanging curious looks.

Three or four more times Richard endured this miserable experience until, his throat and nose stinging from the salt water, his eyes streaming, in despair and almost ready to weep, he suddenly found he was able to keep his head up himself.

"Bravo, Richard!" called Alicia gaily.

"Very good," said Harriet, her expression impassive. "Now you must do the same with your legs."

Once more she held him under the chin and body. But when

she ceased to support the latter, his legs sank again and again.

"Come, Richard," she said impatiently, "you must do better than that!"

"I'm trying, Miss . . . Really I am."

But once again, for the fifth or sixth time, he was unable to keep his legs from sinking.

Harriet drew herself up. "You are obstinate today," she said coolly. "For the last time, Richard, will you do as I tell you? Or will you have the whip?"

He gasped. At his guardian's words, uttered in a clear, almost casual tone, a shocked silence had fallen on the three girls. Alicia, flushing with indignation, was seeking his eyes; but he could not meet her gaze.

"We shall try just once more," said Harriet blandly. "Come, now."

He struggled desperately, his legs beating the water with all his strength.

"Very well, Richard. Come with me, please." She gestured towards the bathing-machine.

He opened his mouth, trying to voice a protest, a plea. He was aware of Harriet's gray eyes fixed on him, wide and hypnotic in their compulsion; at that moment her face seemed terrible and strangely familiar: the cheeks, swollen and darkly reddened by the tight rubber cap, the lips that seemed curiously thicker, the flaring nostrils—all these features he had seen before, in the cell of the Breton château. Stricken with terror, he was unable to speak.

"Did you hear me?"

Under the fascinated gaze of the three girls, governess and pupil entered the bathing-machine and the door closed behind them . . .

The trio outside, drawn as if by some spell to the little building which had been so unexpectedly pressed into service as a place of correction, maintained a tense silence. Alicia, her hand at her mouth, inclined her ear towards the thin wooden wall; the others had approached as closely as they dared.

They heard the low tones of the governess' voice, and the youth's almost inaudible reply; then, with no further warning, the sound they awaited reached them—the sharp report of whipcord on naked flesh, muffled but unmistakable. Alicia's two friends glanced at each other, their breath quickening . . . The sound of the strokes continued, regular and unhurried, and all at once a smothered cry was heard. Alicia, her expression changing from incredulity to outrage, clenched her hands involuntarily . . . As the cries became louder and more shameless, her face became quite pale. Five minutes went by before the shocking sounds of punishment ceased; by that time the girl's delicate features were rigid as stone.

Then the door of the bathing-machine opened, and she received, like a slap in the face, the spectacle of the young man she had meant to make her husband, the spectacle of Richard Lovel stumbling into the sunlight—his head low, his face streaked with tears and still twisted with pain, sobbing, trembling, displaying a pair of loins that were swollen, crisscrossed with deep scarlet welts, and still quivering from the efforts of his sinister guardian.

She stared at him in dismay, still half unable to believe in the shameful sight. "Why, Richard!" she cried. "How could you— how could you let. . . ?" She was unable to finish her question. All at once she was obliged to suppress an hysterical inclination to laugh.

Richard stood before her in silence, gasping with the intensity of his misery. And then suddenly, added to his awareness of the marks on his loins, to his recollection of the cries which he had been unable to stifle, he was conscious of the real humiliation of the costume he was wearing—the childish display of his bathing trunks, the ignominy of the rubber bathing-cap. Putting his face in his hands, he burst into a flood of tears.

Alicia's face suddenly softened. She extended her hand towards her friend for an instant; then she checked the gesture of compassion and drew herself up.

"I think I should be going now, Richard," she said cooly. "Miss Marwood, I am glad to have had the pleasure of meeting you, and the satisfaction of observing the . . . the influence you have over your ward. It has been most instructive. But now I must go."

Harriet smiled, and bowed to her without a word. She passed

her arm around Richard's trembling shoulders and drew him close
to her as the young girl, followed by her two friends, walked
slowly away.

The two following days saw a sudden change in the weather, and
it rained almost continuously. This change served Alicia and her
mother with the necessary excuse for cutting short their seaside
visit; they left Bournemouth on the evening of the day after the
scene on the beach. Richard was profoundly grateful for their departure, for he neither wished, nor indeed was he able, to look his
young friend in the face again.

The weather also furnished Harriet with the pretext she needed
to discontinue the swimming lessons and to replace them by long
walks: she was constitutionally unwilling for her ward to acquire
any accomplishments that might render him more self-reliant; and
in any event the first lesson had served its purpose.

The boy was relieved that Alicia was not a witness to the
effeminate appearance he presented in the walks he now took in
the rain with his implacable guardian; she, at least, he thought
thankfully, was not present to see him in the hooded rubber cape
which Harriet had secured for him, and which he was now obliged
to wear out of doors not only when it was raining but even when
the sky held the slightest hint of a shower.

But if Alicia had left Bournemouth, her two friends had not.
And it was soon apparent to Richard that the matter of his subjection was being thoroughly aired among the young people in
the holiday crowd. He became aware of quizzical looks directed
at him, of words uttered behind hands, of veiled glances marked
by interest and amusement. The youths of his own age showed
themselves frankly curious and full of wonder; the girls revealed
a mixture of sympathy and contempt. He began to feel that his
appearance on the parade with Harriet evoked an air of tension;
when they approached a group of young people the latter would
fall silent, studying them covertly, and when they had passed
Richard was conscious of the stares that followed them. It was not

only the rubber cape he was wearing, he realized at last; the story of his swimming lesson must be familiar to everyone. With this realization he developed an attitude of haughtiness and defiance. After all, he thought, what do I care what they say or think or know? I have Harriet—and that is enough for me.

He was as yet unaware of a crowd's capabilities for cruelty.

But one afternoon, when the sky was still gray and lowering, he was walking with Harriet past the long line of shops, on the way to the deserted bluffs above the town. He saw a knot of young girls approaching, and had already set his face in the expression of pride and aloofness which he reserved for such occasions, when Harriet stopped abruptly before one of the shops, and bidding him wait while she made a purchase, disappeared inside.

He paused, irresolute now that he was alone, and turned in the pretense of an examination of the shop-window. He heard the girls coming closer, heard their whispered colloquy, and from the corner of his eyes recognized one of Alicia's companions on the beach. His cheeks burning, he turned his back; but he could not help hearing the mocking voices.

"Oh dear, I'd no idea it was going to rain!"

"I must run for my umbrella!"

"Oh Pamela, don't be a sissy."

The little group had halted behind him; there were smothered giggles. Richard trembled, not knowing what to do. Suddenly an impulse of anger and desperation seized him, and he half turned to face his tormentors. But before he could speak he heard Alicia's friend exclaim, in admirable mimicry of Harriet's accents:

"Richard! Richard! Have you had the whip today, sir?"

And a half-dozen young voices burst into peals of laughter as the girls strolled past him.

He remained where he was, huddled in his cape. His life, as we have seen, had been unusually rich in humiliations and affronts; but this last experience left him dazed. In that moment a feeling of utter desolation swept over him; he had the sensation, for the first time in his life, of being cut off from all womankind—from every woman, in fact, but Harriet. That night, when his guardian came to kiss him goodnight in bed, he looked at her in wide-eyed

misery and suddenly burst out: "Oh Harriet, Harriet, please let us
leave this place! I am so unhappy here . . . Let us go anywhere,
anywhere where there will be only the two of us! Just you and I,
Harriet . . ."

Looking down at the youth, who had seized her hand and was
kissing it appealingly, Harriet let her lips curve in a triumphant
smile.

"We shall leave tomorrow for Christchurch," she said quietly,
as if her plans had been already made. "I see that your disposition
requires quietness and solitude above everything, my dear Richard, and that these places of public resort are not good for you.
From now on you will live a much more sequestered life with me.
Have no fear, Richard. From now on we shall be alone together
and without interruption, as in the past." Above his head, her
beautiful face was still smiling and pensive. Yes, she was thinking,
that little interlude is over, and we can resume the course. "Yes,
dear boy," she said softly, stroking his hair, "henceforth it will be,
as always, just you and I . . ."

From the living-room he heard Harriet and Sir Robert exchanging
greetings in front of the house. A few minutes earlier, sitting with
Harriet, he had seen the baronet arriving on horseback and leading
the mare with him as usual; his guardian had started up, her face
brightening with pleasure, and with a word of farewell to him had
hastened outside, her long riding-habit caught up in one hand.
Now, he could visualize the scene between them: the long, warm
handclasp, the flattering looks, and then the little ceremony of
Harriet's mounting, her foot cupped by Sir Robert's strong hands
as he lifted her effortlessly into the saddle. He had seen it often
enough, indeed, in the past. But this time, contrary to custom, he
could hear Harriet's voice, unusually clear and vibrant, reaching
him through the open windows.

"Ah, Hartrey, what a divine day for a ride! And this morning I
intend to show you the way, for a change. Yes, to the loveliest
little pond you can imagine . . ."

Richard started back, pierced through with such distress that for a minute he could scarcely breathe; numbly he heard the horses' footfalls receding down the avenue.

It was only fifteen minutes later that he rose and, hatless and clad as he was in his shirt, set out in a kind of trance . . .

The afternoon sun beat down mercilessly on his bare head; the air was hot and dry, and the powdery dust from the roads was choking. The loping run at which he had set off soon slowed to a walk, and he had gone little more than a mile before he was obliged to rest in the shade of a tree. But he had no thought of going back. The terrible fever of curiosity, the insensate craving to discover what would take place between the man he hated and the woman he loved, in the spot consecrated in his mind to his own intense though short-lived ecstasy, drove him on like a beast in harness. By the time he reached the branching lane, his shirt stuck to his back, his face was streaked with sweat and dust, and his breath came in short, panting bursts; so confused and ex- hausted was he that he almost failed to see the wooded footpath itself, and it was only the sight of hoof-marks in the soft ground that arrested him, and at the same time aroused him to the need for caution and concentration.

Suddenly cool and alert, he took his way slowly and with infinite care along the little path. The hoof-marks soon became more pronounced, and then, as the wood grew thicker, he saw be- side them the accompanying marks of boots, and understood that the riders had dismounted; with a quiver of detestation he noted the deep imprint of Hartrey's riding-boot, and in its wake the lighter indentation of Harriet's dainty heels. The next moment he caught sight of the tethered horses, and beyond them the blue flicker of the pond itself. At once he crouched down; then, altering his course to avoid the horses, he worked his way carefully through the trees and around to the side of the pond.

Arriving within sight of it, he caught his breath, feeling a hideous pang pass through him: Harriet and the baronet were leaning against the great pine tree, and his arm was around her shoulders. He wanted to cry out with pain, but checked himself, and sinking down on his knees braced his trembling frame behind a fallen tree-trunk. Then he heard Hartrey's soft voice, throbbing with the intensity of passion, but pitched so low he could not distinguish the words; the voice went on and on, then wavered and stopped.

Harriet's voice broke the silence at last; it was clear but tremulous, with a tone Richard had never heard before. "I shall have to consider of it, Sir Robert . . . Indeed, I have a great regard for you, and I am deeply flattered by the honor you have done me, but . . . "

"But nothing!" Hartrey's voice was still soft, but now the words were easily overheard. "This is no time to speak of flattery or honor, Miss Marwood. Harriet—yes, I must call you so!—know that I am determined, and my determination will brook no resistance. Come, you have only to say a word, to make me the happiest man alive, and yourself—Lady Hartrey. Ah, it is not inconsiderable what I am offering you! My love, my name, whatever settlement you desire, and the assurance of my lifelong devotion and care . . . Harriet, my own dear girl, can you hesitate?"

In the silence that ensued Richard could bear the tension of waiting no longer. He raised his head above the fallen tree, and found himself gazing straight at Harriet. It seemed that she also, her head half turned, was looking him directly in the face. For an instant he was certain that she saw him; but then he was aware, with a terrible sinking of his heart, that she was passing her arm around her companion's neck. He saw her sink slowly backwards, her head raised to receive the lips so close to her own, her whole body straining upwards; the next moment their lips were joined and Richard, uttering a cry of agony, fell backwards to the ground.

He had fainted for a few seconds only, but when he recovered he found Hartrey beside him; the baronet was glaring down at him with exasperation and contempt.

"So, you have appointed yourself a spy on Miss Marwood and me, have you?" he said.

Richard made no reply. An instant later he saw Harriet also standing above him; her expression was calm, absolutely inscrutable.

"What are you doing here, Richard?" she asked quietly.

"Oh Harriet, Harriet . . . " he cried brokenly; he could find no other words, and burst into tears.

Hartrey's lip curled. "The beggar should be horsewhipped," he said.

"Yes," said Harriet, nodding her head slowly. "He should be horsewhipped."

With a single movement Hartrey seized Richard by the arm and dragged him upright; it was only then that the boy saw the heavy riding-crop looped to his rival's sinewy wrist.

"And horsewhipped he shall be!" said Hartrey. With the words he raised the crop and struck Richard savagely across the shoulders. The boy screamed.

"Yes, that is right," said Harriet. "Again, Robert, please . . . No, do not spare him. Whip him well, I beg you."

Hartrey needed no urging; the heavy leather thong whistled again and again around the boy's shoulders, his back, flanks and arms. Howling with pain, Richard writhed and twisted, trying in vain to break free of the iron grip on his wrist. After a minute he fell to the ground, where the strokes still continued to fall on him brutally. All at once he heard Harriet's voice raised sharply.

"That is enough, Robert! Enough, I said. I shall finish this myself."

The blows ceased, and Hartrey released his grip on Richard's wrist.

"Richard," said Harriet. "You will stand up, please."

He made an effort, half rising to his knees, then crumpled again to the ground.

"Did you hear me? Stand up, sir. At once!"

With a sensation of absolute horror, Richard saw Harriet's own slender riding-whip raised above him. He closed his eyes, and felt the lash cutting agonizingly across his loins.

"For the last time, Richard, I order you to stand up."

He stumbled to his feet, swaying; all at once he felt his guardian's firm hand supporting him by the arm. When she spoke he almost failed to understand her words.

"Very well, Richard," she said quietly, "we will go home now. Sir Robert, I wish you a good afternoon. My ward and I will return on foot."

Hartrey stared at her blankly. "Harriet . . . " he began.

"Excuse me, but I must beg you not to address me so. I do not believe my future husband approves of it. Come, Richard, let us go."

Hartrey's voice came, cold as ice. "Did you say, your future husband, madam?"

"I did, sir. A few minutes ago you asked me to be your wife. I have thought of your proposal since then, and this is my answer. Yes, Richard Lovel is the only man I will accept as my husband, if he will have me. I bid you goodbye."

Richard, feeling as if he were in a dream, was aware of the pressure of Harriet's arm drawing him away—away from his rival, away from all the terrors and misery of the last week, drawing him out of the nightmare of what he had seen and heard into a clime of undreamed of bliss and the miraculous shelter of her smile.

Back in the house, Harriet, still in her riding habit, had undressed her ward and was sponging his shoulders and loins as he lay prone on his bed. Scarcely a word had been exchanged between them since they had left the wood.

"There now, Richard," she said at last in a pleasant tone, "your back is looking better, at any rate. Is it still very sore?"

He sighed deeply. "No—I mean, it is much better . . . " But feeling her hands themselves touch his flesh, he could not keep back a groan.

"Yes, it will still be painful for some time. Those are very ugly bruises, you know. Now, you must brace yourself while I apply some salve. It will hurt, but it is the only treatment for cuts like those . . . "

Clenching his teeth, he endured the torment of the friction of her fingers; her hand had become infinitely gentle, but his martyred flesh was a mass of pain. At last it was over, and Harriet stood up.

"You will be quite recovered in a day or two, Richard," she said. "Now, I shall leave you to rest for a few hours."

But as she moved away he turned weakly and called to her. "Harriet," he whispered, "please do not go . . . right away. I . . . I must speak to you . . ."

She paused, then returned slowly to his side. "Yes?" Her voice was low and quiet, but it had an undercurrent of emotion.

"Oh, Harriet, was . . . was I dreaming, when I heard you speaking in the wood? When you said . . . that you would be my . . . my wife . . . and no one else's?"

"No, you were not dreaming."

He stared at her, wide-eyed, still half unbelieving. Her gray-violet eyes met his, frank and unabashed, and for an instant he could not speak; then his words came, breathless, importunate, desperate.

"Then . . . then, Harriet, will you be my wife? Dear God, will you not say so? Will you not marry me, Harriet?"

"Yes, Richard."

"Oh, my darling . . ." He tried to turn, reaching for her hand, but a searing pain through his shoulders made him arrest the gesture; he gasped with the depth of his suffering. Harriet bent down and herself took his hand in both her own, then remained gazing at him, her eyes misted but unwavering.

"No, do not move, Richard," she said. "You will only hurt yourself." She smiled at him tenderly, like a mother. "Yes, Richard, I will be your wife. I think we will be very happy together, my dear."

For almost half a minute he could not utter a word, but remained gazing at her in speechless adoration. Then, "And we will be married soon, very soon, will we not?"

"Yes. As soon as possible. It would be wiser, I think. But we will talk of that this evening. I must leave you now, but only for an hour or two."

But as if still doubtful of his happiness, still uncertain of his possession of her, he could not relinquish her hand. He began to blush, trying to speak.

Harriet looked at him indulgently. "Well, what is it, Richard?" she said.

"There . . . there is only one thing I cannot understand," he whispered. "I . . . I saw something, in the wood . . . You and Sir Robert . . . you . . . you let him kiss you . . ."

Harriet laughed; with her free hand she stroked his hair lightly before replying.

"Yes, I let him kiss me." Her expression became merry, almost mischievous. "He is in many ways an attractive man, you know, and I, Richard, had grown a little tired of waiting . . . for you. After all, my dear, if you have the appetites of a man, as I have told you, why, I also am flesh and blood . . . Or did you not know? You see, Richard, although I am your governess and your guardian, I am . . . also . . . only a woman . . ."

Even as she was speaking Richard had risen from his bed and seized her in his arms; now, heedless of his suffering flesh, of the pains which ran along his shoulders and loins like streams of liquid fire, he strained her to him and pressed his lips to hers, commingling his agony and rapture in an embrace which was a sheer ecstasy.

FROM
OH! CALCUTTA!

by Several Hands
1969

"Who: Whom"°

MAN *is discovered center stage in armchair, relaxed, legs crossed. To his right: a Victorian chaise longue, upholstered in leather. He lights a cigarette. As he does so* GIRL A *enters right. She is dressed like a Victorian parlor maid—black dress, high button shoes, maid's cap. She carries a birch rod.* MAN *watches her as she crosses to the chaise longue and kneels on it, placing the birch rod near her feet. She bends forward, resting her head on her folded arms. She raises her skirt and tucks it above her waist. She is wearing Victorian drawers. Her rear faces the audience as she bends again.* MAN *exhales, still watching her.* GIRL B *is now lowered from the flies, slightly to the left of* MAN. *She is encased in a net of stout rope, which dangles five feet above stage level. She is wearing a bikini. Her wrists and ankles are tied, her mouth is gagged, and she is doubled up.* MAN *watches her descent with impassive interest. Rising, he taps the ash from his cigarette and addresses the audience.*

MAN (*easy, slow, conversational tone*): Like most civilized people, I believe in democracy. I thought I'd better make that clear right from the beginning. I don't believe that any one person

° The two skits presented here were rarely performed. New York: Grove Press, 1969.

is essentially more important than any other. Or less. On the other hand, there are obviously differences between people. Some are taller or thinner or more redheaded than others. And some are what you might call more resonant.

He walks toward GIRL B.

For example, Susan here has resonance. I call her Susan because that's the name of the character she is playing. Susan is a pert English girl of good background, who has been captured and trussed up by a tribe of savages in Sumatra. Indignities of many kinds—some nameless, others specific—are in store for her. Susan has resonance because many people respond to her. They love reading books about her or looking at pictures of her, or seeing films about her. From time to time she's trussed up by Martians or Vikings or Gauleiters. But she's always the same old Susan, always defenseless, always known to her admirers as a damsel in distress. And she strikes a chord. Can you hear it? (*Pause.*) It's a statistical fact that some of you can. That makes Susan a resounding person. Let's hope it comforts her in bondage—against which (GIRL B *wriggles desperately*) she struggles in vain.

He walks over to GIRL A.

This is Jean. Jean also has resonance. She is a parlor maid employed in a Scottish mansion during the middle years of the nineteenth century. The master of the house is an attractive widower, brushed with gray at the temples, and his regime is stern but just, like the glint in his ice-blue eyes. Jean has been caught stealing bottled plums, and now awaits chastisement at the hands of her master. She will now formally present herself.

GIRL A *pulls down her drawers to mid-thigh.*

She will now arch and offer.

GIRL A *arches her back.*

Jean is now fully disclosed. From between her buttocks, the puckered rim of a virgin target tremulously peeps.

Like Susan, she is known in many disguises—as a wayward novice in an Irish cloister, or an indolent prefect at a strict finishing school. Many thousands of people respond to her plight, often quite vividly. Let us not blink at the facts. A high degree of resonance attaches to Jean. May it solace her in her humility, that lovely, well-built girl.

He takes up a position between the two girls.

Remember Lenin—the great Lenin—who said that the world was divided into the "who" and "whom"? He was talking about those who do, and those to whom it is done. Wouldn't you say that Susan and Jean, in their very different ways, were a classic pair of whom?

He turns and stubs out his cigarette. He then faces the audience again.

You'll have noticed I said they were different. But how do they differ? In my view very significantly.

He indicates GIRL B.

Have a good squint at Susan. This girl is where she is as a direct consequence of physical coercion. Brute force and nimble fingers have been at work. The principle of choice—the very heartland of liberty—has been rudely violated. It's an outrage to the human spirit.

He turns to GIRL A.

Now let's take another look at Jean. She kneels there—or squats there—in a posture that must be profoundly embarrassing. You might even call it humiliating. However, if the spirit moves her, she is at liberty to get up and go. Jean, the submissive household servant in temporary disgrace, is a free agent.

He picks up the birch rod and fingers it.

And she is free not only as a parlor maid but as a human being. The girl you are watching—the docile squatter—is Eleanor Brown. (*Or whatever her real name is.*) Born 1941, trained at

R.A.D.A., professional debut with Oldham Rep—you can see the details in the program. If Miss Brown, the employed female performer, decides now—tonight, this moment—to get up and leave the stage, there will be no reprisals. Neither I, nor the author, nor the director will hold it against her. She will return to the theater tomorrow night with her professional reputation untarnished. Whatever happens, she is the master of her fate.

He turns toward GIRL B.

Susan, for all her resonance, is dependent on the will of others. (*He shouts at the wings.*) Take Susan away! Whereas Eleanor —aged 25, divorced with one daughter, favorite food lobster chop suey—remains her own mistress. She is free to stop blushing and go.

He moves closer to her.

Are you listening to me, Eleanor?

She does not move.

Eleanor—do you want to leave the stage?

She does not move.

For the last time, will you please make a sign if you wish to leave the stage?

She does not move. Pause.

As I was saying, I am a strict believer in democracy.

SLOW FADE TO BLACKOUT

FROM
OH! CALCUTTA!

by Several Hands
1969

"St. Dominic's, 1917"°

GWEN, FAUVETTE, MORVYTH: *Fifth Form Girls*
ELSPETH: *Fifth Form Monitor*
MISS BEESLEY: *Headmistress*

*Dropcloth of cover of girls' school books circa 1917. Recorded
sound of girls singing school song. Superimpose projection caption:
"*THE FIFTH FORM AT ST. DOMINIC'S, 1917.*" Fade caption. Superimpose second caption: "*CHAPTER ONE.*" Fade caption. Superimpose third caption: "*GWEN MAKES A BAD START.*" Meanwhile, over
the public address system:*

VOICE (*female*): In the depth of every Englishman's subconscious
   there is a cat-o'-nine-tails and a schoolgirl in black stockings.
   Remark attributed to the French humorist, Pierre Daninos.

*The school song, which has faded for the announcement, swells
up and ends. The dropcloth rises. Behind it are three dormitory
camp beds, occupied by GWEN, FAUVETTE, and MORVYTH. A
bell rings. ELSPETH, the dormitory prefect, enters, dressed in
school uniform—gymslip, black stockings, white blouse, and
school tie.*

° New York: Grove Press, 1969.

ELSPETH: Come on, girls! Stir your old bones! Don't want to treat you to a jaw-wag on the first day of term. Let's have no monkey tricks, or Miss Beesley'll be down on us like a ton of bricks!

GWEN (*sitting up in bed*): Must you be so jinky, Elspeth? This child's fagged out entirely!

ELSPETH: Stop frivolling, you silly young blighter, or I'll spliflicate you!

FAUVETTE (*to audience*): Fumed Elspeth.

GWEN: You needn't be so peacocky, just because you're a monitor!

FAUVETTE (*to audience*): Chirruped Gwen, with a grin on her impish face.

ELSPETH (*to* GWEN): Now listen to me, you young scalawag. You may have been the firebrand of the Fourth, but this is your first day in the Fifth, and you'll have a grizzly time of it unless you mind your manners!

GWEN (*jumping out of bed and slipping dark blue knickers under her nightie*): No use expecting me to knuckle under, Elspeth, I'm as used to scolding as eels to skinning!

ELSPETH: Any more chat from you, and I'll report you to Miss Beesley. And a summons from that worthy rarely bodes good fortune to the recipient. (*To audience.*) Gwen's gauche and brusque, but at heart she's unimpeachable!

MORVYTH, *still curled up in bed, suddenly bursts into tears.*

(*Going to* MORVYTH's *bed.*) Hello! Whence this thusness? Gracious, girl, turn off the waterworks! We don't care for this sickly sort of stuff at St. Dominic's.

MORVYTH: I'm sorry, Elspeth, but I'm dreadfully homesick!

FAUVETTE (*to audience; by now she is languidly dressing and washing*): Wailed Morvyth.

ELSPETH: For goodness' sake bottle it up, Morvyth!

MORVYTH: But my brother's volunteered to be a Tommy, you see, and they're sending him out to the front!

ELSPETH: Then you ought to be proud of him, you silly goose! I've met some of the lads who've come back blinded from the war, and they're twice as cheerful and patient as you.

MORVYTH (*hugging* ELSPETH): You are a trump, Elspeth!

ELSPETH (*extricating herself*): Don't, Morvyth!

FAUVETTE (*to audience*): Said Elspeth huskily.

ELSPETH (*to audience*): Morvyth is a dear, delightful lovable lazy-bones, with sweetly coaxing little ways, and a helpless confiding look in her blue eyes. Her fossils form the nucleus of the school museum.

All the girls are now out of bed and dressing. They follow the same procedure: having pulled on their knickers, they remove their nighties and put on white blouses, gymslips, school ties, and black stockings held by garters.

GWEN (*to audience*): The spiciest character in the form is Fauvette, otherwise known as "The Kipper," and rumored to be the richest girl in school.

FAUVETTE (*to audience*): Some of the girls are fearfully down on me because my wealthy parents send me postal orders. They tease me and call me "Proudie" or "Madam Conceit."

Bell rings.

ELSPETH: Oops! Two minutes to go before Assembly. Scooterons-nous this very sec! I'll nip ahead. Fauvette, I'm counting on you to see to it that the Fifth is there on time in full fig! (ELSPETH *exits.*)

FAUVETTE: *Strafe* the dear old Fifth as far as I'm concerned! Elspeth may be in a rush, but it's not this child's usual way of proceeding!

GWEN: Fauvette!

FAUVETTE (*to audience*): Interposed Gwen, her dark eyes dancing.

GWEN: Will the Bumble Bee be taking us for English composition?

All three, fully dressed, have come downstage. The dropcloth falls behind them.

FAUVETTE: The Bumble Bee? Great Minerva, how ignorant the new bug is! My poor babe, let me initiate you into the shibboleths of the Fifth. Be it known to you that our respected Head, Miss Beesley, vulgarly known as the Bumble Bee, is among our elect set yclept Lemonade—partly owing to her habit of fizzing over, and partly owing to a certain acid quality in her temper.

GWEN: But why shouldn't I call her the Bumble Bee if I want to?

FAUVETTE: Because, old sport, you mustn't correct your betters.

GWEN: And what makes you better than I am?

MORVYTH (*to audience*): Sniffed Gwen in her forthright way.

FAUVETTE: Because, frabjous child, your parents are humble folk, whereas mine are bearing the nation's burdens on their shoulders.

MORVYTH: Do stow it, Fauvette!

FAUVETTE (*to* GWEN): Make no mistake, I shall take care to keep my weekly postal order locked up in my desk, in case you snaffle it!

GWEN: I wouldn't touch anything of yours with a pair of tongs!

MORVYTH (*to audience*): Flared Gwen.

FAUVETTE: And I wouldn't touch anything of yours *except* with a pair of tongs. You're so unwashed!

GWEN: You old bluebottle!

GWEN *throws herself on* FAUVETTE. *They pummel each other, rolling around the stage.* MORVYTH *looks aghast. Suddenly* ELSPETH *re-enters, looking fierce.*

ELSPETH (*separating the combatants*): Peace, turbulent herd! Fauvette, tell me what happened.

FAUVETTE: Please don't think me a rotten sneak, Elspeth, but Gwen set upon me!

GWEN (*hotly*): I say . . .

MORVYTH (*to audience*): Interjected Gwen.

ELSPETH: Did you start this imbroglio, Gwen?

GWEN: Great heavens, no, Fauvette egged me on!

ELSPETH: Then let me give you both a word of advice, my lofty Pharaohs! Pride frequently comes before a fall.

ELSPETH *seizes* GWEN *by the ear.* FAUVETTE *looks smug.*

MORVYTH (*to audience*): I see breakers ahead.

All four girls freeze in this grouping.

VOICE (*female; over public address system*): You have now met Gwen, Fauvette, Morvyth, and Elspeth. At the end of this sketch, one of them will be publicly spanked. By a process of elimination, you, the audience, will decide on the victim. You can now eliminate either Gwen or Fauvette. Please indicate your choice by raising your right hand. Is it Gwen?

GWEN *steps forward from group and faces audience.*

Or Fauvette?

FAUVETTE *does the same.*

(*Using whichever name gets the most votes*)——is hereby exonerated.

BLACKOUT

School song is heard again. Dropcloth appears with projected caption: "HIGH JINKS AND HOT WATER IN THE OFFING." *Dropcloth rises. Lights go up to reveal classroom with desks and blackboard.* FAUVETTE, GWEN, *and* MORVYTH *are seated, chattering.* ELSPETH *enters.*

ELSPETH: *Cave*, all concerned! Miss Beesley's approaching in full sail.

All sit demurely upright. MISS BEESLEY *enters in scholastic gown.*

MISS BEESLEY: Good morning, girls!

ALL: Good morning, Miss Beesley!

ELSPETH (*to audience*): Miss Beesley is a handsome and imposing woman with a stern cast of features.

MISS BEESLEY: Members of the Fifth! I have some remarks to address to two of your number. First of all, Morvyth.

MORVYTH *rises.*

It's come to my ears that you have been acting like a weeping cherub on a monument. Now that won't do at all—we've no patience with grousers at St. Dominic's. It's your bounden duty to be bubbling and girlish so that you can carry away happy memories of your lighthearted schooldays when you go out into the world to be a woman. Do you understand, Morvyth?

MORVYTH: Yes, Miss Beesley, I'll do my uttermost. (*She sits.*)

MISS BEESLEY: There's a gallant girl. And now for the egregious madcap of the Fourth, lately translated to more august surroundings.

GWEN *ruefully rises. The other girls giggle.*

It's been brought to my attention that the aforementioned young scamp has celebrated her arrival in the Fifth by indulging in pugilistic practices with one of her senior bedfellows. Now Gwen, it's A-1 to be high-spirited, but if you overstep the mark again, there'll be a painful reckoning behind my green baize door. *Compris?*

GWEN (*flushed*): Oui—I mean, yes, Miss Beesley! (*She sits.*)

ELSPETH (*to audience*): It's an open secret that Miss Beesley, strict disciplinarian though she is, has a sneaking weakness for Gwen.

MORVYTH (*to audience*): "The Bumble Bee rows Gwen but she likes her," is the general verdict.

FAUVETTE *has meanwhile been rummaging through her desk.*

FAUVETTE: Miss Beesley!

MISS BEESLEY: What is it, child?

FAUVETTE: Somebody or other has nabbed my postal order! It's vanished from my desk!

MORVYTH: Great jumping Jehosephat!

Continue below if GWEN *has been eliminated earlier:*

FAUVETTE: And what's more, I told Morvyth only this morning that I was going to put it there.

Everyone stares at MOR-VYTH *who looks appalled.*

Continue below if FAUVETTE *has been eliminated earlier:*

FAUVETTE: And what's more, I told Gwen only this morning that I was going to put it there!

Everyone stares at GWEN, *who looks appalled.*

GWEN (*to audience*):
Morvyth stood aghast, utterly dumbfounded at the defalcation.

MORVYTH: Fauvette's a fibber! She's just trying to make me blub!

The four girls and MISS BEESLEY freeze in a group.

VOICE (*female; over public address system*):
Three girls are still eligible for punishment.

The girls in question step forward.

In precisely four minutes, one of them will be whipped. We now invite you to eliminate either Fauvette or Morvyth. Please raise your right hand if you wish to spare Fauvette. (*Pause for vote to be noted.*) Or Morvyth. (*Another pause.*)————is hereby exonerated.

MORVYTH (*to audience*):
Gwen stood aghast, utterly dumbfounded at the defalcation.

GWEN: I loathe pointing the finger at a chum, but you told Morvyth as well as yours truly.

The four girls and MISS BEESLEY freeze in a group.

VOICE (*female; over public address system*):
Three girls are still eligible for punishment.

The girls in question step forward.

In precisely four minutes, one of them will be whipped. We now invite you to eliminate either Morvyth or Gwen. Please raise your right hand if you wish to spare Morvyth. (*Pause for vote to be noted.*) Or Gwen. (*Another pause.*)————is hereby exonerated.

BLACKOUT

School song again. Dropcloth appears with caption: "A BEANO IN THE DORM AT WHICH A SCORE IS SETTLED." *Dropcloth rises. Lights up to reveal dormitory setting as in the first scene. The four girls are onstage, slipping out of gymslips and changing*

*into nighties. Other girls could also be present, already wearing
pyjamas, nightdresses, and other kinds of schoolgirl deshabille.*

ELSPETH: Who's in favor of tripping the light fantastic before we
broach the ginger beer?

FAUVETTE: What a perfectly chubby wheeze!

GWEN: Absolutely slap-bang!

All the girls cheer.

ELSPETH: Right-ho! Combs and paper at the ready! One-two-three!

*Some of the girls produce combs and paper and start to play a
popular waltz. The others choose partners and dance.* ELSPETH
approaches MORVYTH, *who looks lonely.*

ELSPETH: Care to borrow my bedjacket, young Morvyth?

MORVYTH: You're a brick, Elspeth, but I'm not sure that lilac's my
color.

FAUVETTE (*to audience*): Mumbled Morvyth, turning hot with
pleasure at the bare idea.

ELSPETH: Never mind, baby, you look nice in anything.

FAUVETTE (*to audience*): Returned Elspeth soothingly.

ELSPETH: And your white petticoat's a perfect dream. I always said
it was a shame to hide it under a dress. ELSPETH *and* MORVYTH
*waltz together. The mood and tempo are dreamy and roman-
tic. Everyone except* FAUVETTE *and the comb-and-paper
players are dancing.*

FAUVETTE (*to audience*): Gwen's cheeks were scarlet and Morvyth's long fair hair floated out picturesquely as she twirled
around in Elspeth Moseley's arms.

FAUVETTE *moves towards* GWEN's *bed. Suddenly,* MISS BEESLEY,
in a dressing gown, marches into the dormitory.

ALL: *Cave*—the Bumble Bee!

MISS BEESLEY (*genially*): I hope I'm not turning up like the pro-
verbial bad penny! It's not my intention to be the specter at the
feast. I was deeply impressed by your doughty efforts in the

end-of-term exams, and I thought it might not be taken amiss if I put in an appearance at your beano.

The girls cheer.

Let the festivities continue.

ELSPETH: In honor of the Bumble Bee's—I mean Miss Beesley's—presence, may I propose a toast in foaming flagons of ginger pop! (*She offers* MISS BEESLEY *a glass.*) Here's to the health of St. Dominic's, the grandest school of all!

The girls all raise their glasses, but before they can drink, FAUVETTE *cries out.*

FAUVETTE: Just a jiffy, you fellows! I've found my postal order—and it's here, in Elspeth's locker.

General cry of astonishment. FAUVETTE *points at the locker.* ELSPETH *goes over and snatches the postal order from inside it.* GWEN *looks abashed. The girls freeze in a group.*

VOICE: Your final choice between Elspeth (ELSPETH *steps forward.*) . . . and Fauvette/Morvyth/Gwen. (*The other victim steps forward.*) Do you eliminate Elspeth? (*Pause for vote.*) Or Fauvette/Morvyth/Gwen? (*Pause for vote.*)————is hereby exonerated.

The group unfreezes and the action continues.

FAUVETTE: I hate being a tattle-tale, but her locker was open, and there it was!

MISS BEESLEY (*to* ELSPETH): Can you explain how Fauvette's postal order came to be in your locker?

ELSPETH: It's not an atom of use asking me, I haven't the ghost of a notion!

GWEN (*to audience*): Was any wretched girl ever in such a fix?

MISS BEESLEY: Things will go easier for you if you make a clean breast of it.

ELSPETH: I'm sorry, Miss Beesley, but I have nothing to confess.

GWEN (*to audience*): Hot tears came welling up, but Elspeth brushed them away angrily.

MISS BEESLEY: Theft is an ugly word, Elspeth. In all the years of my headmistressship, incidents such as this have very seldom occurred. I have had unruliness and disobedience before, but in the whole of my experience never a girl more brazen than you. It is of course impossible for me to allow you to remain at St. Dominic's.

Continue as follows if ELSPETH *is the victim:*

I will deal with you myself in the morning. In the meantime, I shall hand you over to the tender mercies of Gwen—the new monitor of the Fifth—who has full disciplinary powers. (*She exits.*)

GWEN (*to audience*):
The Bumble Bee always reminds me of an ancient Roman—the State first and foremost in her estimates, and herself nowhere. (*She seats herself on one of the beds.*) Hairbrush if you please, Elspeth, or are you going to show the white feather?

Continue as follows if GWEN *is the victim:*

MISS BEESLEY *turns to leave. As she does so,* MORVYTH *rushes forward.*

MORVYTH: Please, Miss Beesley, may I speak?
MISS BEESLEY: What is it, Morvyth?
MORVYTH: I'll take my oath Elspeth's telling the truth. The real culprit is Gwen. She's green with envy because Elspeth's top dog and she'll go to any lengths to do her down. I saw her putting the postal order into Elspeth's locker!
MISS BEESLEY: Is this true, Gwen?

GWEN *is silent.*

Continue as follows if MORVYTH *is the victim:*

MISS BEESLEY *turns to leave. As she does so,* GWEN *rushes forward.*

Continue as follows if FAUVETTE *is the victim:*

MISS BEESLEY *turns to leave. As she does so,* MORVYTH *rushes forward.*

GWEN: Please, Miss Beesley, may I speak?

MISS BEESLEY: What is it, Gwen?

GWEN: I'll take my oath Elspeth's telling the truth. The culprit is Morvyth. She's green with envy because Elspeth is top dog, and she'll go to any lengths to do her down. I saw her putting the postal order into Elspeth's locker.

MISS BEESLEY: Is this true, Morvyth?

MORVYTH *is silent.*

ELSPETH: I may be a blighter, but at least I don't funk!

MORVYTH: Please, Miss Beesley, may I speak?

MISS BEESLEY: What is it, Morvyth?

MORVYTH: I'll take my oath Elspeth's telling the truth. Fauvette's green with envy because Elspeth's top dog, and she'll go to any lengths to do her down. The real culprit is Fauvette herself! I saw her putting the postal order into Elspeth's locker.

MISS BEESLEY: Is this true, Fauvette?

FAUVETTE *is silent.*

Are you willing to swear that it's false?

GWEN *shakes her head.*

In that case, I must apologize to Elspeth, who has undeservedly borne the brunt of my strictures. As for you, Gwen, you have set a most pernicious example, and I will deal with you myself in the morning. In the meanwhile, I shall hand you over to the tender mercies of your monitor, who has full disciplinary powers.
(*She exits.*)

GWEN (*to audience*):
The Bumble Bee always

reminds me of an ancient Roman—the State first and foremost in her estimates, and herself nowhere.

ELSPETH (*seating herself on one of the beds*): Hairbrush, if you please, Gwen, or are you going to show the white feather?

GWEN: I may be a blighter, but at least I don't funk!

Are you willing to swear that it's false?

MORVYTH *shakes her head.*

In that case, I must apologize to Elspeth, who has undeservedly borne the brunt of my strictures. As for you, Morvyth, you have set the most pernicious example, and I will deal with you in the morning. In the meanwhile, I shall hand you over to the tender mercies of your monitor, who has full disciplinary powers.

(*She exits.*)

GWEN (*to audience*):

The Bumble Bee always reminds me of an ancient Roman—the State first and foremost in her estimates, and herself nowhere.

Are you willing to swear that it's false?

FAUVETTE *shakes her head.*

In that case, I must apologize to Elspeth, who has undeservedly borne the brunt of my strictures. As for you, Fauvette, you have set a most pernicious example, and I will deal with you myself in the morning. In the meanwhile, I shall hand you over to the tender mercies of your monitor, who has full disciplinary powers.

(*She exits.*)

GWEN (*to audience*):

The Bumble Bee always reminds me of an ancient Roman—the State first and foremost in her estimates, and herself nowhere.

ELSPETH (*seating herself on one of the beds*): Hairbrush, if you please, Morvyth, or are you going to show the white feather?

MORVYTH: I may be a blighter, but at least I don't funk.

ELSPETH (*seating herself on one of the beds*): Hairbrush, if you please, Fauvette, or are you going to show the white feather?

FAUVETTE: I may be a blighter, but at least I don't funk!

The VICTIM *fetches a hairbrush from her washstand, gives it to the* MONITOR *and bends over her knee. The* MONITOR *slowly raises the* VICTIM's *nightie to the waist and, even more slowly, pulls down her knickers. The other girls gather round to watch the spanking. It takes place in slow motion, with the* VICTIM *ritualistically wriggling as each blow falls. The girls count in unison. We should feel that this is a kind of tribal ceremony— the sacrifice of the willing victim. As the* MONITOR *spanks, it might be a good idea to project on the backcloth a moving close shot of the* VICTIM's *bottom. The counting grows louder and the pace increases. At about the count of ten, we hear electronic "take-off" music, possibly like the sound used by the Beatles in "A Day in the Life." As this sound and the spanking reach a climax, we*

BLACKOUT

FROM
P. N. DEDEAUX, ed.

The Tutor: Being the Reminiscences of Thomasina Wragg°
1970: original, n.d.

It was lovely that summer in the sun. Everything seemed easier and slower, more relaxed and mazed in warmth. I was happy, helping both in the hall and on the estate; and I sneaked off more than ever to the bounding shore in my hour off in the afternoon though I was never more late. My hiding had had that effect, at least. Mrs. Wilson pointed out the moral more than once.

"A good whipping never did a girl no harm. It quickens the senses and, I believe, even whets the appetite. Ye're growing to a big girl, Thomasina, but you need not put on ways just because milady has taken a fancy to you. Upstairs or below, ye'll mind y'r place else I'll see you leathered on that trestle in a trice."

Poor Molly, a woman approaching thirty, suffered so several times, I knew, Mrs. Wilson always picking on her, and some of the other help, too, but Prendergast, or "Prendy," as she was known, Lady Julia's personal maid, was above this personal discipline, as she was above us in her life at the top of the house in a cozy dormer room I had seen on several occasions.

So I would strip off my clothes in the cave and run full-tilt into the sea, my new breasts bouncing and my bottoms joggling behind. The sting and slap of the waves made me gasp as I flung myself into them pell-mell, and came out with breasts aching, breath spluttering, drenched and swamped with the salt. It was

° New York: Grove Press, 1970.

doing so one late August afternoon that I had my shock; my clothes were no longer there.

I had been delegated that day to help with the early harvest, pitching and stooking the barley. I came off the field around five, dusty with chaff, my ankles scratched by the stubble and my shoulders and arms weary as if with weights. Excused by the bailiff, I was making for a wash-off under the pump in the yard when I bethought me that my steps could innocently lead by the cliff, whence I could drop to the sands and bathe. Nobody was ever there. No one ever watched. I left my clothes in their usual place, on a ledge of rock at the back of the cave, and rinsed the day out of me delightfully enough in the brine. Minutes later I stood shivering and aghast, staring on the empty sill of stone. Where had my things gone? Who had been?

Heart in mouth I scampered to the back where the cave took a turn. It was a darkness I had not explored.

"Hands up, Thomasina," said a voice, and a boy of fourteen, well grown, with tousled hair, came forward into the half-light, smiling. "Caught'ee," he said, doing so and trying to plant a kiss on my lips and landing it on my twisting neck. I wriggled wetly free and stood ducked, hiding myself with my hands.

"Give me my clothes, you wretch," I told him. "Come on, where are they?"

For the boy was Reggie Shore, of course. The Hon. Reginald Shore, I should have said, only son of the widowed and dark-haired Lady Mildmount, whose lands at one point adjoined our own. He had been at school a year, I believe, and the reason for our relative intimacy was not distant. He was often coming to our house with his mother, a woman I cordially dreaded, or riding past on his pony, but since helping me over a stile between fields had contrived to come in my way more often. He was cheerful and good-looking, with an open, sandy face and an infectious grin. He was a great tease. He put his hand up my skirts more than once, and then had come the day when he'd helped with some haying. After the others had gone we had slid in the stuff, giggling and laughing, and playing like puppies, finally nuzzling into each other like such, too, bumping and romping. His hands had roamed my body and in the sunset I had not minded. Red of face and scant of breath I had scuffled back and suddenly felt his manhood stiff under its stuff. It leapt fishlike to my touch and I confess I found occasion to palm it more than once before we parted. We had played "Touch" in the loft of the barn several times after that, growing more daring and loving, and while his lingering fingers had traced me quite utterly I perfectly learnt the shape of a penis, one stout and bellicose for its few years, too. There was more than one of us ready to boil over as a result of those coltish wrestlings. Now I knew that he had been spying on me bathing.

"Give me back my clothes at once, Master," I hissed, huddling. "Come on, I can't stand here for ever now."

"You look awful pretty doing so, Tommy. I say, you have been getting hairy lately, an't you."

My hand came out and smacked his smiling face, letting one breast swing full in view as it did so.

"What do you expect?" I said. "Feathers? Come on. I'll be in a frightful scrape at the house if you don't, quickly."

"Ah, that's just it," he said, miming an imposingly grave manner. "I'm afraid you've been a naughty girl, Tommy." He was tapping one toe with a peeled willow switch. "And will have to pay the consequences, Miss Wragg."

"Don't play the schoolmaster with me, Reggie Shore."

"You know you're not supposed to be down here, are you?"

"Nor are you," I retorted hotly. Lady Mildmount was rumored to bring him up like a tartar, afeared lest in the absence of a father he might be raised too "soft." He winced wryly but did not change his grin. "Where are they, Reg? Please." I changed my tone of voice. "Oh, do give me my things and have done with it."

"Take your hands away and let me look at you first," he said. "No."

He sighed and then sat down on the ledge, humming and looking away with that infuriating smile. I was at the wall of the cave opposed to him.

"All right," I said with sudden decision, turning. "But only my back, then." I was proud of my back.

I let him look at it in silence a while, dripping with spray as it was, and comely thighs tight; even so I knew that a tendril or two showed back, beneath my seat.

"My clothes, please."

"Legs apart first, Tommy, and lean forward."

"No! Absolutely not."

"Then I shall throw them all into the sea and you shall either have to return to the house buck naked or fetch them in and go back soaked. In either case, you'll get a whipping."

"And so will you, if I tell on you. And 'twould do you much good, to have the spunk well whipped out of you, young man. I'll wager that thing of yours doesn't stick out quite so stiff and proud after your mother has given you a licking."

"Turn round and let's see your front, Tommy."

There was a long silence and then I breathed out, "Damn you," and turned, my eyes on the wall above his head, my face crimson. He had me in his power, I knew, and the sooner this was done with the better. I did not want to see what he was doing. Anyway I was proud of my front by now as well.

"Hands right by your sides, mind."

"No touching, then. Promise?"

"Promise." He stared and stared. I could feel his eyes fairly boring through me, and mainly in one place, needless to add. At last he said in a hoarse tone, "God, but you're lovely, Thomasina, and I do love you, y'know." I was touched, and braced up my breasts and sucked in my belly, but perhaps it was only schoolboy talk for he went on, "It's such a sweet fat little slice, isn't it, and after that dip your nips are stiff as soldiers, I'd give anything just to be able to nibble one of them a moment, mayn't I, Tom?"

"No. Now give me back my clothes. I've done what you said and you've seen me all over. Nobody except mother has ever seen me naked."

"I shall treasure it for ever, Tommy," he said but with a mock sigh went on; "however, I fear there is one more penalty to pay for your indiscretion." His wand made a juicy whistle through the air. "You have to have a taste of this for your sins."

I looked at him with mute imploring.

"Reg. Please."

"Four," he said shortly.

"No," I said, "it'll tingle terribly."

But my time was running out and I was beginning to feel giggly with him, shielding my breast and self once more and seeing his thing stiff in its trousers. Frankly, I longed to touch it and feel it.

"Come on, naughty Tommy, 'tisn't such a souse. Four quick licks is all I ask. Lord, if we only got as little at school, in the bill. Why, it's never less than a dozen with the birch, and a good rod is seven or eight of these." He swung it whirringly again. "Lord, how those first cuts sting. But you have to stick it through."

"Does you good," I said, pouting.

"But I'd rather have a dozen at the block than my mater's switch any day. It cuts like a razor, that does. Come on, I dare you."

I was shivery and excited and suddenly I said, "Three."

"Four."

"No, three only."

"Four it is."

"Three," I stuck out.

"Three and a half, then, cowardy."

I giggled nervously and acceptingly. What was a half of a cut, I wondered?

"Where?" I asked then.

"Across the bum, of course, where did you think?"

"No, I mean where. I'm not going to bend over like this for you, Reggie Shore."

He stood up and went to a patch of sand where the sun came in and thrashed it. The bendy switch wrote a long weal there. Had I bitten off more than I could chew? This was obviously going to hurt.

"Here." The limb pointed and I lay down. I did so on the hot moist sand with my legs together, and put my head in my folded arms; I was determined he should not make me flinch.

There was a lengthy wait.

"Come on," I said, mouth muffled.

"You do have such tender buns, you know, Tommy, so soft and close and jouncy; it seems a pity to . . ."

"Don't comment," I got out primly. "Get on with it, if you must."

"I'm afraid this is going to hurt you more than me, Thomasina."

As there was another long pause I stole a glance back. He was doffing his jacket on the ledge for the job. The switch looked unspeakably licky. Up the line of one leg I saw his manhood most manifest; it seemed to stretch itself, like some snoozing cat, as he sighed and came forward again. I hid my head instantly.

"The chaps at school say it's twice as bad wet."

The willow rested on my posteriors then, before it lashed across them with a long singing sweep—*Pfffuikk!* I gasped and stretched quickly. The pain came to me at once, much more stingy if not as brutal as Mr. Jorrocks' thong. I pressed into the sand, striving not to satisfy that throbbing thing of his in front by any writhing or wriggling. He paused so long I hissed out angrily, "Come on. You don't have to draw it out so."

"You mark nicely, Tommy. This one's going to be tighter."

I was aware of him rising to his toes to gain full height for the second, which really slashed across me excruciatingly. I gasped again and twisted like a worm for a second.

"You don't have to . . . *that* hard."

"Get straight. Don't try to turn off your right side so."

Pfffuikk!

The third was even harder and drove me burrowing into the sand which I suddenly realized had filled my mouth as well. It stifled my cry, but I knew he had the pleasure of my motions after it. It was impossible not to writhe.

"Now," I heard, "for the half."

I was expecting a stroke half as hard, but my curiosity was piqued when he said gently, "Legs apart now, a little."

My twistings made the command unnecessary in fact. I felt his hand palp my left cheek lightly as if to steady it there, and "Here's the half," he said.

With which he brought that fiendish switch whistling down

precisely across my single sinister buttock. I jacked with a cry, fairly grabbing where he had cut. This was cruelty itself. The blade-like limb had buried itself about my separated left cub with the result that its timed tip, the agonizing part, had bitten like an adder inside my division, welting into the puppyish flesh just by, and beneath, my seam. I had never known such pain and turned, speechless, in the wet sand, doubled and rubbing. Then I heard myself saying, "No" and again "No!"

The Cyclops eye of his urgent young manhood, ready and rubicond, was staring angrily at me. I was bestridden yet oblivious to all but that single scalding weal.

"No, Reggie, no . . . please."

But I was on my back, my legs parted and lifted and my hands could go nowhere but to my smarting seat; so he impaled me easily enough, wet as I evidently was within and without, cutting my hymen as sharply as he had my bottom and with far less fuss or pain. To be truthful, I felt more when his ramming drove me to a rock, on which I scratched one shoulder. His inexperienced quick strokes were oddly merciless and shook me to the marrow; I squirmed back but he dug into me deeper. Then as the worst of the pain in my flesh subsided I realized I was coming to that lightning-like consummation again, only that this time it was to be ten times as racking, and twenty more sweet. My feet pounded, my fingers clawed the sand, which threatened to squeeze into me everywhere, ears, nostrils, and quaking quim.

"I've always wanted to do this to you Tommy," I heard in the blue blaze over my head. "I hope you didn't mind."

I reflected that there was little I might do about it now.

"You're the first for me, my love, and I can't w-w-wait much longer."

And a voice that must have been my own responded: "Give it to me, Reggie . . . yes, my angel, yes . . . aaaaah!"

There was some blinding sense of sun and the spasm so contracted me that for a second I do believe I rested only on feet and head. Mine lasted much longer than his; compounded of the double rodding, switch and prick, it was for a minute eternal bliss, absolute sensation, pure consciousness.

FROM
FRANÇOISE DES LIGNERIS

Fort Frédérick
1960

The great summer heat had come. One evening Anne returned exhausted from having worked in the sun all day. She had put sulfate on the vines hanging along the kitchen garden wall, had watered the beds of beans and eggplants, picked the last little peas suitable for canning.

On the threshold of her bedroom she hesitated a second. Awful, she said to herself. Pretty soon I won't dare walk in this place, or be able to touch a thing!

The blond parquet glimmered with reflections now. There was a smell of wax. Freshly washed curtains hung on either side of shining windows. In its ancient, polished frame the mirror over the mantel pitilessly picked out Anne's earth-incrusted shoes, her old mannish slacks marked with fresh mud, the nails of her strong brown hands dark with compost.

"Jacqueline!" she called.

An extraordinary maid-servant appeared. Jean Gedeon was unrecognizable. Clean black head-bands circled his head. Round the black knee-length uniform an old-fashioned apron had been tied, with a prettily embroidered hem. But the real beauty of the disguise lay in two small gilt earrings whose fragility, and futility, made a sharp contrast with the man's torpid face.

Gedeon had lost his gender without, at the same time, acquiring anything feminine. He possessed the chaste ugliness, the lack of grace, of a governess.

Anne threw down her half-smoked cigarette and watched the zeal with which Gedeon-Jacqueline picked it up, wiping away all ash left by the butt.

"Take my shoes off and polish them," she ordered. Without a word he did as told.

Anne lit another cigarette and stretched out on the bed.

It was delicious to be able to relax like this after a hard day's work. In the old days she'd no sooner come in than she'd have to see to her mother, get dinner ready. Ever since the appointment of her new house-maid she had scarcely had to worry a moment about running the château. At first she had had to give him certain orders, explain things. He'd caught on quickly. Now Gedeon knew how to get the meals ready as well as she did, and the house was cleaned from top to bottom.

Gedeon came back, carrying her shoes.

Anne barely bothered to give them a glance.

"Very badly done," was all she said. "Really, you must be joking. Go and brush them again and do it harder this time."

The door closed behind him. Anne smiled and threw her head back on one arm. She thought of Gedeon sweating blood and tears over those awful old shapeless, worn-out, earth-colored garden shoes, trying like mad to give them a shine they'd lose in a second tomorrow. Useless labor—one of the most degrading of punishments. She stretched out slowly and voluptuously. It was interesting to have purloined a criminal from M. Hélyon and to let him live under the nose, in the very face, of the village. It was more interesting still, much, much more interesting, to follow up this bizarre experience fate had started for her. To tell the truth, the experience exceeded her. It was like nothing she had ever known before. She found herself led into fields for which no map marked the boundaries. It was by no means disagreeable. One would see.

Gedeon returned with her shoes. Anne didn't look at them.

"Put them away," she said.

She went on smoking, lying back on the bed.

"The windows are dirty," she commented. "You're slipping, Jacqueline."

"I can't get them any cleaner than they are," Gedeon murmured huskily.

"Ah but I'm afraid you're going to have to," Anne said. "Go and get your cleaning rags . . ."

A few minutes later Anne heard the rubbing of the duster on the glass, the tiny hiss of the glass itself. The man did not rub with the rabid energy of a worker watching the clock. He had that infinite calm, that patience, of a person who has lost all possession of personal time. Now he was working away at the marks left by the flies since yesterday, rubbing off the minutest seams of their sticky stuff. Indeed, this was no laughing matter for Jean Gedeon!

When she'd listened to the rustle of his rags for long enough she told him to stop. Then she glanced at the creature who waited there, in the precise spot where he'd received her order, his arms dangling.

"Go and wash your hands."

"Shall I take the rags away?"

"No."

And when he came back, with that comic, almost imperceptible frou-frou of his woman's garments, she said: "Now you can remove the rags. Then go and wash your hands again. After that come back here."

She thought: To make this really possible . . . to make it strong and alive . . . to prevent any degeneration . . . She became aware that the man was there again, turned her head. Her look met Gedeon's. His eyes were filled with adoration and reproach. Why are you doing this to me? those eyes seemed to be saying. Is there any point now, between us two?

"Well?" Anne inquired.

He lowered his lids, left the room.

I must, she thought, I must . . .

But she couldn't find the words that would have succeeded in articulating that need she felt to play—to be—the stronger being.

Hearing Gedeon come in again she did not at first look up.

"Get me my skirt," she said, pointing to the closet.

She observed that his hands were still wet. Either he had wanted to show her how carefully he carried out her orders or else he'd washed over-hastily in order to hurry back to her more quickly.

He brought her old skirt embroidered with gray flowers, which she had bought one market day and wore about the house every now and then.

"Take my slacks off."

Suddenly inexpert and clumsy, Gedeon's hands attacked the buttons. Looking in the mirror she saw her cotton chemise emerge, then her long hard thighs. The man was breathing harshly.

"Brush them and then hang them up."

Half-nude as she was, she sat down on the bed, wearing only her slip and faded poplin blouse, with its boyish collar and sleeves rolled over the elbows.

The brush slid more and more gently over the corduroy slacks, then fell to the floor, striking a bed-post. The man must have forgotten he was holding the trousers, their legs draggled over the floor. Ashen-faced, distracted, he approached the bed.

"Well done, Jacqueline," Anne remarked in a tone of soft mockery. "You seem to be breathing more normally now. Put my skirt on for me."

He appeared not to have heard. He remained motionless in front of her, quite close, watching her with panting breath.

Two slaps rang out.

"I don't think you quite understand," she said slowly when, an instant later, he had dropped to his knees behind her and hooked up the skirt with its wan gray flowers.

She turned and took his head in her hands in a gesture of possessive familiarity. Gedeon's arms were round her skirt without pressing it, without so much as touching her body.

For some moments she gently and absently stroked his hair. Then she bent over him: "Listen. You're going to put on a pair of trousers I'll give you. You're going to cross the park from the back and come up by the road leading to the Piquette place. You'll tell the woman there that you're a worker from the forest, that you've been hired for the summer, that you're thirsty and that she's very attractive."

There was silence between them. Gedeon's arms slid down her body. His head hung very low.

"Do you understand?" she demanded. "Or must I repeat it?"

She wanted to compel him to lift his head. Since he refused she gripped him firmly by the scruff of his neck, forcing his head back until he had to stare her in the face.

Two tears rolled down his cheeks but the eyes fastened on hers were as full of adoration as her horse Fleur-de-Maï's.

"May I ask something of you?" said Gedeon.

It was the first time he had summoned up the courage to put a request to her.

"Yes," Anne answered. "You're going to beg me not to call you Jacqueline any more, isn't that it?"

He bent his head.

"It's a very pretty name, Jacqueline," Anne went on reflectively. "Probably she was a very pretty girl, too. Was she blonde? Answer me. No? She wasn't blonde. Then she was dark. Did she wear a ribbon in her hair? What color ribbon?"

Gedeon had got to his feet. He stepped back in a baffled way.

"You hate me?" he asked.

"Do I hate you?"

She said nothing for a second, then shook her head.

"Why, no," she said.

But the scene had lasted too long. She cut it short, in a sharp, cold, detached voice: "I won't call you Jacqueline any more. Now on your way, Jean Gedeon, and go find Germaine."

FROM
BLAKE TREMAINE

New At It[*]
1972

Why, Victoria irritatedly asked herself, as the FASTEN YOUR SEAT-BELTS sign reduced her mini to a mere cummerbund, did she always feel erotic in airplanes? Especially airplanes that hovered as if eternally stationary above endless blue depths—like those of the Mediterranean. They would be getting into Nice in a half hour. Beside her, Joy dreamt like some succulent single length of nylon—no Bothington girl's stockings were worthy of the name unless they looked as if they would have to be peeled off with a paring knife. And no garter tabs kept The Bottom on the edge of its seat, So since Joy was dreaming, Victoria duly dreamt, too. Before long she would have to face her father sputtering into his porridge across the table.

She dreamt of one of the most yummy memories of her young life. It had happened last hols and Victoria sincerely hoped it would happen again. Her parents had been up in town for some pony show or other and the great house had been deserted but for the usual, rather somnolent servants. She had been boredly wondering if it was going to have to be another vibrator afternoon when the telephone rang and a woman who lived a few miles away called Audrey Lumsden telephoned. Victoria knew her imperfectly, from chance meetings at hunt balls and local point-to-points. She did recall the woman had a snotty and spotty son whom she had twice sent over to her father, the Earl, for chastisement, she being a widow. Her father, the Earl, had duly chas-

* New York: Grove Press, 1973.

tised. Victoria had enjoyed seeing the young puppy squirming his way out of the study thereafter.

"Neither my mater nor my pater are at home, I fear," Victoria said, down her end of the ancient phone.

"Never mind," came the determined and increasingly interesting, if disinterested, accents from the other end, "the boy needs a hiding and I've got another of these cruel goes of arthritis. Can't lift a fork to my mouth. You do it at Bothington, don't you?"

"We do," said Victoria, quietly.

"Well then, that's settled. I'll simply send him over. Lay into him hard as you like, he's turned fifteen now and needs it more than ever. Uppish. Take him down a peg or two and you'd be doing me a favor. I'll see the weals with relish. Don't let him off now."

"I won't," said Victoria, as her heart thudded its message, Play up School.

She was utterly, totally ready when the crunch of gravel under bicycle wheels came to her through the open windows of the drawing room twenty minutes later. For a second she had toyed with the idea of some floor-length evening gown, but now she felt she had decided right. The boy should be thrashed by an all-girl girl; the open display of nubile nether limbs would do him no harm at all. It might even do him good.

She had chosen a very violet T-bone shift of crepe, snug as a glove and sunshine short. A gem of a bare-armed nothing that would give her every freedom. What's more, she was, in Bothington lingo, *baring up below*. For she had discarded the idea of pantyhose and from her sky-high steeple heels to the very top of her vulnerable, tender, and so extroverted thighs taupe nylon sheathed her with all the tension she felt inside her skin as well. She had chosen these multi-denier stretch sheers, with their dark tops, to express personality and allure. They were tethered by the tiniest of scarlet garter-belts (four snaps to each thigh), and so ship-shape and ultratight were all of their surfaces that, as she sat, Victoria could see the twin white patches indicative of tension on each round knee. The tiny bumps under the hem of her skirt looked the height of chic, and these delicate indentations of the

garter snaps even showed when she stood, as she did now, at the
sound of the front door bell. She was of course pantyless, and had
prepared all in advance with her customary care. A thin maid
came in.

"Young genn'lemun to see you, Miss."

"Very well, Bella. Tell him I'll be right out."

She ran a tongue over her lips, a hand over one bursting buttock, and was so. Her surprise was extreme. The boy, whom she
remembered but dimly, had grown and straightened. He was
about her height, with floppy fair hair, and he had left his acne
far behind, being warmly bronzed. All in all, in his ivory cricket
shirt and gray flannel shorts, he looked the picture of British boyhood. And British boyhood about to get it. His hands twisted
nervously as he stood in the long hall. Victoria's eyes sharpened
at the sight. He held out a letter to her.

"I was told to give you this."

"You're Lumsden, aren't you?" she said.

"Yes, Miss."

Her being quickened yet further at the term, which he had
obviously been told by his mother to employ. This was all proceeding highly delightfully. He looked in a perfect misery of
intense nervous shyness, compounded of apprehension and humiliation.

Victoria read in a shaky scrawl "GIVE BEARER 8 MORE IF NEC
THX AUDS."

She frowned her downy brows.

"You know why you're here, don't you?"

"Yes, Miss."

"Shall we get on with it, then?"

"Yes . . . thank you."

She went to a stick and umbrella rack, beside some gun cases.
Deliberately she leant and took one of the two long yellow canes
there. Testing its whirry whip on the air she saw him blink; then
she went to an upright leathern chair and walloped the rod into
its back. The lad looked positively aghast at her speed of stroke.
Dust filled the anxious air.

Then she tried the other one, finally selecting the first.

"No, this one's best. It's a little thinner but it's also stiffer at the tip. I think it'll do the job, don't you? It's the last three inches that really hurt. All right, follow me."

As she began slowly, even majestically, up the main staircase, with the boy behind her, a maid came by, short and this time chubby. She grinned to herself at the cortège and Victoria was rewarded to see a deeper color suffuse the boyish cheeks.

She took care to ascend the steps with a hieratic hip-roll, really regal, that moved the material rustlingly over each thigh. She was careful also to keep three steps ahead of her victim, certain that above the taut stocking-tops he would be able to see the white of her sulcal fold fattening out of each stride. She felt the silken stuff rasping sweetly between her thighs. Pressing the elastic cane at the carpet as she mounted, she said in a pleasant, even friendly tone, still without looking back: "I suppose you get swished at school pretty often."

"Yes, Miss," she heard, hoarsely.

"Tight?"

"Yes."

"How many, as a rule?"

"Six."

"I'm sorry to have to say this is going to be eight. Though perhaps your mother told you that."

"Y-yes, Miss."

"Bare bum."

They were at a turning in the stair. As she said it, she bent down to retrieve an inexistent bobby pin. She did not flex her knees to do so, but bent slowly and sumptuously, feeling the thin crepe ride pleasantly up her legs as she did so. If that doesn't make him hard, she thought, nothing will. Peeking back, she was gratified to see the boy bug-eyed; he was staring at the most solid girlish seat he had ever seen, buck bare but for the transversal lines of the scarlet garters. Victoria took her time shifting from one foot to the other, and transferring the silken rod to her left hand also. She uncoiled like a cobra, unleashing, when erect, an open-handed slap with all her weight that set The Bosom bounding and boy reeling, with a cry and hands to ears, across the corridor.

"If I catch you looking at me again there," she breathed ominously, "I'll call your mother and tell her. I'll tell her you tried to rape me. Now follow me and keep your eyes in the boat."

The boat swayed and churned, as the half-blubbering youth obeyed. There were two more staircases to negotiate and then a short spiral wooden one to the long, disused attic Victoria had chosen for infliction. He was breathing stertorously as they approached it. Never had he seen such glibness of surface, such solidity of girl-ass—so close, so tantalizing *there*. The spiral stair was narrow and abrupt. Looking up, the boy saw heaven: under the shadow of the skirt hem the great masses of buttock-cheek moved mesmerically above him. At the top he was gasping. Victoria led him into the long musty attic, lined with relics of the Wrenches, old trophies, ancestral portraits, much red bunting.

She turned dreamily, creamily. Twice she tapped her own bursting right calf with the cane, then she placed its holding knob beneath the trembling chin of the boy before her—yes, he was a shade shorter than she, in her heels.

"Did you look up my skirt again just then?"

"I ... I ... !"

"You did, didn't you? Come on, look me in the eyes."

"I couldn't help ... I didn't mean. . . ."

"Shall I call up your mother and tell her . . . what I just said? Or will you take an extra six from me? Only, it will be necessary for you to graduate to the cord for them, you see. Yes, a nice waxy riding switch we keep up here. Whalebone wound in gut, with a braided trainer. Well. Which is it?"

The boy ducked his head. "I'll . . . I'll take your punishment, Miss."

"All right, Lumsden, help me clear this place a bit. I want to get a nice long run at you. The full length, in fact." Together they pushed back wicker chairs and old shrimping nets, until the floor was almost bare. At the far end, where rose a misty window, ecclesiastical in shape if not in cleanliness, they wrestled into place an antique heavy upright oaken chair. It slammed into position, facing the window. "Good. I'll take you over that. First, I'll change my shoes and God help you, Lumsden, if you look up my skirt

again while I do." As she put on the gym plimsolls she chuckled
to herself to see the boy actually turning away his face to resist
the temptation. When she stood up and confronted him she was
exactly his height and could stare balefully into the depths of his
straying blue eyes. Her face was dead white, though sweat pearled
at her forehead and even beaded her upper lip. She felt perfectly
ferocious and hoped she looked it, too. Lightly she tapped his
nearest buttock. "Off. Take everything off below your waist and
fold them up neatly over there. Then you can knot your shirt in
front so that it stays above your buttocks."

She smiled at what she saw, as his trembling hands obeyed her.
Though boyish, the cheeks were chubby apples and there was a
pronounced manly curve to the fattening prick in front. So she had
not been wrong, after all. Gracefully she went to the chair-back
and draped herself over it, reaching right down to grasp the legs in
front, hiking her skirtlet halfway up her butt in the process. She
spoke to him in the manner of an X-ray technologist adjusting her
patient: "I want you right over like this. Hold on to the legs and
don't let go. Get all your weight right forward, so. Legs a little
apart and well braced back. Are you watching me, Lumsden?
Any clenching," (she clenched) "and you get the cut over. Any
flinching or silly wincing," (she did both, dramatically) "the same.
Three for getting up before permission. Keep your ass right up
and out like this." Slowly she straightened, smoothing down her
skirt and confronting the bobbing prong of his prick. In an amused
tone of voice she said, "Do you usually get an erection before a
beating?"

The boy was almost weeping as he answered, "Ner-no, Miss."

"Then why have you got one now?"

"I dunno, Miss. It's . . . I'm rather afraid."

She laughed mirthlessly. "Does fear make you hard? Anyway,
I didn't say you could, so get it down. Quick."

"I . . . I . . . it . . . I don't think I can, Miss."

"I give you exactly one minute by my Piaget to reduce that
disgusting erection; if it's not down by then," her eyes roamed
ruminatively, "Daddy has a strong cattle-prod up here somewhere
and, if the battery's still working, it might be fun to try it on the

back of your balls. After which"—but the threat had had its effect. The tool limpened a little, as the boy hung his head hangdog, almost puce with embarrassment. "There. That's better. Now then for this hair. I like to see the expression of someone I'm swiping." Taking a tortoiseshell slide off her own locks she applied it to the boy's, drawing up his crop behind his face. "Now let's get this over. Eight tight juicy beauties, just as hard as I can. Bend over and lean right forward and turn your toes a little in, to spread out your cheeks. Fine. That's lovely just like that."

It was. She stood well back and watched it. The chubby boy-meat was braced and bent and she would enjoy lacing into it, as a panther devours its prey. She stood well back—too far, in fact, some ten yards in all. Twice she bounded forward and flashed at air, saying that he had flinched before she cut him. The third time she lashed his shrinking skin with all her stinging skill and was rewarded by a swart line of purple weal, low down. The caning had started in earnest.

She cut as hard as she could and very low. After the third, which elicited a gasped "Christ!" she paused by his head.

"Beginning to tingle a bit?"

"God, yes. Miss!"

"I'm afraid you're going to have an awfully uncomfy bike ride back. Anyway, your hard-on's gone, which is something."

She strolled leisurely back, flexing the cane. It was true, these thin ones stung like hell. He had one pencil-wide weal across his underbum and two others, very close, on the backs of his thighs. Boys were said to dislike it on their legs even more than their bum, and she intended to broaden these into a single scorching band of swollen purple bruise. The tip marks were already black. She let him wait for it, then squelched forward on her gym shoes and cut. With a whacky smack the wood bit in, asplike.

She had to admit he was taking it stoically. His chief symptom was some satisfactory panting. She made him take the fifth over, for flinching. The tip had now made a thick blood-dark welt on his right. She stood staring at his quivering bum, tremoring all over herself like a mare in heat. She wanted to lash him with an intensity of volition she had never ever experienced. She felt pitiless to the depths of her soul. It was all she could do to keep from flaying him alive with cut after cut. She was pouring with sweat. She gave him two more on the legs and stood back, watching. After half a minute she heard a faint whine, like a kitten being distantly strangled.

"What's wrong now, Lumsden?" she asked.

He barely breathed out, clutching to the chair legs as if for dear life. "It hu-u-uuuurts so, oh my God how it huuuuurts!"

"This is a Sunday school picnic compared to what you'll feel with the switch." She gave him the last with every atom of her being and watched. "All right, you can get up now and take a rest."

He stood up, grabbing hold of his upper legs as if trying to wring them dry, his face speechless with contorted agony. Seeing him squirm and prance with the still mounting pain, she felt the moment of honey storm up inside her and pressed her thighs tightly, seething, as it came. He was groaning and moaning as he staggered from the chair. She turned hastily, plucking at herself, and went for the long rapier of the riding switch—used for breaking in ponies: a pure whalebone cord, indeed!

She said evenly: "Do fifty squat-bends and then start running on the spot. Keep the circulation going in those bruises. I'll give you five minutes. With a bit of luck I'll break that blister on your right."

The youth miserably shook his head: "You'll have to tie me, Miss. I can't take any more like that."

She nodded, sensibly. "We have straps. But for the luxury of being fastened down it'll have to be two extra."

"It'll have to be, then."

"Start running. Come on, knees up high."

When he had finished, perspiring, she went level with him: "You didn't think I could hit as hard as that, did you, Lumsden? I thought I could knock the stuffing out of you a bit. Well, you'd better start saying your prayers. I'm going to truss you till you can't twitch and then I'm going to skin you with a nice slow six. We have all the afternoon to ourselves."

He squealed at the second. The fourth made him howl and at

the fifth he began to blubber in a panic. The braided trainer chewed into the tipweals and drew blood in two places. When it was all over and she had unfastened him, he lay on the floor, moaning.

With feigned nonchalance Victoria tossed out: "When you're feeling better, come down to my room on the second floor. It's in this wing. I'll put a bandaid on those grazes and I do have a fridge with some cold beer."

Fifteen minutes later came a timid tap at her bedroom door.

"Come in!"

Tousled, still with the slide in his hair, the boy looked up with sheepish nervousness at the radiant version and vision of girlhood that greeted him there. Victoria had put on a totally transparent pale blue shortie nightie, whose bottom frothed about hers, while her mammoth bosom shelved out, studded, before her. She minced forward towards him on her mules, openly grinning.

"I just showered and freshened up after all that exercise," she explained. "Come on in and don't be shy. It's all over now. No hard feelings—except where they hurt most, eh?" Suddenly she flung her arms about him and gave him a wet and messy kiss. The boy was dumbfounded. "Would you go for a Tuborg?"

"Thanks," he said uncertainly.

While she bent for it in the refrigerator he had a ringside view of the second plumpest ass in the Home Counties. She seemed to have powdered herself all over and was swimming in a mist of Carven's *Ma Griffe*.

"I think I'll have one, too." Bringing the glasses over, beaded and foamy, she gave him a mischievous twinkle. "Sorry if I laid in a bit at the end like that, but if I hadn't your mother would have complained."

"It was the tightest beating I've had for ages."

"Tighter than at school?"

"I thought so."

"Thank you, kind sir." She tilted him a mock-curtsey, dimpling—and when Victoria dimpled, she dimpled all over. "Cheers!"

"Cheers!" he said, draining the glass in one.

"Actually, I thought you took it damn well. Tell me," she

asked thoughtfully, "did I make it hurt because of my stroking, my timing, or by hitting your legs?"

"All three, I think. It hurt like bloody hell." He paused—"Even your pater doesn't hit as low as that."

"Daddy's a real Turk, isn't he. He always takes me in the fold. You see, with a girl, with a fatter overhang, the skin there rubs more and is more tender. In the crease, right under the butt—here." She turned . . . and bent . . . and showed him. The boy heaved a sigh.

"Does he beat you often?"

"Enough."

"And you get it at school too?"

"Yes, Miss."

"Actually," Victoria returned haughtily, "I tend to be in the dishing-out department there these days. Though that's not to say I haven't had some fantastic shellackings in my time. Tell me, is it true your Prefects bugger you afterwards?"

"Sometimes."

"When the bum is all tingly and toasted?"

"Sometimes."

"Um. Well, that's one thing we don't have to go through at Bothington, thanks. Though sometimes our Pre's will pee on us afterwards. Or else wee into our panties and make us wear them wet for the rest of the day. Ugh! All messy and icky. I always hated that. Incidentally, I hope you didn't think I was unjust in punishing you for looking up my skirt on the way?"

"It was your prerogative. I just felt I couldn't help it," the boy said, coloring again.

"Yes, I had to, really. It was a matter of self-respect and pride. Now, of course, it wouldn't matter; in fact, I'd consider it a compliment. I only hope"—and here she paused dramatically—"you got a good view of ass and pussy for your sixer."

"I did," he assured her.

"Worth it?"

"Every nook and cranny."

"Well now you hardly have to look at all, do you? It's all too obviously on display."

"You do have the most marvelous chest I've ever seen."

Victoria looked down. "It is rather massive, isn't it? I sometimes wonder if it could get any bigger, without the skin there bursting. They get in the way a bit when I beat, but I think the extra *avoirdupois* lends weight. Here, would you care for a feel?" Gingerly, gently, the boy advanced a palm and balanced one slick-skinned chubbie, whose nipple darkly stubbed the thin stuff, thumblike. "Go on," she urged, "grab yourself a good piece of tit while you can. There. Heavy, eh?"

"Fantastic," he barely breathed, constriction clear in what was left of his voice.

She drained her beer and said briskly, "Well now then, let's get at the sore spots. Still stinging?"

"Like billyho."

"Drop 'em off and let's see you." She plumped herself down on a pouffe by her dressing table and took the top off some cold cream while the boy once more took off his shorts and pants, the latter showing a spot of blood on the right. When he turned she saw his manhood at almost full-mast, quite powerful in its upward curve and with a nice fatted corona. "You know, you've grown since I saw you last—and *so has this!*" She pulled him forward playfully by the thick tube and was gratified by the troutlike leap it made in her hand as she did so. This was all very promising. "Why don't you lie across my lap while I put some of this on you?"

"Why not?" he grinned, obeying, and, having obeyed to the letter, ass up, felt the cool silk of her full thighs either side his now wholly stiffened gristle. They moved, gently masturbating him as she talked on in her best no-nonsense tone of voice and the boy stood on the sill of bliss. He was drowned in her perfume. Her fingers slipped in the cream she put on his buttock cheeks, massaging them gently, tips caressing their divide from anus to ball-bag. Looking up he could see, since she had perched herself on the edge of her pouffe, the haired seam of her self, the plump lozenge of her person, shaped just like a tiny rugby football, at the junction of her incredible thighs. He felt he was going out of his mind and his breathing harshened once more.

"Ouch! You really caught it, didn't you? What a beauty this

one was. Was that the third, or the fourth, do you remember? I say, I really whacked your legs. I can't remember when I've seen such a set of weals. Miss Nicholson couldn't do better." Finally, when she stood him up like a doll, or toy soldier, one of the best erections she had seen in a boy stared, glared, blared right into her face. Gently her fingers cooled his bum cheeks, and then she palmed his balls. "Heavens! They feel absolutely loaded with spunk."

"They are," he gasped, grinning.

"Well, we can't let you go home all stiff like this, can we? Do you wank off a lot at school?"

"A lot. But it was never like that just then. I damn nearly spurted all over your Aubusson or whatever it is."

"That would have been a waste, wouldn't it?" Her eyes roved as she held the silky-skinned member, weighing it approvingly. "Would you like me to melt this down for you a bit, do you think?"

"I would."

"Um. Just a mo'." She went to the door, softly locked the lock. "If Daddy ever got to hear of this I'd be in for a positively dismal time in the south south-west. That damn Army cane of his. Trouble is, he enjoys doing it. I wish he'd take it out on Mummy instead." In a lithe movement she shed her shortie and stood straddle-legged, thick-bushed, arms akimbo (or the nearest to it) before him. "Have you ever ever had a girl, by the way? Slept with her? Fucked her cunt, I mean?"

He ruefully shook his head.

"Well, there's always a first, isn't there. I suppose you've buggered boys?"

This time he nodded briskly.

"Well, you aren't going to me. I don't want that big brute up my anus, thanks. But you can put it up my adorable, panting, mushy twat! Which can hardly wait to feel it inside. *Quick!*" she hissed, enlacing him with her arms. "How do you want it? Me writhing on my monumental back or simply standing on my head munching grapes? Possibly it'd be fun with you sitting down and me. . . ."

"I'd prefer to stand, thanks all the same."

"How 'bout this?" She turned and grabbed her ankles. The upside-down cock looked perfectly colossal as it approached, bobbing. "Ah, I thought you would. Jee-suss!"

"Please observe," came the silky accents of the airline stewardess, *"the* NO FUCKING *sign."*

Victoria awoke with a start. Joy was plucking at her skirt, or what was left of it.

"Wakey, wakey, we're landing in Nice, dear."

Victoria turned and stretched and stared into the bottomless mauve orbs of her companion in crime.

"Darling. I was just about to come. Fantastic sexy dream. But you don't think that . . . I mean . . . you do realize that neither of us has a single mark on our sumptuous skins despite all that happened to us at the camp."

Joy was thoughtfully gazing at a knuckle, where a puckered scab was healing.

"So that was real," Victoria nodded slowly. "Ibrahim was real. He felt real . . . *and so do you!"*